THE STATE OF PRESCHOOL 2008

STATE PRESCHOOL YEARBOOK

© 2008 The National Institute for Early Education Research
By W. Steven Barnett, Ph.D.
Dale J. Epstein, Ph.D.
Allison H. Friedman, Ed.M.
Judi Stevenson Boyd, Ed.M.
Jason T. Hustedt, Ph.D.

ISBN 0-9749910-5-8

Table of Contents

VISIT OUR WEBSITE FOR ACCESS TO ALL DATA WWW.NIEER.ORG

United States

PERCENT OF NATIONAL POPULATION ENROLLED

AVERAGE STATE SPENDING PER CHILD ENROLLED
(2008 DOLLARS)

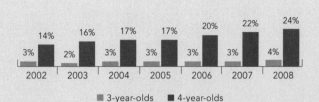

■ 3-year-olds ■ 4-year-olds

The 2007-2008 year was one of impressive progress for state-funded preschool education. Overall, state programs made major progress in expanding enrollment and continued to raise quality standards. For the second year running per-child funding increased, reversing the prior downward trend in expenditures. However, despite the modest upward trend in spending overall, fewer states were confirmed as providing sufficient funding per child to meet our benchmarks for quality standards. In current economic circumstances, this shortfall is especially worrisome.

In the United States today, more than 80 percent of all 4-year-olds attend some kind of preschool program. About half of those (39 percent of all 4-year-olds) are enrolled in some kind of public program (state pre-K, Head Start or special education), with the other half enrolled in a private program. Most of the 4-year-olds in public programs attend state pre-K, which enrolls almost a quarter of the population at age 4. Unfortunately, these numbers vary tremendously by state. In Oklahoma nearly 90 percent of the 4-year-olds receive a free public education. At the other extreme, as few as 10 percent are enrolled in public programs in some states. Private enrollment does not make up the differences in enrollment between these extremes.

Pre-K enrollment at age 3 is much more limited, primarily because public provision is so much lower. Enrollment in private programs is very similar at ages 3 and 4. Only 14 percent of 3-year-olds attend some type of public program, with barely 4 percent of 3-year-olds attending a state-funded pre-K program. Enrollment also varies dramatically by state, but most states serve less than 1 or 2 percent of their 3-year-olds outside of special education and Head Start.

WHAT'S NEW?

• Enrollment increased by more than 108,000 children. More than 1.1 million children attended state-funded preschool education, 973,178 at age 4 alone.

• States' pre-K enrollment of 3- and 4-year-olds approaches 1.4 million in both general and special education.

• Thirty-three of the 38 states with programs increased enrollment.

• When general and special education enrollments are combined, 28 percent of 4-year-olds and 6.3 percent of 3-year-olds are served nationally.

• Nine states improved on NIEER's Quality Standards Checklist. Only one state fell back.

• State pre-K spending per child rose to $4,061; spending from all reported sources rose to $4,609 per child.

• Total state funding for pre-K rose to almost $4.6 billion. Funding from all reported sources exceeded $5.2 billion, an increase of nearly $1 billion (23 percent) over last year.

• In most states the level of funding per child reported from all sources appears to be too low for programs to meet all 10 benchmarks for quality standards.

NATIONAL ACCESS

Total state program enrollment, all ages 1,134,687

States that fund preschool .... 38 states

Income requirement .... 31 state programs have
an income requirement

Hours of operation .... 10 full-day, 10 half-day,
30 determined locally

Operating schedule .... 37 academic year,
13 determined locally

Special education enrollment, ages 3 & 4 408,426

Federal Head Start enrollment, ages 3 & 4 .... 752,023[1]

Total federal Head Start and .... 906,992[1]
Early Head Start enrollment, ages 0 to 5

State-funded Head Start enrollment, ages 3 & 4 .... 18,122[2]

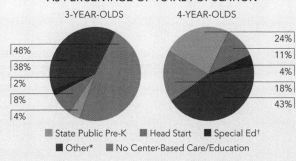

STATE PRE-K AND HEAD START ENROLLMENT AS PERCENTAGE OF TOTAL POPULATION

3-YEAR-OLDS: 48%, 38%, 2%, 8%, 4%

4-YEAR-OLDS: 24%, 11%, 4%, 18%, 43%

■ State Public Pre-K ■ Head Start ■ Special Ed[†]
■ Other* ■ No Center-Based Care/Education

[†] This number represents children in special education
who are not enrolled in state-funded pre-K or Head Start.

*This includes local public education as well as
private child care and other center-based programs.

NATIONAL QUALITY STANDARDS CHECKLIST SUMMARY

POLICY	BENCHMARK	OF THE 50 STATE-FUNDED PRE-K INITIATIVES, NUMBER MEETING BENCHMARKS
Early learning standards	Comprehensive	46
Teacher degree	BA	27
Teacher specialized training	Specializing in pre-K	40
Assistant teacher degree	CDA or equivalent	12
Teacher in-service	At least 15 hours/year	41
Maximum class size 3-year-olds 4-year-olds	20 or lower	44
Staff-child ratio 3-year-olds 4-year-olds	1:10 or better	45
Screening/referral and support services	Vision, hearing, health; and at least 1 support service	36
Meals	At least 1/day	21
Monitoring	Site visits	38

NATIONAL RESOURCES

Total state preschool spending .... $4,596,040,309[3]

Local match required? .... 12 state programs
require a local match

State Head Start spending $151,679,773

State spending per child enrolled .... $4,061[3]

All reported spending per child enrolled* $4,609

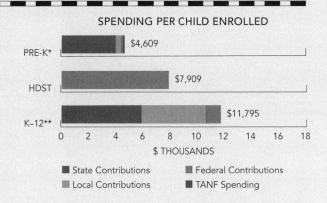

SPENDING PER CHILD ENROLLED

PRE-K*: $4,609
HDST: $7,909
K–12**: $11,795

0 2 4 6 8 10 12 14 16 18
$ THOUSANDS

■ State Contributions ■ Federal Contributions
■ Local Contributions ■ TANF Spending

* Pre-K programs may receive additional funds from federal or local sources
that are not included in this figure.

** K–12 expenditures include capital spending as well as current operating
expenditures.

Data are for the '07-'08 school year, unless otherwise noted.

---

[1] The enrollment figure for federal Head Start, ages 3 and 4, is limited to children
served in the 50 states and DC, including children served in migrant and
American Indian programs. The enrollment figure for total federal Head Start
and Early Head Start, ages 0 to 5, includes all children served in any location,
including the U.S. territories, and migrant and American Indian programs.

[2] This figure includes 14,602 children who attended programs that were
considered to be state-funded preschool initiatives. These children are also
counted in the state-funded preschool enrollment total.

[3] This figure includes federal TANF funds directed toward preschool at states'
discretion.

TABLE 1: STATE RANKINGS AND QUALITY CHECKLIST SUMS

STATE	Access for 4-Year-Olds Rank	Access for 3-Year-Olds Rank	Resource Rank Based on State Spending	Resource Rank Based on All Reported Spending	Quality Standards Checklist Sum (Maximum of 10)
Alabama	36	None Served	14	21	10
Arizona	34	None Served	35	37	4
Arkansas	14	2	11	6	9
California	26	9	20	26	4
Colorado	23	12	36	29	6
Connecticut	22	11	5	2	6
Delaware	30	None Served	7	12	8
Florida	2	None Served	34	36	4
Georgia	3	None Served	15	22	8
Illinois	11	1	24	28	9
Iowa	20	20	29	18	6.7
Kansas	21	None Served	31	34	7
Kentucky	13	6	23	19	8
Louisiana	12	None Served	9	15	7.9
Maine	18	None Served	38	31	5
Maryland	9	19	19	3	9
Massachusetts	27	5	30	25	5
Michigan	19	None Served	16	23	8
Minnesota	38	21	3	5	8
Missouri	35	18	33	35	7
Nebraska	33	16	32	13	8
Nevada	37	24	27	32	7
New Jersey	15	4	1	1	8.5
New Mexico	25	None Served	28	33	9
New York	8	25	18	24	6
North Carolina	16	None Served	10	11	10
Ohio	29	15	4	9	4.3
Oklahoma	1	None Served	17	8	9
Oregon	31	14	2	4	8
Pennsylvania	28	8	8	14	6.2
South Carolina	10	13	37	38	8
Tennessee	17	22	13	17	9
Texas	5	10	21	27	4
Vermont	4	3	25	30	6.8
Virginia	24	None Served	22	16	7
Washington	32	17	6	10	9
West Virginia	6	7	12	7	7
Wisconsin	7	23	26	20	5.1
Alaska	No Program	No Program	No Program	No Program	No Program
Hawaii	No Program	No Program	No Program	No Program	No Program
Idaho	No Program	No Program	No Program	No Program	No Program
Indiana	No Program	No Program	No Program	No Program	No Program
Mississippi	No Program	No Program	No Program	No Program	No Program
Montana	No Program	No Program	No Program	No Program	No Program
New Hampshire	No Program	No Program	No Program	No Program	No Program
North Dakota	No Program	No Program	No Program	No Program	No Program
Rhode Island	No Program	No Program	No Program	No Program	No Program
South Dakota	No Program	No Program	No Program	No Program	No Program
Utah	No Program	No Program	No Program	No Program	No Program
Wyoming	No Program	No Program	No Program	No Program	No Program

Executive Summary

STATE-FUNDED PRESCHOOL EDUCATION: PAST, PRESENT, AND FUTURE

The 2007-2008 year was one of impressive progress for state-funded preschool education. Overall, state programs made major progress in expanding enrollment and continued to raise quality standards. For the second year running per-child funding increased, reversing the prior downward trend in expenditures. However, despite the modest upward trend in spending overall, fewer states were confirmed as providing sufficient funding per child to meet our benchmarks for quality standards. In current economic circumstances, this shortfall is especially worrisome. As the dark clouds and storms of a troubled economy worsen, we recall the words of Ebenezer Scrooge in Charles Dickens' *A Christmas Carol*: "Are these the shadows of the things that Will be, or are they shadows of things that May be, only?" We do not yet know, but the decisions of state and federal policymakers over the next several months, and next year, are likely to answer that question and could profoundly affect the future of early education in the United States.

WHAT'S NEW?

- Enrollment increased by more than 108,000 children. More than 1.1 million children attended state-funded preschool education, 973,178 at age 4 alone.
- States' pre-K enrollment of 3- and 4-year-olds approaches 1.4 million in both general and special education.
- Thirty-three of the 38 states with programs increased enrollment.
- When general and special education enrollments are combined, 28 percent of 4-year-olds and 6.3 percent of 3-year-olds are served nationally.
- Nine states improved on NIEER's Quality Standards Checklist. Only one state fell back.
- State pre-K spending per child rose to $4,061; spending from all reported sources rose to $4,609 per child.
- Total state funding for pre-K rose to almost $4.6 billion. Funding from all reported sources exceeded $5.2 billion, an increase of nearly $1 billion (23 percent) over last year.
- In most states the level of funding per child reported from all sources appears to be too low for programs to meet all 10 benchmarks for quality standards.

GROWING DISPARITIES

As some states move forward rapidly, others fall further behind. Oklahoma remains the only state where virtually every child can start school at age 4, but other states are approaching that goal. In at least eight other states, more than half of 4-year-olds attend a public preschool program of some kind. At the other end of the spectrum, 12 states have no regular state preschool education program. In eight states, less than one in five children are enrolled in a public preschool program at age 4 even taking into account preschool special education and Head Start.

Top 10 States Serving 4-Year-Olds				No-Program States
State	**Percent of 4-Year-Olds Served**			Alaska
	State Pre-K	State Pre-K and Special Education	State Pre-K, Special Education, and Head Start	Hawaii
Oklahoma	71	72	88	Idaho
Florida	61	65	74	Indiana
Georgia	53	54	61	Mississippi
Vermont	50	56	65	Montana
Texas	45	46	55	New Hampshire
West Virginia	43	44	65	North Dakota
Wisconsin	40	42	51	Rhode Island
New York	39	44	54	South Dakota
Maryland	37	42	49	Utah
South Carolina	35	40	50	Wyoming

Other important disparities across the states include:

• State pre-K spending ranges from zero in 12 states to more than $10,000 per child.

• In five states, combined state and local spending exceeds $8,000 per pupil, while in five others it falls below $3,000 per pupil.

• Most states meet a majority of the benchmarks for program quality standards, but 5 states meet less than half. These states include three of the four states with the largest populations and numbers of children in pre-K— California, Texas and Florida.

• There are no maximum class sizes or limits on staff-child ratios in Texas, the only state that fails to set either. California and Maine have limits on staff-child ratios but no class size limit. Most other states limit classes to 20 or fewer children with a teacher and an assistant.

GAINS FOR 3-YEAR-OLDS

Enrollment of 3-year-olds continued to rise, though in smaller numbers than at age 4. This year the national, combined general and special education enrollment was comparable to Head Start enrollments at age 3. This is an important development. Nevertheless, enrollment at age 3 remains far below enrollment at age 4, even though the effects of inadequate educational opportunities are clearly evident by age 3 for many children. Only a handful of states make substantial efforts to serve 3-year-olds without disabilities. The leader in serving 3-year-olds in state pre-K is Illinois, which is the only state committed to serving all 3-year-olds, but it is closely followed by Arkansas. Four states, Illinois, Arkansas, Vermont and New Jersey serve at least 20 percent of children at age 3 in general and special education programs.

Top 5 States Serving 3-Year-Olds			
State	Percent of 3-Year-Olds Served		
	State Pre-K	State Pre-K and Special Education	State Pre-K, Special Education, and Head Start
Illinois	20	24	32
Arkansas	18	21	32
Vermont	16	20	29
New Jersey	16	20	24
Massachusetts	10	14	21

QUALITY IMPROVES

The growing enrollment in state pre-K, documented by NIEER, is valuable to children and the nation only if program quality is high enough to produce meaningful gains in learning and development. Thus, it is notable that states have continued their progress toward higher quality standards. In 2007-2008, improvements in program standards enabled nine states (including two with new programs) to meet more benchmarks on NIEER's Quality Standards Checklist, while only one state moved backwards.

SHADOWS OF THINGS THAT MAY BE

As states consider their fiscal year 2010 budgets, the nation may be experiencing its worst economic downturn since the Great Depression. In the fourth quarter of 2008, the gross domestic product declined by nearly 4 percent, unemployment reached a 15-year high, and state tax revenues fell dramatically. Many states are anticipating their worst budget deficits in a generation. Local government revenues are falling as well. This economic decline will deepen before it improves.

All of this may produce dire consequences for state pre-K programs. In most states, expenditures on pre-K are entirely discretionary and therefore easier to cut than expenditures for some other program. Even states that have not announced cuts to pre-K are considering contingency plans for enrollment cuts, reductions in program standards, and postponing plans for expansion. What eventually happens will depend on the extent to which the federal government provides states with temporary financial assistance, states' commitments to use their own funds, and any new federal funds to maintain and even expand pre-K.

As important as a response to the current economic crisis seems now, the long-term response of the federal government to the educational needs of young children is even more important. High-quality pre-K can help improve the educational success of all children and by doing so, decrease school failure and dropout, and crime and delinquency. In addition, high-quality preschool education has been found to improve economic productivity and health. The bulk of federal early education funding now goes to Head Start and to the Child Care Block Grant, which provides child care subsidies for poor families. As these programs are not designed to serve all young children, a new federal initiative is needed to support early learning and development more broadly.

At the most favorable growth rate that could be expected based on past experience (about 100,000 children per year), it will take another 20 years for the United States to achieve universal access for 4-year-olds. At current growth rates it will take 150 years for the United States to achieve universal access for 3-year-olds. If the nation's political leaders are serious about providing every American 4-year-old with access to a quality preschool education without another generation passing by, it will require a major commitment from the states *and* the federal government. Similarly, no living American is likely to see access guaranteed to all 3-year-olds without increased state and federal commitment.

We propose that the federal government commit to doubling the rate of growth in state pre-K while raising quality standards in the states so that by the year 2020 all 4-year-olds in America will have access to a good education. To do this, the federal government should match state spending with up to $2,500 for every additional child enrolled in state pre-K programs meeting basic quality standards. These should at least include teacher qualifications, class size and ratio, and some system for continuous improvement of teaching and learning. In addition, the federal government should facilitate increased integration of child care, Head Start, and state pre-K. If the federal government adopts such a course, *all* of our children will have a brighter future. If it does not, disparities in early education and school readiness will continue to increase, and another generation will pass without the benefits of quality pre-K for all.

ACCESS: A TALE OF TWO TRENDS

Enrollment in state-funded prekindergarten continued to increase during the 2007-2008 school year, serving 1,134,687 children in 38 states, including 1,122,478 3- and 4-year-olds. Access to state pre-K programs expanded due to the development of new initiatives in three states (Pennsylvania, Iowa, and Ohio) and increased capacity in 30 other states. As a result, enrollment increased by more than 100,000 children compared to the 2006-2007 year. Enrollment in pre-K by state is reported in Tables 2 and 3, and Head Start and special education enrollment are reported in Table 4. For the first time, in this *Yearbook* we calculated an unduplicated percentage of children enrolled in special education, separate from those enrolled in state pre-K and Head Start. Some of the key findings on state pre-K from the 2007-2008 school year include:

• Approximately 24 percent of 4-year-olds and 4 percent of 3-year-olds were served across the country.

• During the 2007-2008 school year, 32 states increased their enrollment of 4-year-olds, compared to 2006-2007 when 30 states increased enrollment. Several states made huge gains in enrollment. Alabama more than doubled its enrollment of 4-year-olds, and with the additions of new programs, Iowa increased enrollment by 348 percent and Ohio by 184 percent.

• Only four states decreased enrollment of 4-year-olds, most by less than 5 percent.

• Overall, enrollment for 4-year-olds increased by 11 percent and enrollment for 3-year-olds increased by 14 percent from the previous year. Since the 2001-2002 school year, enrollment for 4-year-olds has increased by 73 percent while 3-year-old enrollment has increased by 45 percent.

• Oklahoma continues to serve the largest percentage of 4-year-olds at 71 percent, followed by Florida (61 percent) and Georgia (53 percent). These three states with pre-K for all continue to be the only states to serve more than half of their 4-year-olds in state pre-K.

• Although the percent of 3-year-olds in state pre-K continued to climb slowly, approaching 4 percent for the first time during 2007-2008, access to state pre-K for 3-year-olds continues to lag behind. As in the previous year, only five states served more than 10 percent of their 3-year-olds outside of preschool special education. Illinois, Arkansas, Vermont, and New Jersey are the only states to serve more than 15 percent of 3-year-olds in state pre-K programs.

FIGURE 1: PERCENT OF 4-YEAR-OLDS SERVED IN STATE PRE-K

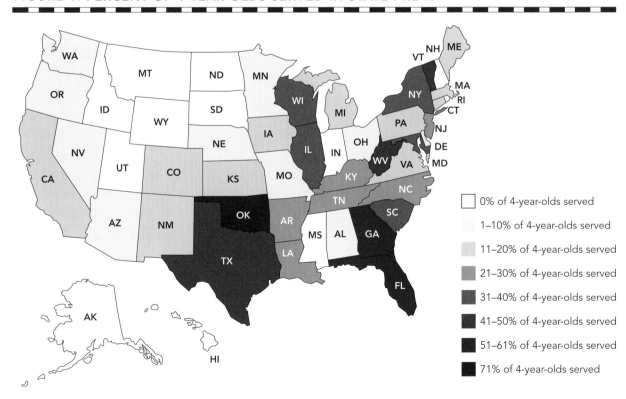

0% of 4-year-olds served

1–10% of 4-year-olds served

11–20% of 4-year-olds served

21–30% of 4-year-olds served

31–40% of 4-year-olds served

41–50% of 4-year-olds served

51–61% of 4-year-olds served

71% of 4-year-olds served

QUALITY STANDARDS: MEETING GREAT EXPECTATIONS

The quality of a preschool program determines how effective it is in helping children learn and develop, with consequences for later success in school and economic benefits to its community. Nevertheless, there are still many preschool education programs across the country that are of poor or mediocre quality. The establishment of specific quality standards in state-level policy helps to ensure that programs can reach higher levels of quality. Each state-funded prekindergarten program has its own quality standards and requirements in place for its classrooms. A research-based checklist of 10 quality benchmarks is used in the *Yearbook* to compare quality standards across the states and their prekindergarten programs.

The tables below show the total number of quality benchmarks met by state pre-K programs from 2001-2002 to 2007-2008. As depicted, state pre-K programs have increased the number of quality benchmarks met over the years. A list of the benchmarks and summary of the supporting research is provided beginning on page 24.

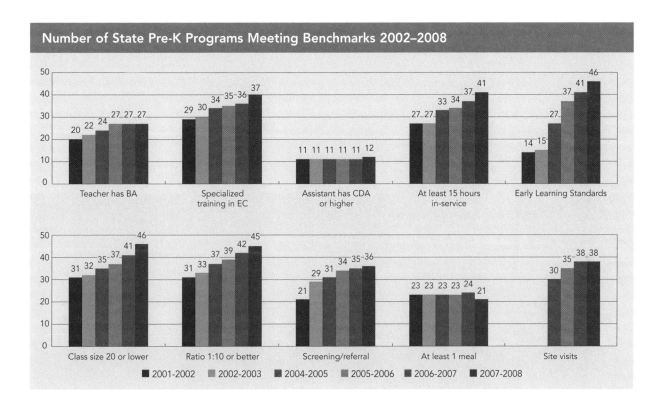

It is important to note that while each benchmark is important in defining quality, they are not all equally important, and not every aspect of quality is encapsulated in these 10 benchmarks. Instead, the benchmarks are preconditions for quality, and attention should be paid to the specific benchmarks met and not just the total number. The quality benchmarks offer evidence of a state's commitment to provide every child enrolled in a state-funded preschool program with an effective educational experience. Lastly, it is important to acknowledge that the benchmarks focus on policy requirements of the prekindergarten program rather than actual practice. Therefore some classrooms may exceed state-level policy requirements (as they represent minimum standards) or fail to meet state-level policy (if programs do not adhere to requirements).

Overall, states increased the number of benchmarks met, indicating an improvement in program quality standards. For the 38 states with prekindergarten programs, the median number of benchmarks rose to 7.1 out of 10, compared to 6.8 the previous year. Nine states (including two with new programs) increased the number of benchmarks met, while only one state decreased in the number of benchmarks. Other key findings for the 2007-2008 school year include:

- North Carolina and Alabama remain the only two states to meet all 10 benchmarks. Louisiana NSECD and Maryland's prekindergarten initiative increased their quality standards and met nine out of 10 benchmarks for the first time. Seven other states continued to fund programs that met nine out of 10 benchmarks—Arkansas, Illinois, New Jersey, New Mexico, Oklahoma, Tennessee, and Washington.

- Kansas greatly improved the quality of its prekindergarten program and now meets four more benchmarks, raising its total met from three to seven. For the 2007-2008 school year, there were only five states that continued to meet fewer than half of the 10 benchmarks.

- Only two benchmarks are met by fewer than half of all programs: just 12 programs require assistant teachers to have at least a CDA credential (or equivalent) and only 21 require at least one meal to be offered to children.

- There are no limits on maximum class sizes or staff-child ratios in Texas, the only state that fails to set either. California and Maine have limits on staff-child ratios but no class size limits. Most other states limit class sizes to 20 or fewer children with a teacher and an assistant.

Despite continued progress, state standards continue to vary a great deal. Children in Georgia or Alabama will have access to a program that meets eight or 10 of the NIEER quality benchmarks, respectively, whereas programs in neighboring Florida are required to meet only four of the benchmarks. For a complete summary of the benchmarks met by each state pre-K initiative during the 2007-2008 school year, see Table 5 on page 18.

RESOURCES: HARD TIMES AHEAD?

During the 2007-2008 school year, states increased spending for prekindergarten, enough to support both increases in enrollment *and* improvements in quality standards. Adequate funding is one key to providing children with a high-quality education. Unfortunately, securing adequate funding for pre-K may become even more challenging in the next few years as the country struggles to cope with a tough economic climate. Some states provide enough funding to provide a high-quality education in their state pre-K programs using only state dollars. Other states rely on a combination of state, local, and federal dollars to adequately fund their state pre-K programs. And still other states do not appear to adequately fund their state pre-K programs based on the figures reported to NIEER. However, since not all states are able to report all of the federal and local dollars that are spent on their programs there is uncertainty in some states about the adequacy of funding levels.

• In 2007-2008, states spent $4.6 billion on state preschool initiatives, an increase of $872 million (without adjusting for inflation), or 23.4 percent, from the previous year. State pre-K spending ranged from $3.25 million in Nevada, a state with about 75,400 3- and 4-year-olds, to more than $694 million in Texas, which has about 784,000 3- and 4-year-olds.

• Three states, Iowa, Ohio and Pennsylvania, contributed slightly more than $200 million to new state pre-K initiatives during the 2007-2008 school year.

• Average state spending per child enrolled increased for the second consecutive year and reached $4,061. This is an increase of $419 per child without adjusting for inflation (an increase of $204 when adjusted for inflation).

• States varied greatly in their per-child spending. New Jersey was the top ranked state, spending $10,989 per child. Three states, New Jersey, Oregon and Minnesota, spent more than twice the national average. Two states, Maine and South Carolina, spent less than $2,000 per child. Twelve states continued to spend nothing on state pre-K, and on average, states still spent much less per child on a year of pre-K education than on a year of K–12 education.

• All reported spending for state pre-K programs exceeded $5.2 billion dollars, an increase of $989 million (without adjusting for inflation), or 23.4 percent, from the previous year. The majority of this increase is accounted for by the increase in state spending.

• The national average of per-child spending was $4,609 when combining state, local, and locally allocated federal funds, despite incomplete data. This is an increase of $475 per child without adjusting for inflation (and an increase of $232 adjusted for inflation). The majority of this increase is accounted for by the increase in state spending. Despite incomplete data for some states, we estimate that at least 17 of 38 states spend enough money to meet all 10 of NIEER's quality benchmarks.

• More than 60 percent of 3- and 4-year-olds in state pre-K were served in six states—Texas, Florida, New York, California, Illinois, and Georgia—none of which reported enough per-child funding from all sources to adequately fund a high-quality preschool program.

Inflation-adjusted spending per child enrolled increased for the second time in *Yearbook* history and for the second year in a row. However, increases over the past two years do not entirely offset previous declines, and inflation-adjusted per-child state spending is still down more than $500 from 2001-2002. Spending per child enrolled increased in more than half of the states offering state pre-K programs compared to the previous year. Since 2001-2002, while only five states have decreased nominal per-child spending, a total of 22 states have failed to keep up with inflation. Table 6 on page 19 provides more detailed information on spending.

For the second year, the *Yearbook* includes two resource rankings for state preschool programs. States are ranked based on (1) the amount of funds states spent for each child enrolled and (2) all reported funds spent for each child enrolled. This second resource ranking was added because some states rely on local dollars and locally allocated federal dollars, in addition to state dollars, to completely fund their state pre-K initiatives. Not all states are able to fully report on the non-state resources used to fund their state pre-K initiatives, and therefore this second ranking may underestimate spending for some states. There are a few states with large differences in their positions on the two resource rankings, including Nebraska, Iowa and Maryland, where local and federal dollars make up a large percentage of total reported spending on pre-K in the state. As a result, each of these states earns a higher ranking once spending from all reported sources is considered. The national average of per-child spending from all reported sources was $4,609, though this figure surely underestimates the true national average if all spending could be identified. Tables 6 and 7 (page 20) show the per-child spending in each state, using all known sources.

Also for the second time, the Yearbook includes an analysis of which states funded their prekindergarten initiatives sufficiently to be able to meet the NIEER quality benchmarks. This year, fewer than half of states had pre-K programs that could be determined to be sufficiently funded to meet all 10 benchmarks. Of the 17 states that were determined to sufficiently fund their pre-K program, six met seven or fewer of the NIEER benchmarks. These states, we would suggest, could reasonably raise standards without increasing funding per child. Six of the programs that did not sufficiently fund their state pre-K programs (as judged by all reported spending), met eight or more NIEER benchmarks. These include Alabama and North Carolina, the two states that meet all 10 NIEER benchmarks. Both states provided sufficient funding to meet all 10 NIEER benchmarks last year. We are concerned that unless funding per child increases in North Carolina, programs will be forced to undercut quality in some other ways (with unreasonably low teacher pay for their qualifications, for example). Alabama may actually be adequately funded as discussed below. However, Alabama was unable to report its local funding this year and also had the highest increase in percentage of 3- and 4-year-olds served of any state, with the exception of Iowa and Ohio, which both added new programs.

Some of the 21 states that could not be confirmed as adequately funding their state preschool initiatives based on all reported spending were not able to provide complete spending information beyond state spending. These states may actually adequately fund or come close to adequately funding their preschool programs, depending on the extent of the additional local and/or federal sources that could not be identified. Alabama is an example of such a state. For 2007-2008, Alabama was only able to report state spending, although it also requires a local match. Our calculations suggest that a full-day pre-K program in Alabama should cost $6,971 per child, but the state only spent $4,415 per child. It is likely that with the addition of Alabama's local match the state is able to adequately fund the program. Florida on the other hand does not appear to sufficiently fund its preschool program, and it is unclear whether the state uses anything but state dollars to fund the program. Florida would need to spend $4,023 per child to adequately fund its program but currently only spends $2,500 per child. Most preschool providers in Florida are in the private sector and therefore may find it difficult to come up with additional funding.

TABLE 2: PRE-K ACCESS BY STATE

ACCESS FOR 4-YEAR-OLDS RANK	STATE	PERCENT OF CHILDREN ENROLLED IN STATE PREKINDERGARTEN (2007-2008)			NUMBER OF CHILDREN ENROLLED IN STATE PREKINDERGARTEN (2007-2008)		
		4-year-olds	3-year-olds	Total (3s and 4s)	4-year-olds	3-year-olds	Total (3s and 4s)
1	Oklahoma	71.0%	0.0%	35.2%	35,231	0	35,231
2	Florida	61.3%	0.0%	30.4%	134,583	0	134,583
3	Georgia	53.4%	0.0%	26.4%	76,491	0	76,491
4	Vermont	49.6%	16.5%	33.0%	3,327	1,096	4,423
5	Texas	44.9%	4.5%	24.7%	175,468	17,895	193,363
6	West Virginia	42.6%	6.2%	24.4%	9,095	1,331	10,426
7	Wisconsin	40.1%	0.7%	20.4%	28,471	517	28,988
8	New York	38.9%	0.1%	19.4%	91,202	315	91,517
9	Maryland	36.7%	1.2%	18.8%	26,827	892	27,719
10	South Carolina	35.4%	3.7%	19.4%	20,394	2,196	22,590
11	Illinois	31.1%	19.8%	25.4%	54,756	35,355	90,111
12	Louisiana	29.9%	0.0%	14.7%	17,788	0	17,788
13	Kentucky	28.4%	10.1%	19.3%	15,800	5,685	21,485
14	Arkansas	28.1%	17.6%	22.9%	10,880	6,896	17,776
15	New Jersey	25.7%	15.8%	20.7%	29,035	17,969	47,004
16	North Carolina	22.5%	0.0%	11.2%	27,788	0	27,788
17	Tennessee	21.1%	1.0%	11.0%	17,014	791	17,805
18	Maine	18.5%	0.0%	9.3%	2,675	0	2,675
19	Michigan	18.2%	0.0%	9.0%	23,134	0	23,134
20	Iowa	17.4%	1.1%	9.3%	6,787	438	7,225
21	Kansas	16.1%	0.0%	8.1%	6,281	0	6,281
22	Connecticut	16.0%	4.2%	10.1%	6,907	1,792	8,699
23	Colorado	15.6%	4.0%	9.8%	10,752	2,721	13,473
24	Virginia	13.0%	0.0%	6.4%	13,125	0	13,125
25	New Mexico	12.8%	0.0%	6.3%	3,570	0	3,570
26	California	12.4%	5.2%	8.8%	63,758	27,035	90,793
27	Massachusetts	11.4%	10.2%	10.8%	8,666	7,703	16,369
28	Pennsylvania	10.8%	5.5%	8.1%	15,910	8,027	23,937
29	Ohio	9.6%	2.8%	6.2%	14,136	4,141	18,277
30	Delaware	7.3%	0.0%	3.7%	843	0	843
31	Oregon	6.9%	3.6%	5.3%	3,217	1,667	4,884
32	Washington	6.3%	2.0%	4.1%	5,117	1,684	6,801
33	Nebraska	5.7%	2.4%	4.1%	1,468	642	2,110
34	Arizona	5.6%	0.0%	2.8%	5,401	0	5,401
35	Missouri	4.0%	2.0%	3.0%	3,088	1,552	4,640
36	Alabama	3.7%	0.0%	1.9%	2,265	0	2,265
37	Nevada	2.2%	0.5%	1.4%	829	193	1,022
38	Minnesota	1.6%	1.1%	1.3%	1,099	767	1,866
No Program	Alaska	0.0%	0.0%	0.0%	0	0	0
No Program	Hawaii	0.0%	0.0%	0.0%	0	0	0
No Program	Idaho	0.0%	0.0%	0.0%	0	0	0
No Program	Indiana	0.0%	0.0%	0.0%	0	0	0
No Program	Mississippi	0.0%	0.0%	0.0%	0	0	0
No Program	Montana	0.0%	0.0%	0.0%	0	0	0
No Program	New Hampshire	0.0%	0.0%	0.0%	0	0	0
No Program	North Dakota	0.0%	0.0%	0.0%	0	0	0
No Program	Rhode Island	0.0%	0.0%	0.0%	0	0	0
No Program	South Dakota	0.0%	0.0%	0.0%	0	0	0
No Program	Utah	0.0%	0.0%	0.0%	0	0	0
No Program	Wyoming	0.0%	0.0%	0.0%	0	0	0
50 States Population		24.0%	3.6%	13.8%	973,178	149,300	1,122,478[1]

For details about how these figures were calculated, see the Methodology section and Roadmap to the State Profile Pages.

[1] Nationwide, an additional 12,209 children of other ages were enrolled in state prekindergarten, for a total enrollment of 1,134,687.

TABLE 3: CHANGE IN PRESCHOOL ENROLLMENT OVER TIME

STATE	ENROLLMENT CHANGES FROM 2001-2002 TO 2007-2008				ENROLLMENT CHANGES FROM 2006-2007 TO 2007-2008			
	Change in 3-year-olds		Change in 4-year-olds		Change in 3-year-olds		Change in 4-year-olds	
	Number	Percent	Number	Percent	Number	Percent	Number	Percent
Alabama	0	NA	1,509	199.6%	0	NA	1,203	113.3%
Alaska	0	NA	0	NA	0	NA	0	NA
Arizona	0	NA	1,124	26.3%	0	NA	325	6.4%
Arkansas	5,954	632.1%	8,656	389.2%	2,828	69.5%	2,732	33.5%
California	16,111	147.5%	19,224	43.2%	717	2.7%	7,504	13.3%
Colorado	1,991	272.7%	2,432	29.2%	637	30.6%	968	9.9%
Connecticut*	257	16.7%	2,490	56.4%	-115	-6.0%	282	4.3%
Delaware	0	NA	0	0.0%	0	NA	0	0.0%
Florida	0	NA	134,583	NA	0	NA	10,193	8.2%
Georgia	0	NA	12,878	20.2%	0	NA	2,336	3.2%
Hawaii	0	NA	0	NA	0	NA	0	NA
Idaho	0	NA	0	NA	0	NA	0	NA
Illinois	21,257	150.8%	15,854	40.8%	2,644	8.1%	7,648	16.2%
Indiana	0	NA	0	NA	0	NA	0	NA
Iowa	-73	-14.3%	5,231	336.2%	-80	-15.4%	5,272	348.0%
Kansas	0	NA	4,051	181.7%	0	NA	310	5.2%
Kentucky	813	16.7%	2,983	23.3%	-130	-2.2%	-8	-0.1%
Louisiana	0	NA	10,269	136.6%	0	NA	3,245	22.3%
Maine	0	NA	1,235	85.8%	0	NA	412	18.2%
Maryland	-516	-36.6%	8,453	46.0%	43	5.1%	2,002	8.1%
Massachusetts*	-1,729	-18.3%	-766	-8.1%	550	7.7%	619	7.7%
Michigan	0	NA	-3,343	-12.6%	0	NA	1,333	6.1%
Minnesota	-48	-5.9%	-171	-13.5%	-97	-11.2%	-146	-11.7%
Mississippi	0	NA	0	NA	0	NA	0	NA
Missouri	-994	-39.0%	-598	-16.2%	-158	-9.2%	-174	-5.3%
Montana	0	NA	0	NA	0	NA	0	NA
Nebraska	518	418.5%	1,112	312.2%	146	29.4%	491	50.3%
Nevada	82	73.9%	508	158.3%	53	37.9%	30	3.8%
New Hampshire	0	NA	0	NA	0	NA	0	NA
New Jersey	5,184	40.5%	5,154	21.6%	710	4.1%	795	2.8%
New Mexico	-470	-100.0%	3,200	864.9%	-242	-100.0%	1,073	43.0%
New York	-5,520	-94.6%	27,703	43.6%	-840	-72.7%	7,697	9.2%
North Carolina	0	NA	26,548	2141.0%	0	NA	9,827	54.7%
North Dakota	0	NA	0	NA	0	NA	0	NA
Ohio*	-5,573	-57.4%	251	1.8%	2,271	121.4%	9,157	183.9%
Oklahoma	0	NA	9,352	36.1%	0	NA	856	2.5%
Oregon	558	50.3%	628	24.3%	464	38.6%	982	43.9%
Pennsylvania*	8,027	NA	13,360	523.9%	4,772	146.6%	5,581	54.0%
Rhode Island	0	NA	0	NA	0	NA	0	NA
South Carolina	1,846	527.4%	4,744	30.3%	1,847	529.2%	-973	-4.6%
South Dakota	0	NA	0	NA	0	NA	0	NA
Tennessee	-51	-6.1%	15,256	867.8%	38	5.0%	4,721	38.4%
Texas	-1,846	-9.4%	47,885	37.5%	970	5.7%	5,155	3.0%
Utah	0	NA	0	NA	0	NA	0	NA
Vermont*	727	197.0%	2,707	436.6%	68	6.6%	419	14.4%
Virginia	0	NA	7,247	123.3%	0	NA	624	5.0%
Washington	535	46.6%	332	6.9%	521	44.8%	446	9.5%
West Virginia	-437	-24.7%	4,010	78.9%	258	24.0%	-491	-5.1%
Wisconsin*	-171	-24.9%	14,967	110.8%	-33	-6.0%	3,593	14.4%
Wyoming	0	NA	0	NA	0	NA	0	NA
50 states	46,432	45.1%	411,058	73.1%	17,842	13.6%	96,039	10.9%

* At least one program in these states did not break down total enrollment figures into specific numbers of 3- and 4-year-olds served. As a result, the figures in this table are estimates.

TABLE 4: 2007-2008 ENROLLMENT OF 3- AND 4-YEAR-OLDS IN STATE PRE-K, PRESCHOOL SPECIAL EDUCATION, AND HEAD START

STATE	Pre-K + Pre-K Special Education				Pre-K + Pre-K Special Education + Head Start			
	3-year-olds		4-year-olds		3-year-olds		4-year-olds	
	Number Enrolled	Percent of State Population	Number Enrolled	Percent of State Population	Number Enrolled	Percent of State Population	Number Enrolled	Percent of State Population
Alabama*	607	1.0%	3,489	5.8%	6,716	10.9%	12,781	21.1%
Alaska	286	2.9%	356	3.8%	1,453	14.7%	1,903	20.2%
Arizona	2,690	2.7%	9,050	9.4%	8,341	8.5%	20,518	21.3%
Arkansas	8,071	20.6%	13,248	34.2%	12,642	32.3%	18,515	47.9%
California	37,040	7.1%	78,297	15.2%	71,249	13.7%	135,559	26.3%
Colorado	4,599	6.7%	13,768	20.0%	8,031	11.7%	19,122	27.7%
Connecticut	3,312	7.7%	9,130	21.1%	6,232	14.6%	12,891	29.8%
Delaware	429	3.7%	1,485	12.8%	1,133	9.9%	2,420	20.9%
Florida*	4,985	2.2%	143,214	65.2%	18,101	8.1%	163,568	74.4%
Georgia	1,776	1.2%	77,875	54.3%	14,173	9.7%	87,401	61.0%
Hawaii	506	3.1%	626	4.2%	1,544	9.5%	2,255	15.2%
Idaho	871	3.7%	754	3.3%	1,837	7.8%	3,156	13.7%
Illinois	42,337	23.7%	65,640	37.2%	57,388	32.1%	84,767	48.1%
Indiana	3,723	4.2%	4,906	5.6%	8,288	9.4%	12,212	14.0%
Iowa	1,334	3.4%	8,122	20.8%	3,836	9.9%	11,603	29.7%
Kansas	1,492	3.9%	8,862	22.7%	4,518	11.7%	12,338	31.6%
Kentucky	6,431	11.4%	17,095	30.8%	12,313	22.0%	25,987	46.8%
Louisiana	433	0.7%	20,054	33.7%	11,235	18.3%	29,454	49.5%
Maine*	537	3.7%	3,514	24.5%	2,026	14.1%	5,591	38.6%
Maryland	3,143	4.2%	30,247	41.5%	8,341	11.2%	35,757	49.0%
Massachusetts*	10,820	14.3%	13,335	17.4%	15,835	20.9%	19,667	25.4%
Michigan	3,874	3.0%	27,382	21.4%	16,714	13.0%	47,370	37.2%
Minnesota	3,102	4.4%	4,552	6.6%	6,977	9.9%	10,152	14.7%
Mississippi	223	0.5%	603	1.4%	10,642	24.6%	15,536	36.9%
Missouri	3,625	4.6%	7,393	9.6%	9,989	12.8%	15,775	20.5%
Montana	101	0.9%	229	2.0%	1,699	14.7%	2,549	22.1%
Nebraska	1,674	6.4%	2,706	10.6%	3,439	13.3%	5,267	20.6%
Nevada*	1,270	3.5%	2,748	7.4%	2,386	6.5%	4,400	11.8%
New Hampshire	321	2.1%	810	5.3%	891	5.9%	1,615	10.4%
New Jersey	22,273	19.6%	34,911	30.9%	27,502	24.2%	41,911	37.1%
New Mexico	1,030	3.6%	5,135	18.4%	3,388	12.0%	9,535	34.2%
New York	14,962	6.3%	103,069	43.9%	33,804	14.2%	127,543	54.4%
North Carolina	2,844	2.3%	30,994	25.0%	9,386	7.4%	42,017	33.9%
North Dakota	147	1.9%	191	2.5%	1,293	16.6%	1,915	25.5%
Ohio	7,743	5.2%	20,096	13.6%	22,138	14.9%	38,352	26.0%
Oklahoma	263	0.5%	35,646	71.9%	7,244	14.5%	43,686	88.1%
Oregon	2,905	6.5%	4,694	10.1%	6,908	15.0%	11,081	23.8%
Pennsylvania	13,164	8.9%	22,142	15.1%	25,993	17.6%	40,849	27.8%
Rhode Island	463	3.7%	739	6.1%	1,540	12.2%	2,449	20.2%
South Carolina*	3,388	5.8%	23,072	40.1%	9,215	15.7%	28,925	50.3%
South Dakota	268	2.4%	476	4.5%	1,694	15.1%	2,646	24.9%
Tennessee	2,129	2.6%	18,101	22.4%	8,016	9.8%	27,682	34.3%
Texas	21,148	5.5%	177,470	45.5%	51,293	13.0%	212,943	54.5%
Utah	1,777	3.5%	2,188	4.4%	3,462	6.8%	5,964	12.0%
Vermont	1,360	20.5%	3,736	55.7%	1,929	28.9%	4,372	65.1%
Virginia*	2,801	2.7%	17,891	17.7%	7,986	7.7%	25,027	24.7%
Washington	3,961	4.7%	8,137	10.0%	8,410	10.1%	15,189	18.6%
West Virginia	1,512	7.0%	9,431	44.2%	4,077	19.0%	13,895	65.1%
Wisconsin	2,531	3.5%	29,857	42.1%	9,064	12.7%	36,237	51.1%
Wyoming	500	7.2%	820	11.7%	1,157	16.6%	1,773	25.2%
50 States	256,780	6.3%	1,118,284	27.6%	573,471	14.0%	1,554,116	38.3%

* These states serve special education children in their state pre-K programs but were not able to provide an unduplicated count; the unduplicated percentage served could be less.
For details about how these figures were calculated, see the Methodology section and the Roadmap to the State Profile Pages.

TABLE 5: 2007-2008 STATE PRE-K QUALITY STANDARDS

STATE	Comprehensive early learning standards	Teacher has BA	Specialized training in pre-K	Assistant teacher has CDA or equiv.	At least 15 hrs/yr in-service	Class size 20 or lower	Staff-child ratio 1:10 or better	Vision, hearing, health, and one support service	At least one meal	Site visits	Quality Standards Checklist Sum 2007-2008
Alabama	✔	✔	✔	✔	✔	✔	✔	✔	✔	✔	10
Arizona	✔					✔	✔			✔	4
Arkansas	✔		✔	✔	✔	✔	✔	✔	✔	✔	9
California			✔		✔		✔			✔	4
Colorado	✔		✔		✔	✔	✔			✔	6
Connecticut	✔		✔		✔	✔	✔	✔			6
Delaware	✔		✔		✔	✔	✔	✔	✔	✔	8
Florida	✔					✔	✔			✔	4
Georgia	✔		✔		✔	✔	✔	✔	✔	✔	8
Illinois	✔	✔	✔	✔	✔	✔	✔	✔		✔	9
Iowa (Shared Visions)	✔		✔			✔	✔	✔	✔		6
Iowa (SVPP)	✔	✔	✔		✔	✔	✔	✔			7
Kansas	✔	✔		✔		✔	✔	✔		✔	7
Kentucky	✔	✔	✔		✔	✔	✔	✔	✔		8
Louisiana (8g)	✔	✔			✔	✔	✔		✔	✔	7
Louisiana (LA4)	✔	✔			✔	✔	✔	✔	✔	✔	8
Louisiana (NSECD)	✔	✔		✔	✔	✔	✔	✔	✔	✔	9
Maine	✔	✔	✔	✔	✔						5
Maryland	✔	✔	✔	✔	✔	✔	✔	✔		✔	9
Massachusetts	✔				✔	✔	✔		✔		5
Michigan	✔	✔	✔	✔	✔	✔	✔	✔			8
Minnesota	✔		✔	✔	✔	✔	✔		✔	✔	8
Missouri	✔	✔	✔		✔	✔	✔			✔	7
Nebraska	✔	✔	✔	✔	✔	✔	✔			✔	8
Nevada	✔	✔	✔		✔	✔	✔			✔	7
New Jersey (Abbott)	✔	✔	✔		✔	✔	✔	✔	✔	✔	9
New Jersey (ECPA)	✔	✔	✔		✔			✔		✔	6
New Jersey (ELLI)	✔	✔	✔		✔	✔	✔	✔		✔	8
New Mexico	✔	✔	✔	✔	✔	✔	✔	✔		✔	9
New York			✔		✔	✔	✔	✔		✔	6
North Carolina	✔	✔	✔	✔	✔	✔	✔	✔	✔	✔	10
Ohio (ECE)			✔					✔		✔	3
Ohio (ELI)			✔			✔	✔	✔		✔	5
Oklahoma	✔	✔	✔		✔	✔	✔	✔	✔	✔	9
Oregon	✔		✔		✔	✔	✔	✔	✔	✔	8
Pennsylvania (EABG)	✔					✔	✔	✔		✔	5
Pennsylvania (HSSAP)	✔		✔		✔	✔	✔	✔	✔	✔	8
Pennsylvania (K4)	✔	✔			✔	✔	✔				5
Pennsylvania (Pre-K Counts)	✔		✔		✔	✔	✔			✔	6
South Carolina (4K)	✔	✔	✔		✔	✔	✔	✔		✔	8
South Carolina (CDEPP)	✔		✔		✔	✔	✔	✔	✔	✔	8
Tennessee	✔	✔	✔		✔	✔	✔	✔	✔	✔	9
Texas	✔	✔	✔		✔						4
Vermont (Act 62)	✔	✔	✔		✔	✔	✔	✔			7
Vermont (EEI)	✔	✔	✔			✔	✔	✔			6
Virginia	✔				✔	✔	✔	✔	✔	✔	7
Washington	✔		✔	✔	✔	✔	✔	✔	✔	✔	9
West Virginia	✔		✔		✔	✔	✔	✔		✔	7
Wisconsin (4K)	✔	✔	✔		✔					✔	5
Wisconsin (HdSt)	✔		✔			✔	✔	✔	✔		6
Totals	46	27	40	12	41	44	45	36	21	38	

Note: Alaska, Hawaii, Idaho, Indiana, Mississippi, Montana, New Hampshire, North Dakota, Rhode Island, South Dakota, Utah, and Wyoming are not included in this table because they do not fund state prekindergarten initiatives.

Check marks in green show new policy changes effective with the 2007-2008 school year. For more details about quality standards and benchmarks, see Roadmap to the State Profile Pages.

TABLE 6: RANKINGS OF PRE-K RESOURCES PER CHILD ENROLLED BY STATE

STATE	Resource rank based on state spending	State $ per child enrolled in pre-K	Change in state per child spending from 2006-2007 to 2007-2008 Adjusted dollars	Total state preschool spending in 2007-2008	Resource rank based on all reported spending	All reported $ per child enrolled in pre-K
New Jersey	1	$10,989	-$124	$516,541,421	1	$10,989
Oregon	2	$8,337	$20	$42,500,000	4	$8,337
Minnesota	3	$8,310	$631	$19,520,751	5	$8,310
Ohio	4	$7,260	$4,597	$139,509,323	9	$7,260
Connecticut	5	$7,181	-$981	$62,465,669	2	$9,393
Washington	6	$7,046	$681	$47,919,000	10	$7,046
Delaware	7	$6,795	-$348	$5,727,800	12	$6,795
Pennsylvania*	8	$6,252	$408	$130,548,078	14	$6,252
Louisiana	9	$5,885	$444	$104,674,104	15	$5,997
North Carolina	10	$5,061	$71	$140,635,709	11	$6,954
Arkansas	11	$4,923	$352	$92,895,744	6	$7,979
West Virginia	12	$4,793	$90	$59,452,747	7	$7,778
Tennessee	13	$4,465	$52	$80,000,000	17	$5,578
Alabama	14	$4,415	-$940	$10,000,000	21	$4,415
Georgia	15	$4,249	-$105	$325,000,000	22	$4,249
Michigan	16	$4,230	-$183	$97,850,000	23	$4,230
Oklahoma	17	$3,966	$331	$139,735,130	8	$7,484
New York	18	$3,948	$290	$361,293,769	24	$3,948
Maryland	19	$3,770	$680	$104,509,466	3	$8,558
California	20	$3,607	-$84	$333,507,727	26	$3,607
Texas	21	$3,581	$577	$694,211,195	27	$3,581
Virginia	22	$3,575	-$213	$46,916,828	16	$5,639
Kentucky	23	$3,497	-$183	$75,127,000	19	$4,860
Illinois	24	$3,372	-$146	$309,596,682	28	$3,372
Vermont	25	$3,290	$561	$14,602,206	30	$3,290
Wisconsin	26	$3,161	-$205	$92,212,500	20	$4,737
Nevada	27	$3,130	-$388	$3,251,671	32	$3,130
New Mexico	28	$3,056	-$95	$10,909,000	33	$3,056
Iowa	29	$3,039	-$102	$22,391,481	18	$4,932
Massachusetts	30	$2,853	-$1,045	$54,940,492	25	$3,811
Kansas	31	$2,843	$94	$17,857,511	34	$2,843
Nebraska	32	$2,792	$385	$6,200,647	13	$6,748
Missouri	33	$2,757	$67	$12,794,517	35	$2,757
Florida	34	$2,500	$28	$336,469,116	36	$2,500
Arizona	35	$2,316	-$204	$12,507,717	37	$2,316
Colorado	36	$2,085	-$83	$28,433,185	29	$3,353
South Carolina	37	$1,719	$24	$38,821,515	38	$2,134
Maine	38	$1,686	-$302	$4,510,608	31	$3,281
Alaska	No Program	$0	$0	$0	No Program	$0
Hawaii	No Program	$0	$0	$0	No Program	$0
Idaho	No Program	$0	$0	$0	No Program	$0
Indiana	No Program	$0	$0	$0	No Program	$0
Mississippi	No Program	$0	$0	$0	No Program	$0
Montana	No Program	$0	$0	$0	No Program	$0
New Hampshire	No Program	$0	$0	$0	No Program	$0
North Dakota	No Program	$0	$0	$0	No Program	$0
Rhode Island	No Program	$0	$0	$0	No Program	$0
South Dakota	No Program	$0	$0	$0	No Program	$0
Utah	No Program	$0	$0	$0	No Program	$0
Wyoming	No Program	$0	$0	$0	No Program	$0
50 States		$4,061	$204	$4,596,040,309		$4,609

* Calculations of per-child spending in Pennsylvania include the EABG, HSSAP, and Pre-K Counts programs only, because the K4 program did not provide information on spending.
For details about how these figures were calculated, see the Methodology section and the Roadmap to the State Profile Pages.

TABLE 7: RANKINGS OF ALL REPORTED RESOURCES PER CHILD ENROLLED

Resource rank based on all reported spending	State	All reported $ per child enrolled in pre-K	Estimate of per child spending*	Is the reported funding sufficient to meet the NIEER benchmarks?	Additional per child funding needed	Quality benchmark total
1	New Jersey	$10,989	$8,988 F	Yes	$0	8.5
2	Connecticut	$9,393	$8,751 F	Yes	$0	6
3	Maryland	$8,558	$4,699 H	Yes	$0	9
4	Oregon	$8,337	$3,971 H	Yes	$0	8
5	Minnesota	$8,310	$4,200 H	Yes	$0	8
6	Arkansas	$7,979	$6,549 F	Yes	$0	9
7	West Virginia	$7,778	$3,679 H	Yes	$0	7
8	Oklahoma	$7,484	$3,654 H	Yes	$0	9
9	Ohio	$7,260	$4,162 H	Yes	$0	4.3
10	Washington	$7,046	$4,513 H	Yes	$0	9
11	North Carolina	$6,954	$7,510 F	No	$556	10
12	Delaware	$6,795	$4,419 H	Yes	$0	8
13	Nebraska	$6,748	$3,675 H	Yes	$0	8
14	Pennsylvania	$6,252	$4,141 H	Yes	$0	6.2
15	Louisiana	$5,997	$6,899 F	No	$902	7.9
16	Virginia	$5,639	$8,613 F	No	$2,974	7
17	Tennessee	$5,578	$7,313 F	No	$1,735	9
18	Iowa	$4,932	$3,639 H	Yes	$0	6.7
19	Kentucky	$4,860	$3,839 H	Yes	$0	8
20	Wisconsin	$4,737	$4,124 H	Yes	$0	5.1
21	Alabama	$4,415	$6,971 F	No	$2,556	10
22	Georgia	$4,249	$7,812 F	No	$3,563	8
23	Michigan	$4,230	$4,243 H	Yes	$0	8
24	New York	$3,948	$4,861 H	No	$913	6
25	Massachusetts	$3,811	$4,729 H	No	$918	5
26	California	$3,607	$4,764 H	No	$1,157	4
27	Texas	$3,581	$4,299 H	No	$718	4
28	Illinois	$3,372	$4,485 H	No	$1,113	9
29	Colorado	$3,353	$4,168 H	No	$815	6
30	Vermont	$3,290	$3,675 H	No	$385	6.8
31	Maine	$3,281	$3,628 H	No	$347	5
32	Nevada	$3,130	$4,323 H	No	$1,193	7
33	New Mexico	$3,056	$3,811 H	No	$755	9
34	Kansas	$2,843	$3,677 H	No	$834	7
35	Missouri	$2,757	$3,931 H	No	$1,174	7
36	Florida	$2,500	$4,023 H	No	$1,523	4
37	Arizona	$2,316	$3,981 H	No	$1,665	4
38	South Carolina	$2,134	$3,917 H	No	$1,783	8
No Program	Alaska	$0	$4,125 H	No	$4,125	NA
No Program	Hawaii	$0	$4,116 H	No	$4,116	NA
No Program	Idaho	$0	$3,499 H	No	$3,499	NA
No Program	Indiana	$0	$3,859 H	No	$3,859	NA
No Program	Mississippi	$0	$3,609 H	No	$3,609	NA
No Program	Montana	$0	$3,215 H	No	$3,215	NA
No Program	New Hampshire	$0	$4,044 H	No	$4,044	NA
No Program	North Dakota	$0	$3,484 H	No	$3,484	NA
No Program	Rhode Island	$0	$4,391 H	No	$4,391	NA
No Program	South Dakota	$0	$3,305 H	No	$3,305	NA
No Program	Utah	$0	$3,981 H	No	$3,981	NA
No Program	Wyoming	$0	$3,518 H	No	$3,518	NA

* For each state, a full-day (F) or half-day estimate (H) of per-child spending was used, based on the operating schedule of the state pre-K program. For states that operated both full- and half-day programs, a half-day estimate was generally used. State estimates were constructed from a national estimate adjusted for state cost of education differences. The national estimate was obtained from Gault, B., Mitchell, A., & Williams, E. (2008). *Meaningful Investments in Pre-K: Estimating the Per-Child Costs of Quality Programs.* Washington, DC: Institute for Women's Policy Research. The state cost index was obtained from: Taylor, L. & Fowler, W. (2006). *A comparable wage approach to geographic cost adjustment.* Washington DC: IES, US Department of Education.

For details about how these figures were calculated, see the Methodology section and Roadmap to the State Profile Pages.

WHAT QUALIFIES AS A STATE PRESCHOOL PROGRAM?

NIEER's *Yearbook* focuses on state-funded preschool initiatives meeting these criteria:

- The initiative is funded, controlled, and directed by the state.

- The initiative serves children of preschool age, usually 3 and/or 4. Although initiatives in some states serve broader age ranges, programs that serve only infants and toddlers are excluded.

- Early childhood education is the primary focus of the initiative. This does not exclude programs that offer parent education but does exclude programs that mainly focus on parent education. Programs that focus on parent work status or programs where child eligibility is tied to work status are also excluded.

- The initiative offers a group learning experience to children at least two days per week.

- State-funded preschool education initiatives must be distinct from the state's system for subsidized child care. However, preschool initiatives may be coordinated and integrated with the subsidy system for child care.

- The initiative is not primarily designed to serve children with disabilities, but services may be offered to children with disabilities.

- State supplements to the federal Head Start program are considered to constitute *de facto* state preschool programs if they substantially expand the number of children served and the state assumes some administrative responsibility for the program. State supplements to fund quality improvements, extended days, or other program enhancements or to fund expanded enrollment only minimally are not considered equivalent to a state preschool program.

While ideally this report would identify all preschool education funding streams at the state, local and federal levels, there are a number of limitations on the data that make this extremely difficult to do. For example, preschool is only one of several types of educational programs toward which local districts can target their Title I funds. Many states do not track how Title I funds are used at the local level and the extent to which they are spent on preschool education. Another challenge involves tracking total state spending for child care, using a variety of available sources, such as CCDF dollars, TANF funds, and any state funding above and beyond the required matches for federal funds. Although some of these child care funds may be used for high-quality, educational, center-based programs for 3- and 4-year-olds that closely resemble programs supported by state prekindergarten initiatives, it is nearly impossible to determine what proportion of the funds are spent this way.

AGE GROUPINGS USED IN THIS REPORT

Children considered to be 3 years old during the 2007-2008 school year are those who were eligible to enter kindergarten two years later, during the 2009-2010 school year. Children considered to be 4 years old during the 2007-2008 school year were eligible to enter kindergarten one year later, during the 2008-2009 school year. Children considered to be 5 year olds during the 2007-2008 school year were already eligible for kindergarten at the beginning of the 2007-2008 school year.

Roadmap to the State Profile Pages

How to interpret data on the individual state profiles:

For each state that has a preschool education initiative, we present one page with a description of the state's program followed by a page with data on the program's key features.

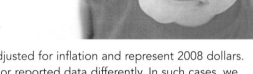

On the top of the first page for each state are two sets of bar graphs:

- The first set shows percentages of the state's 3-year-olds and 4-year-olds enrolled in the state program.
- The second set shows the state's spending per child enrolled in the state preschool initiative.

Both sets of bar graphs depict changes in state prekindergarten over time, from fiscal year 2002 (which corresponds to the 2001-2002 school year) through fiscal year 2008 (the 2007-2008 school year). Most of the 2002-2007 data used for comparison purposes come from NIEER's previous *Yearbooks*, although spending figures are adjusted for inflation and represent 2008 dollars. There are also some exceptions in cases where states revised data or reported data differently. In such cases, we adjusted data to ensure comparability across program years.

The bar graphs are followed by a narrative describing the main features of the state's initiative(s), with details such as the initiative's origins, the types of settings in which state-funded preschool can be offered, and eligibility criteria for children. The narrative also notes unique or particularly interesting aspects of the state initiatives that may not be highlighted elsewhere in the report, along with relevant new developments. Some descriptive information in the narratives was originally included in *Seeds of Success* from the Children's Defense Fund and the *Quality Counts 2002* issue of *Education Week*.

At the bottom of the first page of each state profile are four numbers showing the 38 states with prekindergarten ranking on the following measures:

- The percentage of the state's 4-year-old population enrolled in the state's prekindergarten program (Access Ranking–4s);
- The percentage of the state's 3-year-old population enrolled in the state's prekindergarten program (Access Ranking–3s);
- State expenditures per child enrolled in the program (Resources Ranking–State Spending);
- And, all reported expenditures per child enrolled in the program, including local and federal spending as well as state spending (Resources Ranking–All Reported Spending).

This last measure, Resources Ranking–All Reported Spending, is used for the second time by NIEER and provides a more complete picture of spending in states employing local and federal funding sources than Resources Ranking–State Spending alone. However, because states vary in their ability to report spending from these other sources, the new ranking is imperfect and sometimes underestimates total spending.

For states with more than one prekindergarten initiative, information is presented slightly differently, as is explained on the individual profiles for these states. Iowa, Louisiana, New Jersey, Ohio, Pennsylvania, South Carolina, Vermont, and Wisconsin each have more than one distinct initiative.

The 12 states not funding state prekindergarten initiatives in the 2007-2008 school year are also given state profile pages. For most of these states, the space usually filled by a description of a state's initiative is left blank, and the table on the quality standards is omitted. However, these profiles provide information on enrollment for special education, federally funded Head Start, and state-funded Head Start. Data on spending for K–12 and federal Head Start are also provided. In addition, state Head Start spending is reported when applicable.

The sections below provide an overview of information contained in the data tables on the state profile pages and explain why these elements are important. Data in the tables are for the 2007-2008 program year except where noted.

ACCESS

The first item in the Access data table is total state program enrollment. This is the number of children enrolled at a specific point in time. Following that is the percentage of school districts (or in some cases, counties, communities or parishes) offering state preschool programs. This information shows the extent of the initiative's geographic coverage. Next, the table shows what, if any, income requirement is used in determining eligibility for the program.

Data on the hours of operation (hours per day and days per week) and operating schedule (academic or calendar year) are shown as additional measures of access because working parents may find it difficult to get their children to and from a program that operates only a few hours a day. The number of hours children participate in a preschool program also matters for other reasons, such as influencing the program's effects on children's development and learning.

The Access data table also shows enrollment of 3- and 4-year-old children in two federally funded programs besides the state prekindergarten initiative: preschool special education and Head Start. The Head Start enrollment total includes children in the American Indian/Alaskan Native and migrant regions. The final item in the table reports how many children are participating in state-funded Head Start.

Two Access pie charts illustrate the percentages of 3-year-olds and 4-year-olds in the state enrolled in the state-funded preschool initiative(s), special education, and Head Start. The remaining children are categorized as enrolled in "Other/None." These children may be enrolled in another type of private or publicly funded program (e.g., state-subsidized child care) or may not be attending a center-based program at all. For the 2008 *Yearbook*, we calculated an unduplicated count for special education enrollment in order to more accurately represent the number of children served in the state. The special education percentage represents children who are in special education but not enrolled in Head Start or state pre-K. All other special education children are included in the Head Start and state pre-K enrollment percentages. The Head Start percentage also includes any children supported by state contributions to Head Start.

QUALITY STANDARDS CHECKLIST

State policies in 10 critical areas related to quality are shown. For each area, states receive a checkmark when their policy meets or exceeds the related benchmark standard. On the right-hand side of the page, a box displays the total number of benchmarks met by the state. The Quality Standards Checklist represents a set of minimum criteria needed to ensure effective preschool education programs, especially when serving children at-risk for school failure. However, the checklist is not intended as an exhaustive catalog of all features of a high-quality program and meeting all 10 standards does not necessarily guarantee high quality. On the other hand, each of these standards is essential, and no state's preschool education policies should be considered satisfactory unless all 10 benchmarks are met.

The limitations of research are such that judgment inevitably plays a role in setting specific benchmarks based on evidence. As studies find that the potential benefits from strong preschool education programs exceed costs by 7 to 17 times, we gave more weight to the risk of losing substantial benefits by setting benchmarks too low than to the risk of raising costs by setting benchmarks too high.[1] Costs of many preschool programs are currently quite low; thus, benchmarks steer closer to the characteristics of programs demonstrated to produce reasonably large educational benefits for children in randomized trials and the strongest quasi-experimental studies (e.g., High/Scope Perry Preschool and Chicago Child-Parent Centers) and farther from the characteristics of programs found in rigorous studies to have weak effects.[2]

Four of the items we use to gauge the quality of state prekindergarten programs involve teacher credentials and training. State preschool policies are evaluated based on whether programs require teachers to have a bachelor's degree;[3] whether they require teachers to have specialization in preschool education;[3] whether they require assistant teachers to have at least a Child Development Associate (CDA) or equivalent credential;[4] and whether they require teachers to have at least 15 hours of annual in-service training.[5] Teacher qualifications receive this emphasis in our checklist because research shows this area to be crucial in determining program quality. Better education and training for teachers can improve the interaction between children and teachers, which in turn affects children's learning.

Class size and staff-child ratios are also emphasized in the Quality Standards Checklist, with the expectation that states will limit class sizes to 20 at the most[6] and have no more than 10 children per teacher.[7] With smaller classes and fewer children per teacher, children have greater opportunities for interaction with adults and can receive more individualized attention, resulting in a higher quality program.

---

1 Reynolds, A., Temple, J., Robertson, D., & Mann, E. (2002). Age 21 cost-benefit analysis of the Title I Chicago Child-Parent Centers. *Education Evaluation and Policy Analysis, 24*, 267–303. Belfield, C., Nores, M., Barnett, S., & Schweinhart, L. (2006). The High/Scope Perry Preschool Program: Cost-benefit analysis using data from the age-40 follow-up. *Journal of Human Resources, 41*(1), 162–190.

2 Temple, J., & Reynolds, A. (2007). Benefits and costs of investments in preschool education: Evidence from the Child-Parent Centers and related programs. *Economics of Education Review, 26*, 126–144. Barnett, W.S., & Belfield, C. (2006). Early childhood development and social mobility. *Future of Children, 16*(2), 73–98.

3 Based on a review of the evidence, a committee of the National Research Council recommended that preschool teachers have a BA with specialization in early childhood education. Bowman, B.T., Donovan, M.S., & Burns, M.S. (Eds). (2001). *Eager to learn: Educating our preschoolers*. Washington, DC: National Academy Press. Burchinal, M.R., Cryer, D., Clifford, R.M., & Howes, C. (2002). Caregiver training and classroom quality in child care centers. *Applied Developmental Science, 6*, 2–11. Barnett, W.S. (2003). Better teachers, better preschools: Student achievement linked to teacher qualifications. *Preschool Policy Matters, 2*. New Brunswick, NJ: National Institute for Early Education Research, Rutgers University. Whitebook, M., Howes, C., & Phillips, D. (1989). *Who cares? Child care teachers and the quality of care in America* (Final report on the National Child Care Staffing Study). Oakland, CA: Child Care Employee Project.

4 Preschool classrooms typically are taught by teams of a teacher and an assistant. Research focusing specifically on the qualifications of assistant teachers is rare, but the available evidence points to a relationship between assistant teacher qualifications and teaching quality. There is much evidence on the educational importance of the qualifications of teaching staff generally. Bowman et al. (2001). Burchinal et al. (2002). Barnett (2003). Whitebook et al. (1989). The CDA has been recommended to prepare assistant teachers who are beginning a career path to become teachers rather than permanent assistants. Kagan, S.L. & Cohen, N.E. (1997). *Not by chance: Creating an early care and education system for America's children* [Abridged report]. New Haven, CT: Bush Center in Child Development and Social Policy, Yale University.

5 Good teachers are actively engaged in their continuing professional development. Bowman et al. (2001). Frede, E.C. (1998). Preschool program quality in programs for children in poverty. In W.S. Barnett & S.S. Boocock (Eds.). (1998). *Early care and education for children in poverty: Promises, programs, and long-term results* (pp. 77–98). Albany, NY: SUNY Press. Whitebook et al. (1989) found that teachers receiving more than 15 hours of training were more appropriate, positive, and engaged with children in their teaching practices.

6 The importance of class size has been demonstrated for both preschool and kindergarten. A class size of 20 is larger than the class size shown in many programs to produce large gains for disadvantaged children. Barnett, W.S. (1998). Long-term effects on cognitive development and school success. In W.S. Barnett & S.S. Boocock (Eds.). (1998). *Early care and education for children in poverty: Promises, programs, and long-term results* (pp. 11–44). Albany, NY: SUNY Press. Bowman et al. (2001). Finn, J.D. (2002). Class-size reduction in grades K–3. In A. Molnar (Ed.). (2002). *School reform proposals: The research evidence* (pp. 27–48). Greenwich, CT: Information Age Publishing. Frede (1998). NICHD Early Child Care Research Network. (1999). Child outcomes when child care center classes meet recommended standards for quality. *American Journal of Public Health, 89*, 1072–1077. National Association for the Education of Young Children. (2005). *NAEYC early childhood program standards and accreditation criteria*. Washington, DC: Author.

7 A large literature establishes linkages between staff-child ratio, program quality, and child outcomes. A ratio of 1:10 is smaller than in programs that have demonstrated large gains for disadvantaged children and is the lowest (fewest number of teachers per child) generally accepted by professional opinion. Barnett (1998). Bowman et al. (2001). Frede (1998). NICHD Early Child Care Research Network (1999). National Association for the Education of Young Children (2005).

Early learning standards are also critical to quality,[8] as they offer programs guidance and ensure that they cover the full range of areas essential to children's learning and development. States should have comprehensive early learning standards covering all areas identified as fundamental by the National Education Goals Panel[9]—children's physical well-being and motor development, social/emotional development, approaches toward learning, language development, and cognition and general knowledge. These standards should be state requirements or actively promoted for use in state-funded preschool education classrooms and should be specifically tailored to the learning of preschool-age children so that it is appropriate for their level of development.

The Quality Standards Checklist also addresses the comprehensive services that preschool programs should be expected to offer. Programs should provide at least one meal;[10] vision, hearing, and health screenings and referrals;[11] and additional parent involvement opportunities, such as parent conferences, or support services, such as parent education.[12] These items are included because children's overall wellbeing and success in school involves not only their cognitive development but also their physical and social/emotional health.

It should be noted that the Quality Standards Checklist focuses on state prekindergarten policy requirements rather than practice. A state with good policies may have some programs that fail to comply with these policies; conversely, a state with weak policies may have many programs that exceed state standards. While evaluating implementation of standards is outside the scope of this report, the checklist does include an indicator of whether states are taking steps to monitor programs' implementation of the quality standards. Policies requiring strong state quality standards are essential, but it is also necessary to have a means of ascertaining that programs meet those standards.[13] Through the examination of program practices, monitoring helps to enforce the standards and ensure high-quality education.

---

8 Current practice too frequently underestimates children's capabilities to learn during the preschool years. Clear and appropriate expectations for learning and development across all domains are essential to an educationally effective preschool program. Bowman et al. (2001). Frede (1998). Kendall, J.S. (2003). Setting standards in early childhood education. *Educational Leadership, 60*(7), 64–68.

9 National Education Goals Panel. (1991). *The Goal 1 Technical Planning Subgroup report on school readiness.* Washington, DC: Author.

10 Good nutrition contributes to healthy brain development and for children's learning. Shonkoff, J.P., & Phillips, D.A. (Eds.). (2000). *From neurons to neighborhoods: The science of early childhood development.* Washington, DC: National Academy Press.

11 For some children, preschool provides the first opportunity to detect vision, hearing, and health problems that may impair a child's learning and development. This opportunity should not be missed. Meisels, S.J., & Atkins-Burnett, S. (2000). The elements of early childhood assessment. In J.P. Shonkoff & S.J. Meisels (Eds.). (2000). *Handbook of early childhood intervention* (pp. 231–257). New York: Cambridge University Press.

12 Families are the primary source of support for child development and the most effective programs have partnered with parents. Bowman et al. (2001). Frede (1998).

13 Monitoring of program quality and external accountability for pre-K are essential components of program standards. Bowman et al. (2001).

RESOURCES

A table in the Resources section offers the following information: total state spending for the prekindergarten initiative; whether a local match is required; amount of state Head Start spending (if applicable); state spending per child enrolled in the program; and all reported (local, state and federal) spending per child enrolled in the program. These measures show various views of the resources allocated to prekindergarten, which allows for a more complete picture of a state's commitment to preschool education. For example, total spending by a state may appear low, but may prove to be fairly high relative to the number of children enrolled. On the other hand, a state with a high total funding level may have a low per-pupil spending level if it enrolls a large number of children. In some states, local communities contribute substantial additional funds to state pre-K. In such cases, the figure that includes all reported spending is the best gauge of the level of available resources, to the extent that information about local spending is available.

A bar chart in the resources section compares preschool spending to federal Head Start and K–12 spending. Different colors indicate the different funding sources (local, state and federal). A separate color is used to indicate any TANF funds that a state directs toward its prekindergarten initiative. While TANF funds are federal dollars, it is the state's decision to devote these funds to prekindergarten as opposed to other purposes. Data on the amounts of local and federal pre-K funds used are included in the bar chart when available.

ACCESS

Total state program enrollment ....Number of children in state pre-K program

School districts that offer state program ....Percentage of school districts in state where program is offered
(may include programs not provided by district itself)

Income requirement ....Maximum family income for participants

Hours of operation ....Hours per day and days per week programs operate

Operating schedule ....Annual schedule of operation (academic year or entire calendar year)

Special education enrollment ....Number of 3- and 4-year-olds served by the Preschool Grants Program
of the Individuals with Disabilities Education Act

Federally funded Head Start enrollment ....Number of slots for 3- and 4-year-olds in
Head Start funded with federal money

State-funded Head Start enrollment ....Number of slots for 3- and 4-year-olds in
Head Start funded with state money

QUALITY STANDARDS CHECKLIST

POLICY   STATE PRE-K REQUIREMENT

Early learning standards...National Education Goals Panel content areas covered by state learning
standards for preschool-age children must be comprehensive

Teacher degree ....Lead teacher must have a BA, at minimum

Teacher specialized training ....Lead teacher must have specialized training in a pre-K area

Assistant teacher degree ....Assistant teacher must have a CDA or equivalent, at minimum

Teacher in-service..Teacher must receive at least 15 hours/year of in-service
professional development and training

Maximum class size ....Maximum number of children per classroom must be 20 or lower
   3-year-olds
   4-year-olds

Staff-child ratio...Lowest acceptable ratio of staff to children in classroom
   3-year-olds   (e.g., maximum number of students per teacher) must be 1:10 or better
   4-year-olds

Screening/referral and support services..............................Screenings and referrals for vision, hearing, and health must be required;
at least one additional support service must be provided to families

Meals...At least one meal must be required daily

Monitoring ....Site visits must be used to demonstrate ongoing adherence to state program standards

RESOURCES

Total state pre-K spending ....Total state funds spent on state pre-K program

Local match required? ....Whether state requires local providers to match state monetary
contributions to program and amount of any required match

State Head Start spending (when applicable)................................Total state funds spent to supplement federal Head Start program

State spending per child enrolled ....Amount of state funds spent per child participating in pre-K program

All reported spending per child enrolled ....Amount of all reported funds spent per child participating in pre-K program

GLOSSARY OF ABBREVIATIONS

AA	Associate of Arts
ACF	Administration for Children and Families
BA	Bachelor of Arts
BS	Bachelor of Science
CCDF	Child Care and Development Fund
CD	Child Development
CDA	Child Development Associate credential
DOE	Department of Education
EC	Early Childhood
ECE	Early Childhood Education
ECERS(-R)	Early Childhood Environment Rating Scale (-Revised)
ECSE	Early Childhood Special Education
EE	Elementary Education
ELL	English Language Learner
ELLCO	Early Language and Literacy Classroom Observation
ELS	Early Learning Standards
ESL	English as a Second Language
FPL	Federal Poverty Level
GED	General Equivalency Diploma
HdSt	Head Start
HSD	High School Diploma
IDEA	Individuals with Disabilities Education Act
IEP	Individualized Education Plan
IFSP	Individualized Family Service Plan
K	Kindergarten
LEA	Local Education Agency
MA	Master of Arts
MOE	Maintenance of Effort
N–	Denotes that the age range covered by a teaching license begins at nursery (e.g., N–4 = nursery–grade 4)
NA	Not Applicable
NAEYC	National Association for the Education of Young Children
NCLB	No Child Left Behind
P–	Denotes that the age range covered by a teaching license begins at preschool (e.g., P–4 = preschool–grade 4)
PIR	Program Information Report (Head Start)
Pre-K	Prekindergarten
SMI	State Median Income
SpEd	Special Education
TANF	Temporary Assistance to Needy Families
T.E.A.C.H.	Teacher Education and Compensation Helps (T.E.A.C.H. Early Childhood® Project)

State Profiles

Alabama

PERCENT OF STATE POPULATION ENROLLED

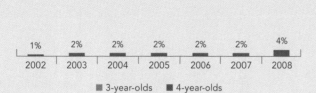

■ 3-year-olds ■ 4-year-olds

STATE SPENDING PER CHILD ENROLLED
(2008 DOLLARS)

*I*n 2000, Alabama began offering state-funded preschool education for 4-year-olds through the Alabama Pre-Kindergarten Program. There are no specific requirements for eligibility beyond meeting the age criteria and being a resident of Alabama. Limited resources for the program have kept statewide enrollment numbers low.

Sites for the Alabama Pre-Kindergarten Program are selected through a competitive grant process. Grantees must provide a local match that represents 50 percent of their grant award. Classroom settings are varied and include public schools, private child care centers, Head Start centers, faith-based centers, and colleges and universities. The state's goal is to have at least one classroom per county and classrooms are currently offered by grantees in all but one county.

The Alabama Pre-Kindergarten Program revised its teacher certification standards to require new hires to have specialized training in early childhood education beginning in the 2005-2006 school year. This change in requirements resulted in the initiative meeting all 10 of the NIEER quality benchmarks. Initially, the state exempted teachers hired under a previous set of requirements, which allowed for a degree in elementary, rather than preschool, education. However, effective in 2009, all teachers in the program will be required to earn a preschool–third grade add-on to their degree or complete additional early childhood education coursework.

In 2007-2008, an increase in state funding enabled the state to provide pre-K to more children, and more technical assistance will be available to programs during the 2008-2009 academic year. In addition, the increase in funding will enable the state, for the first time, to provide scholarships for potential preschool teachers to work toward their degrees.

ACCESS RANKINGS		RESOURCES RANKINGS	
4-YEAR-OLDS	3-YEAR-OLDS	STATE SPENDING	ALL REPORTED SPENDING
36	None Served	14	21

ALABAMA PRE-KINDERGARTEN PROGRAM

ACCESS

Total state program enrollment 2,265

School districts that offer state program.............99% (counties)

Income requirement ....None

Hours of operation ....6.5 hours/day, 5 days/week

Operating schedule ....Academic year

Special education enrollment 3,407

Federally funded Head Start enrollment.......................15,400

State-funded Head Start enrollment 0

STATE PRE-K AND HEAD START ENROLLMENT AS PERCENTAGE OF TOTAL POPULATION

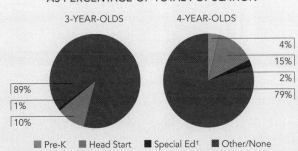

3-YEAR-OLDS

4-YEAR-OLDS

89%
1%
10%

4%
15%
2%
79%

■ Pre-K   ■ Head Start   ■ Special Ed†   ■ Other/None

† This number represents children in special education who are not enrolled in Head Start, but includes children who are enrolled in state-funded pre-K.

QUALITY STANDARDS CHECKLIST

POLICY	STATE PRE-K REQUIREMENT	BENCHMARK	DOES REQUIREMENT MEET BENCHMARK?
Early learning standards	Comprehensive	Comprehensive	☑
Teacher degree	BA	BA	☑
Teacher specialized training	Degree in CD or ECE[1]	Specializing in pre-K	☑
Assistant teacher degree	CDA	CDA or equivalent	☑
Teacher in-service	40 clock hours	At least 15 hours/year	☑
Maximum class size		20 or lower	☑
3-year-olds	NA		
4-year-olds	18		
Staff-child ratio		1:10 or better	☑
3-year-olds	NA		
4-year-olds	1:9		
Screening/referral and support services	Vision, hearing, health, dental; and support services[2]	Vision, hearing, health; and at least 1 support service	☑
Meals	Lunch and snack	At least 1/day	☑
Monitoring	Site visits and other monitoring	Site visits	☑

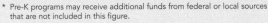

TOTAL BENCHMARKS MET

10

RESOURCES

Total state pre-K spending $10,000,000

Local match required?......................Yes, 50% of grant amount

State spending per child enrolled $4,415

All reported spending per child enrolled* $4,415

SPENDING PER CHILD ENROLLED

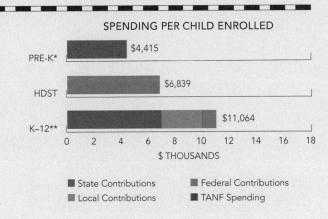

PRE-K* $4,415

HDST $6,839

K–12** $11,064

0   2   4   6   8   10   12   14   16   18
$ THOUSANDS

■ State Contributions   ■ Federal Contributions
■ Local Contributions   ■ TANF Spending

* Pre-K programs may receive additional funds from federal or local sources that are not included in this figure.

** K–12 expenditures include capital spending as well as current operating expenditures.

Data are for the '07-'08 school year, unless otherwise noted.

---

[1] Any preschool teachers with degrees in elementary education who were hired before May 2006 must obtain the P–3 add-on or complete additional early childhood coursework within three years or by 2009.

[2] Support services include two annual parent conferences or home visits, parenting support or training, parent involvement activities, health services for children, and transition to kindergarten activities.

Alaska

NO PROGRAM

Alaska has provided a supplement to federal Head Start programs since the 1980s, but does not have a state-funded preschool education initiative. State funds for the Head Start program are targeted toward school readiness activities and professional development, both in the interest of improving the program's quality. In addition, funds are used to provide access to more children and families whenever possible. State funding through Alaska's Head Start supplement totaled $6,077,200 during the 2007-2008 school year and was available to any federally recognized Head Start program operating in the state. In the 2007-2008 school year, 490 additional children and families were served in Head Start and Early Head Start settings.

For fiscal year 2010, the governor has proposed $800,000 more for Head Start funding and $2 million for a pilot prekindergarten program.

ACCESS RANKINGS		RESOURCES RANKINGS	
4-YEAR-OLDS	3-YEAR-OLDS	STATE SPENDING	ALL REPORTED SPENDING
No Program		No Program	

ACCESS

Total state program enrollment 0

School districts that offer state program........................NA

Income requirement ....NA

Hours of operation ....NA

Operating schedule ....NA

Special education enrollment 1,100

Federally funded Head Start enrollment....................2,340

State-funded Head Start enrollment ....374 [1]

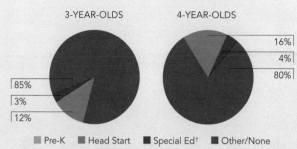

STATE PRE-K AND HEAD START ENROLLMENT AS PERCENTAGE OF TOTAL POPULATION

3-YEAR-OLDS

85%
3%
12%

4-YEAR-OLDS

16%
4%
80%

■ Pre-K   ■ Head Start   ■ Special Ed[†]   ■ Other/None

[†] This number represents children in special education who are not enrolled in Head Start.

QUALITY STANDARDS CHECKLIST

TOTAL BENCHMARKS MET	No Program

RESOURCES

Total state pre-K spending...$0

Local match required? ....NA

State Head Start spending................................$6,077,200

State spending per child enrolled $0

All reported spending per child enrolled*......................$0

* Pre-K programs may receive additional funds from federal or local sources that are not included in this figure.

**K–12 expenditures include capital spending as well as current operating expenditures.

Data are for the '07-'08 school year, unless otherwise noted.

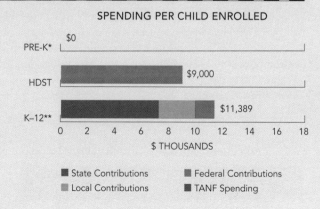

SPENDING PER CHILD ENROLLED

PRE-K* $0

HDST $9,000

K–12** $11,389

0 2 4 6 8 10 12 14 16 18

$ THOUSANDS

■ State Contributions   ■ Federal Contributions
■ Local Contributions   ■ TANF Spending

[1] Alaska does not require a specific amount of slots to be offered using the state funds it provides to federal Head Start programs, although an estimated 374 additional 3- and 4-year-olds were served in 2007-2008. This figure is based on the total number of non-ACF-funded children served and the percentage of 3- and 4-year-olds as reported in the 2007-2008 Head Start PIR.

Arizona

PERCENT OF STATE POPULATION ENROLLED

STATE SPENDING PER CHILD ENROLLED
(2008 DOLLARS)

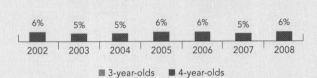

| 2002 | 2003 | 2004 | 2005 | 2006 | 2007 | 2008 |
| 6% | 5% | 5% | 6% | 6% | 5% | 6% |

■ 3-year-olds   ■ 4-year-olds

| $3,040 | $3,138 | $3,023 | $2,681 | $2,523 | $2,520 | $2,316 |
| 2002 | 2003 | 2004 | 2005 | 2006 | 2007 | 2008 |

A rizona began funding state preschool education programs in 1991. In 1996, the state began using the Arizona Early Childhood Block Grant (ECBG) to fund prekindergarten. The ECBG additionally funds supplemental services for full-day kindergarten and first through third grades. To be eligible for an ECBG prekindergarten program, children must be 4 years old by September 1 and must be from a family with an income at or below 185 percent of the federal poverty level. ECBG funds for preschool education are distributed to school districts, which can then provide funding to Head Start or private child care providers if parents prefer those settings for their children. Preschool programs receiving ECBG funding are required to be accredited by organizations approved by the state, such as the National Association for the Education of Young Children.

ECBG prekindergarten teachers are currently required to have only a high school diploma or GED. However, effective July 1, 2009, all new pre-K teachers will be required to have an Arizona Early Childhood Certification, which requires a BA degree and passing a written assessment of early childhood subject knowledge. The Arizona Early Childhood Certification became available for the first time in 2005, but was not required.

A formal evaluation was conducted over a three-year time period and completed in July 2008. It included a review of financial accounting practices, distribution of grant monies, expenditures, and the department's monitoring of preschool providers.

In an effort to further support developmental and health initiatives for young children, in 2006 Arizona established First Things First (FTF), a state agency designed to support local and state level programs to provide high-quality early education services for children from birth through age 5. Working with the Arizona Department of Education, in 2009 FTF plans to allocate $90 million through statewide and regional initiatives to provide information and education to families and to the Early Childhood Education field through quality improvement incentives, a statewide quality rating system, T.E.A.C.H. scholarships, home visiting, mental and dental health services, kith and kin training, and numerous other projects to expand and enhance access to high-quality early childhood services throughout the state.

ACCESS RANKINGS		RESOURCES RANKINGS	
4-YEAR-OLDS	3-YEAR-OLDS	STATE SPENDING	ALL REPORTED SPENDING
34	None Served	35	37

ARIZONA EARLY CHILDHOOD BLOCK GRANT – PREKINDERGARTEN COMPONENT

ACCESS

Total state program enrollment 5,401

School districts that offer state program 17%

Income requirement ....185% FPL

Hours of operation ....Determined locally[1]

Operating schedule ....Academic year

Special education enrollment 8,463

Federally funded Head Start enrollment.........................17,119

State-funded Head Start enrollment 0

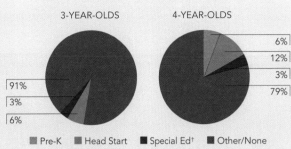

STATE PRE-K AND HEAD START ENROLLMENT AS PERCENTAGE OF TOTAL POPULATION

3-YEAR-OLDS: 91%, 3%, 6%

4-YEAR-OLDS: 6%, 12%, 3%, 79%

Pre-K | Head Start | Special Ed[†] | Other/None

[†] This number represents children in special education who are not enrolled in Head Start but may be enrolled in state-funded pre-K.

QUALITY STANDARDS CHECKLIST

POLICY	STATE PRE-K REQUIREMENT	BENCHMARK	DOES REQUIREMENT MEET BENCHMARK?
Early learning standards	Comprehensive	Comprehensive	☑
Teacher degree	HSD[2]	BA	☐
Teacher specialized training	None[2]	Specializing in pre-K	☐
Assistant teacher degree	HSD[3]	CDA or equivalent	☐
Teacher in-service	12 clock hours	At least 15 hours/year	☐
Maximum class size		20 or lower	☑
3-year-olds	NA		
4-year-olds	20		
Staff-child ratio		1:10 or better	☑
3-year-olds	NA		
4-year-olds	1:10		
Screening/referral and support services	Determined locally	Vision, hearing, health; and at least 1 support service	☐
Meals	Depend on length of program day[4]	At least 1/day	☐
Monitoring	Site visits and other monitoring	Site visits	☑

TOTAL BENCHMARKS MET

4

RESOURCES

Total state pre-K spending $12,507,717

Local match required? ....No

State spending per child enrolled $2,316

All reported spending per child enrolled* $2,316

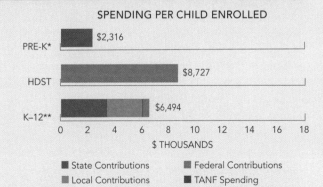

SPENDING PER CHILD ENROLLED

PRE-K* — $2,316

HDST — $8,727

K–12** — $6,494

$ THOUSANDS (0 2 4 6 8 10 12 14 16 18)

State Contributions | Federal Contributions | Local Contributions | TANF Spending

* Pre-K programs may receive additional funds from federal or local sources that are not included in this figure.

** K–12 expenditures include capital spending as well as current operating expenditures.

Data are for the '07-'08 school year, unless otherwise noted.

[1] Most ECBG programs operate 4 hours per day, 3-5 days per week for the academic year. It is recommended that programs operate at least 12 hours per week.

[2] As of July 1, 2009, all pre-K teachers in settings funded by ECBG must hold an early childhood certification, which requires a bachelor's degree. Since 2005, most programs have hired new staff who have or are eligible for the EC certification or endorsement. The Arizona Department of Education is working closely with the community colleges and universities to offer scholarships and onsite classes to allow current teachers to work toward a BA in ECE.

[3] Assistant teachers must have at least a high school diploma. The exception is for assistants in Title I schools, who must have an AA per NCLB requirements.

[4] The state licensing agency requires licensed programs, including all ECBG pre-K programs, to provide meals depending on the length of time and the time of day a child attends. A child present at or before 8 am must be served breakfast; a child present between 11 am and 1 pm must be served lunch; and a child present at or after 5 pm must be served dinner. Children present between 2 and 4 hours must be served at least one snack; if present between 4 and 8 hours, one meal and at least one snack; and if present for 9 or more hours, at least one meal and two snacks.

Arkansas

PERCENT OF STATE POPULATION ENROLLED

STATE SPENDING PER CHILD ENROLLED
(2008 DOLLARS)

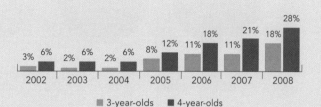

■ 3-year-olds ■ 4-year-olds

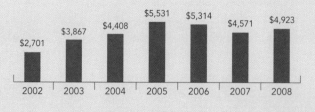

I n 1991, the Arkansas Better Chance (ABC) program began as part of a state education reform initiative. Since its inception, ABC has been funded through a dedicated sales tax. Beginning in 2001, the program has been partially funded by an excise tax on package beer. Additionally, ABC receives some federal funding, although local contributions must cover at least 40 percent of the total program funding.

The program provides services for children from low-income families from birth to age 5. Additional risk factors for determining eligibility for the ABC program include having a teen parent, developmental delay, low birth weight, limited English proficiency, being in foster care, having a parent on active military duty, and family violence. Arkansas has a diverse pre-K delivery system with about half of all providers being public schools or education cooperatives. The state also permits and funds programs operating through Head Start and private organizations, which comprise the other half.

ABC provides financial resources to its programs for teacher professional development, including college degrees. State legislators have commissioned an interim study to examine the possibility of instituting a birth–5 teaching license that would be required for state pre-K teachers in public schools, including those in multi-classroom sites. The study will be discussed more in depth during the 2009 state legislative session.

In recent years, state funding for prekindergarten has increased steadily, resulting in greater access to the program. In the 2004-2005 program year, the Arkansas Better Chance for School Success (ABCSS) program was established using new state funds. ABCSS and ABC have the same quality standards, but ABCSS is targeted to 3- and 4-year-old children in families below 200 percent of the federal poverty level and who live in school districts that are in school improvement status or in which at least 75 percent of children perform poorly on state benchmark exams in math and literacy. This report combines enrollment and spending figures for the ABC and ABCSS programs.

ACCESS RANKINGS		RESOURCES RANKINGS	
4-YEAR-OLDS	3-YEAR-OLDS	STATE SPENDING	ALL REPORTED SPENDING
14	2	11	6

ARKANSAS BETTER CHANCE/ARKANSAS BETTER CHANCE FOR SCHOOL SUCCESS

ACCESS

Total state program enrollment ....18,870[1]

School districts that offer state program 94%

Income requirement ....200% FPL

Hours of operation..............................7 hours/day, 5 days/week

Operating schedule ....Academic year

Special education enrollment 8,109

Federally funded Head Start enrollment...........................9,838

State-funded Head Start enrollment 0

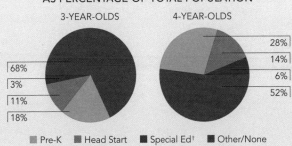

STATE PRE-K AND HEAD START ENROLLMENT
AS PERCENTAGE OF TOTAL POPULATION

3-YEAR-OLDS

68%
3%
11%
18%

4-YEAR-OLDS

28%
14%
6%
52%

■ Pre-K ■ Head Start ■ Special Ed[†] ■ Other/None

[†] This number represents children in special education
who are not enrolled in state-funded pre-K or Head Start.

QUALITY STANDARDS CHECKLIST

POLICY	STATE PRE-K REQUIREMENT	BENCHMARK	DOES REQUIREMENT MEET BENCHMARK?
Early learning standards	...................................Comprehensive	Comprehensive	☑
Teacher degree	.....................BA/BS (single classroom sites); AA/AS (multiple classroom sites)[2]	BA	☐
Teacher specialized training	...................Degree in EC with P–4 license (public single classroom sites); Degree in EC (nonpublic single classroom sites & multiple classroom sites)[2]	Specializing in pre-K	☑
Assistant teacher degree	....CDA	CDA or equivalent	☑
Teacher in-service	.....................60 clock hours (certified staff); 30 clock hours (other staff)	At least 15 hours/year	☑
Maximum class size 3-year-olds 4-year-olds	....20 20	20 or lower	☑
Staff-child ratio 3-year-olds 4-year-olds	....1:10 ....1:10	1:10 or better	☑
Screening/referral and support services	...................Vision, hearing, health, dental, developmental; and support services[3]	Vision, hearing, health; and at least 1 support service	☑
Meals	.............................Breakfast, lunch and snack	At least 1/day	☑
Monitoring	.............................Site visits and other monitoring	Site visits	☑

TOTAL BENCHMARKS MET

9

RESOURCES

Total state pre-K spending ....$92,895,744[4,5]

Local match required? ....Yes, 40% of total funding

State spending per child enrolled ....$4,923[5]

All reported spending per child enrolled* $7,979

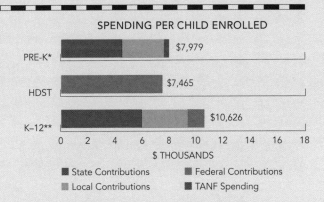

SPENDING PER CHILD ENROLLED

PRE-K* $7,979

HDST $7,465

K–12** $10,626

0 2 4 6 8 10 12 14 16 18
$ THOUSANDS

■ State Contributions   ■ Federal Contributions
■ Local Contributions   ■ TANF Spending

* Pre-K programs may receive additional funds from federal or local sources
  that are not included in this figure.

**K–12 expenditures include capital spending as well as current operating
  expenditures.

Data are for the '07-'08 school year, unless otherwise noted.

[1] This figure includes some infants and toddlers. It represents center-based
  enrollment only and does not include 5,674 children who received home-visiting
  services during 2007-2008.

[2] The P–4 teacher license covers birth–grade 4. In multiple classroom sites, one
  teacher must have a BA/BS in EC and P–4 certification for every three classrooms,
  and the other two classrooms may have a teacher with an AA/AS in EC. This was
  also true in previous years.

[3] Support services include two annual parent conferences or home visits, education
  services or job training for parents, parenting support or training, parent
  involvement activities, health services for children, information about nutrition,
  referral to social services, and transition to kindergarten activities.

[4] Additional state, TANF, and local funds totaling $15,877,743, not included in this
  figure, were allocated to a home-based program option.

[5] These figures include both state and TANF funds.

California

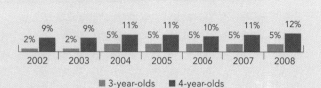

PERCENT OF STATE POPULATION ENROLLED

	2002	2003	2004	2005	2006	2007	2008
3-year-olds	2%	2%	5%	5%	5%	5%	5%
4-year-olds	9%	9%	11%	11%	10%	11%	12%

■ 3-year-olds ■ 4-year-olds

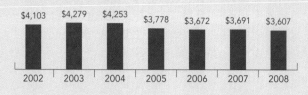

STATE SPENDING PER CHILD ENROLLED
(2008 DOLLARS)

| 2002 | 2003 | 2004 | 2005 | 2006 | 2007 | 2008 |
| $4,103 | $4,279 | $4,253 | $3,778 | $3,672 | $3,691 | $3,607 |

In 1965, California began offering the California State Preschool Program, becoming one of the first states in the nation to make state-funded prekindergarten available. Three- to 5-year-old children are eligible to participate in the program if they are from families with an income below 75 percent of the state median income or if they have experienced or are at risk for abuse, neglect or exploitation. The California State Preschool Program provides funding to school districts, child care providers, and Head Start agencies through a competitive application process. The program usually funds part-day programs but also provides a full-day program and works with other federal and state-funded child care assistance programs to fund extended hours.

In 2007-2008, California published the California Preschool Learning Foundations. These early learning standards focus on social-emotional development, language and literacy, English language development, and mathematics, but have not yet been adopted. The second volume of the standards focus on visual and performing arts, physical development and health, and are currently being developed and expected to be finalized in 2009. The California State Preschool Program uses the Desired Results for Children and Families system to record children's development and to plan curriculum and other developmentally appropriate activities. This system is being aligned with the Learning Foundations and once complete, the Learning Foundations will be implemented by using the Desired Results Development Profile – Revised (DRDP-R).

The Prekindergarten and Family Literacy Program (PKFLP), a new initiative in the 2007-2008 school year, was modeled after the State Preschool Program and provides preschool services along with a literacy component to more than 5,000 4-year-olds in 40 out of 58 counties in California. PKFLP provides either a half- or full-day program for children from families at or below 75 percent of the state median income or for children receiving protective services or who are at risk for abuse, neglect or family violence.

This report focuses on the State Preschool Program and PKFLP as one initiative, combining enrollment and spending figures for the two programs. Additionally, California runs other programs that provide developmental services and child care that are not distinct state-funded prekindergarten programs. General Child Care Programs fund full-time slots for 3- and 4-year-olds, which follow the same requirements and curriculum as the State Preschool Program, but are targeted to working parents who need full-day care for their children. The First 5 initiative funds programs promoting early childhood development, which are used to provide services from prenatal care to age 5, including child health care, parent education, family support, and early care and education. California also provides $200 million for a School Readiness Initiative for a four-year program.

Additionally, in 2008 the California State Preschool Program Act was signed into law, which will create the largest state-funded preschool education program in the U.S. It is anticipated that the state's five main preschool programs providing center-based child development services to 3- and 4-year-old children will be consolidated into a newly formed California State Preschool Program.

ACCESS RANKINGS		RESOURCES RANKINGS	
4-YEAR-OLDS	3-YEAR-OLDS	STATE SPENDING	ALL REPORTED SPENDING
26	9	20	26

CALIFORNIA STATE PRESCHOOL PROGRAM & PREKINDERGARTEN AND FAMILY LITERACY PROGRAM

ACCESS

Total state program enrollment ....92,458[1]

School districts that offer state program ....98% (counties)[2]

Income requirement ....90% (State Preschool Program)
or 80% (PKFLP) of children
must be at or below 75% SMI[3]

Hours of operation.............................3 hours/day (part-day), or
6.5 hours/day (full-day); 5 days/week

Operating schedule ....Determined locally[4]

Special education enrollment 40,266

Federally funded Head Start enrollment 91,471

State-funded Head Start enrollment 0

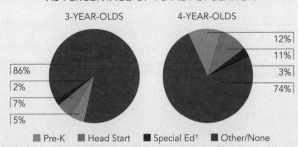

STATE PRE-K AND HEAD START ENROLLMENT
AS PERCENTAGE OF TOTAL POPULATION

3-YEAR-OLDS: 86%, 2%, 7%, 5%

4-YEAR-OLDS: 12%, 11%, 3%, 74%

■ Pre-K   ■ Head Start   ■ Special Ed†   ■ Other/None

† This number represents children in special education
who are not enrolled in state-funded pre-K or Head Start.

QUALITY STANDARDS CHECKLIST

POLICY	STATE PRE-K REQUIREMENT	BENCHMARK	DOES REQUIREMENT MEET BENCHMARK?
Early learning standards	None[5]	Comprehensive	☐
Teacher degree	CDA[6]	BA	☐
Teacher specialized training	Meets CDA requirements[6]	Specializing in pre-K	☑
Assistant teacher degree	CD Asst. Teacher Permit[7]	CDA or equivalent	☐
Teacher in-service	105 clock hours/5 years	At least 15 hours/year	☑
Maximum class size		20 or lower	☐
3-year-olds	No limit[8]		
4-year-olds	No limit		
Staff-child ratio		1:10 or better	☑
3-year-olds	1:8[8]		
4-year-olds	1:8		
Screening/referral and support services	Health, developmental; and support service[9]	Vision, hearing, health; and at least 1 support service	☐
Meals	Depend on length of program day[10]	At least 1/day	☐
Monitoring	Site visits and other monitoring	Site visits	☑

TOTAL BENCHMARKS MET

4

RESOURCES

Total state pre-K spending ....$333,507,727[11]

Local match required? ....No

State spending per child enrolled ....$3,607[12]

All reported spending per child enrolled* ....$3,607[12]

* Pre-K programs may receive additional funds from federal or local sources
that are not included in this figure.

**K–12 expenditures include capital spending as well as current operating
expenditures.

Data are for the '07-'08 school year, unless otherwise noted.

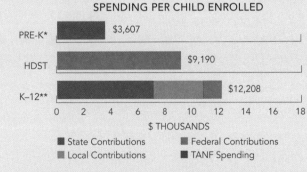

SPENDING PER CHILD ENROLLED

PRE-K*: $3,607
HDST: $9,190
K–12**: $12,208

$ THOUSANDS

■ State Contributions   ■ Federal Contributions
■ Local Contributions   ■ TANF Spending

---

[1] The enrollment figure is a duplicated count as children can be enrolled in both the State Preschool Program and the Prekindergarten Family Literacy Program. Total enrollment is a sum of reported enrollments of both programs, with 87,433 served in the State Preschool Program and 5,025 served in PKFLP.

[2] The State Preschool Program is offered in 98 percent of counties, while the PKFLP is offered in 69 percent of counties, specifically counties with low performing schools.

[3] The income cutoff applies to all children except those who receive protective services or who are at risk for abuse, neglect, or exploitation. For the PKFLP, the income cutoff is 80 percent of children at or below 75 percent SMI.

[4] Part-day programs typically operate for a school or academic year (175-180 days). However, some programs operate fewer than 175 days and some programs operate a full calendar year (246 days) and exceptions to the days per year can be granted.

[5] The Preschool Learning Foundations that include early learning standards were published in the 2007-2008 school year and will be implemented in 2011-2012 school year once they are aligned with the Desired Results Developmental Profile-Revised (DRDP-R).

[6] The Child Development Associate Teacher permit is the minimum requirement for an individual who may function as a lead teacher in the classroom. The permit requires 12 units in ECE or child development and 50 days of work experience in an instructional capacity. It may be renewed one time for a five-year period. A CDA credential issued in California meets temporary alternative qualifications for the Associate Teacher permit. The full Child Development Teacher permit requires a minimum of 40 semester units of education including a minimum of 24 units in ECE or child development, and 175 days of work experience.

[7] The Child Development Assistant Teacher Permit requires 6 credits in ECE or child development.

[8] Three-year-olds are served only in the State Preschool Program.

[9] Decisions regarding vision and hearing screenings are made at the local level. A physical exam including vision, hearing and general health is required for program entry, but not mandated by the state. Health and social services referral and follow-up to meet family needs are required. Other support services include two annual parent conferences or home visits, parent education or job training, parent involvement activities, child health services, referral for social services, and transition to kindergarten activities. PKFLP also offers parent support or training and other support services.

[10] Licensing laws and regulations require that all part-day (3.5 hour) programs provide at least a snack. Lunch and two snacks are required but breakfast is optional for all full-day (6.5 hour) programs. Contractors must meet the nutritional requirements specified by the federal Child Care Food Program or the National School Lunch Program, and programs must provide breakfast or lunch if specified in the original application for services.

[11] This total is a sum of spending from the State Preschool Program ($308,043,436) and PKFLP ($25,464,291).

[12] Per-child spending was calculated using the sum of total enrollments from both programs. However, because enrollment is a duplicated count, per-child spending may be higher than the numbers reported here. These figures reflect state spending for preschool programs only, and do not reflect spending for General Child Care programs.

Colorado

PERCENT OF STATE POPULATION ENROLLED

STATE SPENDING PER CHILD ENROLLED
(2008 DOLLARS)

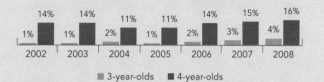

■ 3-year-olds   ■ 4-year-olds

In an effort to reduce school dropout rates, the Colorado Preschool and Kindergarten Program (CPKP) began in 1988 and provides preschool services to at-risk 3- and 4-year-olds and full-day kindergarten children. In order to participate in CPKP, 3-year-olds must have at least three risk factors, while 4-year-olds must have at least one. These risk factors include eligibility for free or reduced-price lunch, low parental education levels, parental substance abuse, homelessness, or participation in the foster care system. Prior to 2008, state legislation permitted 15 percent of the CPKP slots to be used for full-day kindergarten and 5 percent of the slots to be used for full-day preschool. During the 2007-2008 school year, more than 2,000 children were served in the second half of their kindergarten day and 266 children participated in full-day preschool programs.

All CPKP funding is provided to public schools through Colorado's school finance funding formula, although public schools may in turn subcontract with Head Start or community-based agencies. In addition, preschool education programs may use other funding sources, such as federal Head Start money, to supplement CPKP services, extend the program day, or provide wrap-around care.

Starting with the 2006-2007 school year, CPKP sites began implementing and reporting outcomes on approved assessment systems identified in Results Matter. Results Matter, initially funded through a federal grant, involves collecting outcomes data for children from birth to age 5 in early childhood programs in order to build a comprehensive system for reporting data. Currently, 30,000 children across a range of programs in Colorado participate in Results Matter. In addition, Colorado has established a P-20 Education Coordinating Council, which focuses on identifying options to expand, monitor and coordinate preschool through third grade education.

In the 2007 legislative session, CPKP was expanded to serve an additional 2,000 children (1,700 in preschool and 300 in kindergarten). The state also authorized 3,500 more children to be served during the 2008-2009 program year. During the 2008 legislative session, the kindergarten component of CPKP was eliminated and the program's name returned to the Colorado Preschool Program (CPP). With the 3,500 slots authorized and the full-day kindergarten slots converted back to preschool, CPP will experience a 45 percent increase in its capacity to serve preschool children in the 2008-2009 program year.

ACCESS RANKINGS		RESOURCES RANKINGS	
4-YEAR-OLDS	3-YEAR-OLDS	STATE SPENDING	ALL REPORTED SPENDING
23	12	36	29

COLORADO PRESCHOOL AND KINDERGARTEN PROGRAM

ACCESS

Total state program enrollment.....................................13,636[1]

School districts that offer state program 96%

Income requirement ....185% FPL[2]

Hours of operation ....2.5 hours/day, 4 days/week[3]

Operating schedule ....Academic year

Special education enrollment 6,420

Federally funded Head Start enrollment...........................8,786

State-funded Head Start enrollment 0

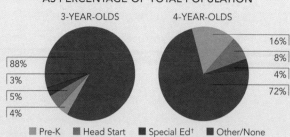

STATE PRE-K AND HEAD START ENROLLMENT AS PERCENTAGE OF TOTAL POPULATION

3-YEAR-OLDS: 88%, 3%, 5%, 4%

4-YEAR-OLDS: 16%, 8%, 4%, 72%

■ Pre-K ■ Head Start ■ Special Ed† ■ Other/None

† This number represents children in special education who are not enrolled in Head Start but may be enrolled in state-funded pre-K.

QUALITY STANDARDS CHECKLIST

POLICY	STATE PRE-K REQUIREMENT	BENCHMARK	DOES REQUIREMENT MEET BENCHMARK?
Early learning standards	Comprehensive[4]	Comprehensive	☑
Teacher degree	CDA or AA in ECE or CD[5]	BA	☐
Teacher specialized training	Meet CDA requirements or AA in ECE	Specializing in pre-K	☑
Assistant teacher degree	None[6]	CDA or equivalent	☐
Teacher in-service	15 clock hours	At least 15 hours/year	☑
Maximum class size		20 or lower	☑
3-year-olds	16		
4-year-olds	16		
Staff-child ratio		1:10 or better	☑
3-year-olds	1:8		
4-year-olds	1:8		
Screening/referral and support services	Health and developmental; and support services[7]	Vision, hearing, health; and at least 1 support service	☐
Meals	Depend on length of program day[8]	At least 1/day	☐
Monitoring	Site visits and other monitoring	Site visits	☑

TOTAL BENCHMARKS MET

6

RESOURCES

Total state pre-K spending ....$28,433,185[9,10]

Local match required? ....No

State spending per child enrolled $2,085

All reported spending per child enrolled* $3,353

* Pre-K programs may receive additional funds from federal or local sources that are not included in this figure.

**K–12 expenditures include capital spending as well as current operating expenditures.

Data are for the '07-'08 school year, unless otherwise noted.

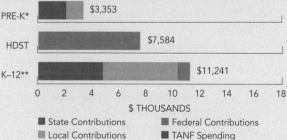

SPENDING PER CHILD ENROLLED

PRE-K* — $3,353

HDST — $7,584

K–12** — $11,241

$ THOUSANDS (0 to 18)

■ State Contributions ■ Federal Contributions
■ Local Contributions ■ TANF Spending

---

[1] In 2007-2008, the Colorado Preschool and Kindergarten Program served 2,454 children in the second half of their kindergarten day. These children are not included in the enrollment total above. In addition, under the Early Childhood Councils, three school districts have waivers to serve children younger than 3 in CPKP. Finally, state statute allows 5 percent of the preschool slots to fund a child to participate in a full-day preschool program using two slots. In 2007-2008, 266 children were served in this way. These children are not included in the enrollment total above.

[2] Income is the most frequently used risk factor for eligibility. Children may also qualify based on other risk factors.

[3] Programs must operate the equivalent of 2.5 hours per day, 4 days per week, though there is flexibility in the length of the program day. Five days per week are funded. Children attend 4 days per week, with the fifth day used for home visits, teacher planning time, completion of child assessments, or staff training.

[4] The Building Blocks to Colorado's Content Standards document has been revised and expanded. The updated standards were in place at the beginning of the 2007-2008 school year.

[5] Teachers must have coursework in child development, developmentally appropriate practices, understanding parent partnerships, and multicultural education and must be supervised by someone with at least a BA in ECE or CD.

[6] Although there is no educational requirement, assistant teachers must meet Colorado Department of Human Services licensing requirements.

[7] Vision, hearing, and dental screenings and referrals are determined locally. Support services include one annual parent conference or home visit, education services or job training for parents, parenting support or training, parent involvement activities, health services for parents and children, information about nutrition, referral to social services, transition to kindergarten activities, and information for referral to immunization and dental care.

[8] Meals and nutritious snacks must be served at suitable intervals. Children who are in the program for more than 4 hours per day must be offered a meal that meets at least one-third of their daily nutritional needs.

[9] Total 2007-2008 funding for the Colorado Preschool and Kindergarten Program, including both preschool and full-day kindergarten, was $53,805,314. The figure above reflects only the portion of these funds provided for the preschool component of the program. This is a change from previous years when the state was unable to break down CPKP funding for preschool and kindergarten.

[10] This figure does not include a contribution of $17,286,849 from local sources which is required by the School Finance Formula.

Connecticut

PERCENT OF STATE POPULATION ENROLLED

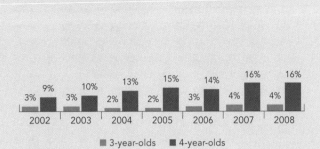

	2002	2003	2004	2005	2006	2007	2008
3-year-olds	3%	3%	2%	2%	3%	4%	4%
4-year-olds	9%	10%	13%	15%	14%	16%	16%

■ 3-year-olds ■ 4-year-olds

STATE SPENDING PER CHILD ENROLLED
(2008 DOLLARS)

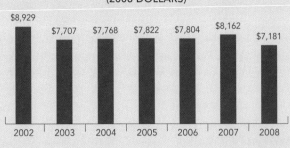

2002	2003	2004	2005	2006	2007	2008
$8,929	$7,707	$7,768	$7,822	$7,804	$8,162	$7,181

Connecticut established the School Readiness program in 1997 to improve preschool access for 3- and 4-year-old children. The program serves children in any town with a priority school and any town in the 50 lowest wealth ranked towns in the state. School Readiness funds are allocated by the state directly to priority school readiness districts, but are awarded to other towns through competitive grants. School Readiness services can be provided through public schools, Head Start programs, and child care centers. In communities participating in the program, the chief elected official and the district school superintendent establish a School Readiness Council to provide direction to the local programs.

The School Readiness program offers different space types in order to accommodate working and non-working families. The space type options include full-day, school-day, and part-day. Full-day spaces are available 5 days per week, 7-10 hours per day for 50 weeks per year. School-day spaces are available 5 days per week, 6 hours per day for 180 days per year. Part-day spaces are available 5 days per week, 2 ½ hours per day for 180 days per year. At least 60 percent of children enrolled in the program must have a family income at or below 75 percent of the state median income.

Connecticut also has a Department of Social Services program that serves approximately 3,700 children up to age 5 with a total fiscal year 2008 spending of $46,934,814. Children may attend for free if their family household income is less than 75 percent of the state median income, but families are required to go through a redetermination of fee every six months so the fee could change for a family within a program year.

In 2007-2008, Connecticut also dedicated $5,500,000 million in state funds to supplement federal Head Start. These funds created approximately 450 additional slots and were also used to provide additional services, extend the program day and year, and support program quality enhancements.

ACCESS RANKINGS	
4-YEAR-OLDS	3-YEAR-OLDS
22	11

RESOURCES RANKINGS	
STATE SPENDING	ALL REPORTED SPENDING
5	2

CONNECTICUT SCHOOL READINESS

ACCESS

Total state program enrollment ....8,699[1]

School districts that offer state program ......38% (communities)

Income requirement ....60% of children must
be at or below 75% SMI

Hours of operation ....Determined by type of slot[2]

Operating schedule........................Determined by type of slot[2]

Special education enrollment 4,764

Federally funded Head Start enrollment..........................6,193

State-funded Head Start enrollment ....489[3]

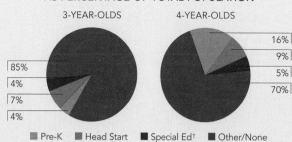

STATE PRE-K AND HEAD START ENROLLMENT AS PERCENTAGE OF TOTAL POPULATION

3-YEAR-OLDS

85%
4%
7%
4%

4-YEAR-OLDS

16%
9%
5%
70%

■ Pre-K   ■ Head Start   ■ Special Ed[†]   ■ Other/None

[†] This number represents children in special education
who are not enrolled in state-funded pre-K or Head Start.

QUALITY STANDARDS CHECKLIST

POLICY	STATE PRE-K REQUIREMENT	BENCHMARK	DOES REQUIREMENT MEET BENCHMARK?
Early learning standards	Comprehensive	Comprehensive	☑
Teacher degree	CDA + 12 credits in EC[4]	BA	☐
Teacher specialized training	Meets CDA requirements	Specializing in pre-K	☑
Assistant teacher degree	None	CDA or equivalent	☐
Teacher in-service	6 clock hours[5]	At least 15 hours/year	☐
Maximum class size		20 or lower	☑
3-year-olds	20		
4-year-olds	20		
Staff-child ratio		1:10 or better	☑
3-year-olds	1:10		
4-year-olds	1:10		
Screening/referral and support services	Vision, hearing, health, dental;[6] and support services[7]	Vision, hearing, health; and at least 1 support service	☑
Meals	Depend on length of program day[8]	At least 1/day	☐
Monitoring	Site visits and other monitoring	Site visits	☑

TOTAL
BENCHMARKS
MET

6

RESOURCES

Total state pre-K spending $62,465,669

Local match required?..No

State Head Start spending $5,500,000

State spending per child enrolled $7,181

All reported spending per child enrolled* $9,393

---

* Pre-K programs may receive additional funds from federal or local sources
that are not included in this figure.

** K–12 expenditures include capital spending as well as current operating
expenditures.

Data are for the '07-'08 school year, unless otherwise noted.

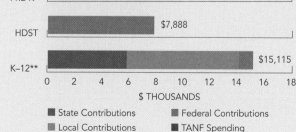

SPENDING PER CHILD ENROLLED

PRE-K* $9,393

HDST $7,888

K–12** $15,115

0   2   4   6   8   10   12   14   16   18

$ THOUSANDS

■ State Contributions   ■ Federal Contributions
■ Local Contributions   ■ TANF Spending

---

[1] The state did not break enrollment into specific numbers of 3- or 4-year-olds, so
all age breakdowns are estimates using the averages from state programs that did
have age counts.

[2] There are four types of slots, including full-day (7-10 hours)/full-year (50 weeks/year);
school-day (6 hours)/school-year (180 days/year); part-day (2.5 hours)/school-year
(180 to 250 days/year); and extended-day (slots that extend the hours, days, and
weeks of a non-School Readiness program to meet full-day, full-year requirements)
All programs operate 5 days per week. Funding levels vary by the type of slot.

[3] This figure is based on the federal PIR total of non-ACF-funded enrollment and
the proportion of all enrollees who were ages 3 or 4.

[4] The majority of public schools with School Readiness classrooms have a certified
teacher present for at least 2.5 hours per day.

[5] All school readiness staff must complete two annual trainings in early childhood
education and one annual training in serving children with disabilities. They must

also document training in emerging literacy, diversity in the classroom, and
licensing requirements for training in nutrition, safety, CPR, First Aid, and health.

[6] All children must have an annual well-child checkup by their health care provider
that conforms to EPSDT standards. Programs must provide vision, hearing, and
dental screenings directly or through contract with another agency.

[7] Support services include education services or job training for parents, parenting
support or training, parent involvement activities, health services for children,
information about nutrition, referral to social services, transition to kindergarten
activities, and family literacy and ESL.

[8] Programs are required to serve one snack to children who attend fewer than 5
hours per day and one snack plus one meal to children in class for 5 to 9 hours
per day. Children attending more than 8 hours per day must be provided one
snack and two meals or two snacks and one meal. Either the program or the
parent may provide the food.

Delaware

PERCENT OF STATE POPULATION ENROLLED

STATE SPENDING PER CHILD ENROLLED
(2008 DOLLARS)

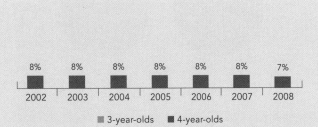

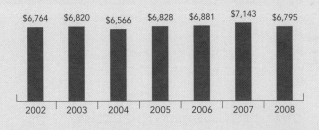

■ 3-year-olds ■ 4-year-olds

I n 1994, Delaware began funding preschool education through the Early Childhood Assistance Program (ECAP), which is modeled after the federal Head Start program. Programs are required to follow federal Head Start Performance Standards. The goal of ECAP is to increase access to comprehensive early childhood services for the state's 4-year-olds who are income-eligible for Head Start. ECAP funds are allocated to private agencies, public schools, and for-profit early care and education programs in addition to Head Start agencies. Ninety percent of enrolled children must come from families with an income at or below 100 percent of the federal poverty level. ECAP children also must have identified medical, developmental or social risk factors and 10 percent of the slots must be made available to children with disabilities. The selection and location of the ECAP grantees is guided by the Community Needs Assessment data. For the 2008-2009 program year, changes to the Head Start Act will require changes in state prekindergarten. One such change allows programs to accept children living in households 101 to 130 percent over poverty and still count them as income eligible, with certain restrictions.

In 2003, the state began using a mandatory curriculum framework for state-funded pre-K programs known as the Delaware Early Learning Foundations. This framework is now under revision and is aligned with K–12 performance indicators and standards. Delaware is working on a quality rating system for its early care and education programs, but it is not yet available to all programs and therefore a minimum rating for each setting is not yet required. A prekindergarten professional development system is also being designed that will be aligned with the state's professional development system for K–12.

ACCESS RANKINGS		RESOURCES RANKINGS	
4-YEAR-OLDS	3-YEAR-OLDS	STATE SPENDING	ALL REPORTED SPENDING
30	None Served	7	12

DELAWARE EARLY CHILDHOOD ASSISTANCE PROGRAM

ACCESS

Total state program enrollment 843

School districts that offer state program..........100% (counties)

Income requirement ....90% of children must
be at or below 100% FPL

Hours of operation............At least 3.5 hours/day, 5 days/week[1]

Operating schedule ....Determined locally[1]

Special education enrollment 1,336

Federally funded Head Start enrollment..........................1,639

State-funded Head Start enrollment ....843[2]

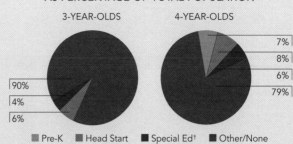

STATE PRE-K AND HEAD START ENROLLMENT AS PERCENTAGE OF TOTAL POPULATION

3-YEAR-OLDS: 90%, 4%, 6%

4-YEAR-OLDS: 7%, 8%, 6%, 79%

■ Pre-K ■ Head Start ■ Special Ed† ■ Other/None

† This number represents children in special education
who are not enrolled in state-funded pre-K or Head Start.

QUALITY STANDARDS CHECKLIST

POLICY	STATE PRE-K REQUIREMENT	BENCHMARK	DOES REQUIREMENT MEET BENCHMARK?
Early learning standards	Comprehensive	Comprehensive	☑
Teacher degree	CDA[3]	BA	☐
Teacher specialized training	Meets CDA requirements	Specializing in pre-K	☑
Assistant teacher degree	HSD[3]	CDA or equivalent	☐
Teacher in-service	15 clock hours[4]	At least 15 hours/year	☑
Maximum class size		20 or lower	☑
3-year-olds	NA		
4-year-olds	20		
Staff-child ratio		1:10 or better	☑
3-year-olds	NA		
4-year-olds	1:10		
Screening/referral and support services	Vision, hearing, health, developmental, dental, behavioral; and support services[5]	Vision, hearing, health; and at least 1 support service	☑
Meals	At least one meal and snack	At least 1/day	☑
Monitoring	Site visits and other monitoring	Site visits	☑

TOTAL BENCHMARKS MET

8

RESOURCES

Total state pre-K spending $5,727,800

Local match required?..No

State Head Start spending ....$5,727,800[6]

State spending per child enrolled..................................$6,795

All reported spending per child enrolled* $6,795

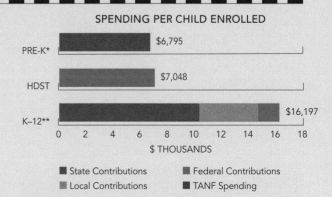

SPENDING PER CHILD ENROLLED

PRE-K*: $6,795

HDST: $7,048

K–12**: $16,197

$ THOUSANDS

■ State Contributions   ■ Federal Contributions
■ Local Contributions   ■ TANF Spending

* Pre-K programs may receive additional funds from federal or local sources
that are not included in this figure.

** K–12 expenditures include capital spending as well as current operating
expenditures.

Data are for the '07-'08 school year, unless otherwise noted.

[1] Half-day programs are funded to operate a minimum of 3.5 hours per day, and
many operate 4 hours per day. Most programs align with public school operating
schedules.

[2] This number represents ECAP enrollment. All state-funded Head Start enrollment
is through ECAP.

[3] New child care regulations came into effect in January 2008 that offer multiple
educational/training combinations to qualify for the position. ECAP follows
Head Start Performance Standards staffing requirements.

[4] All grantees, except school districts, are in licensed programs that are required to
have 18 clock hours per year.

[5] Support services include four annual parent conferences or home visits,
education services or job training for parents, parenting support or training,
parent involvement activities, health services for parents and children,
information about nutrition, referral to social services, transition to kindergarten
activities, and mental health services.

[6] ECAP is a state-funded Head Start model. All state pre-K spending is therefore
directed toward Head Start programs.

Florida

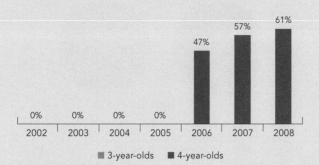

PERCENT OF STATE POPULATION ENROLLED

- 3-year-olds
- 4-year-olds

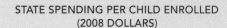

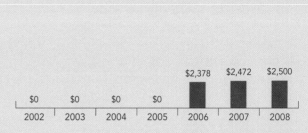

STATE SPENDING PER CHILD ENROLLED
(2008 DOLLARS)

In response to a 2002 state constitutional amendment requiring universal availability of preschool programs for all 4-year-olds whose parents want them to attend, Florida's Voluntary Prekindergarten (VPK) program was established in 2005. VPK became available across the entire state and served more than 100,000 children in its first year of operation.

Services are offered in a variety of settings by providers who meet the program's minimum requirements. These settings include licensed child care centers, licensed family child care homes, accredited nonpublic schools, accredited faith-based providers, and public schools. Participating local providers receive fixed funding based on a per-child amount. Funds are distributed through early learning coalitions, which are the local administrators of the program. Families may enroll children in any participating program where space is available.

Families must choose between two different versions of the VPK program—a school-year program totaling 540 instructional hours or a summer program totaling 300 instructional hours. The 540-hour school year program requires teachers to have a Child Development Associate (CDA) or equivalent credential while the 300-hour summer program requires teachers to hold at least a bachelor's degree.

For the 2007-2008 school year, the number of participating children increased by 10,000, and VPK received a 4.6 percent increase in the base student allocation.

The School Readiness Program, another Florida pre-K initiative, began in 1999 and expanded in 2001 when it incorporated two other state programs, the State Migrant Prekindergarten Program and the Prekindergarten Early Intervention Program. Early learning coalitions distribute federal and state dollars to support a broad range of early childhood programs and services through this initiative. Data in this report focus only on the VPK program.

ACCESS RANKINGS		RESOURCES RANKINGS	
4-YEAR-OLDS	3-YEAR-OLDS	STATE SPENDING	ALL REPORTED SPENDING
2	None Served	34	36

FLORIDA VOLUNTARY PREKINDERGARTEN PROGRAM

ACCESS

Total state program enrollment ....134,583[1]

School districts that offer state program ....100% (counties)

Income requirement ....None

Hours of operation ....Determined locally[2]

Operating schedule......540 hours/year (school-year program);
300 hours/year (summer program)[2]

Special education enrollment 17,790

Federally funded Head Start enrollment.........................33,470

State-funded Head Start enrollment 0

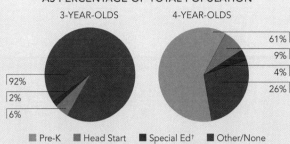

STATE PRE-K AND HEAD START ENROLLMENT AS PERCENTAGE OF TOTAL POPULATION

3-YEAR-OLDS
92%
2%
6%

4-YEAR-OLDS
61%
9%
4%
26%

■ Pre-K   ■ Head Start   ■ Special Ed[†]   ■ Other/None

[†] This number represents children in special education who are not enrolled in Head Start, but includes children who are enrolled in state-funded pre-K.

QUALITY STANDARDS CHECKLIST

POLICY	STATE PRE-K REQUIREMENT	BENCHMARK	DOES REQUIREMENT MEET BENCHMARK?
Early learning standards	Comprehensive	Comprehensive	☑
Teacher degree	BA (summer); CDA or equivalent (school year)[3]	BA	☐
Teacher specialized training	EC or EE certification (public and nonpublic - summer); Meets CDA requirements (school year)[3]	Specializing in pre-K	☐
Assistant teacher degree	40 clock hours[4]	CDA or equivalent	☐
Teacher in-service	10 clock hours/year[5]	At least 15 hours/year	☐
Maximum class size		20 or lower	☑
3-year-olds	NA		
4-year-olds	10 (summer); 18 (school year)		
Staff-child ratio		1:10 or better	☑
3-year-olds	NA		
4-year-olds	1:10[6]		
Screening/referral and support services	Determined locally[7]	Vision, hearing, health; and at least 1 support service	☐
Meals	Depend on length of program day[8]	At least 1/day	☐
Monitoring	Site visits and other monitoring	Site visits	☑

TOTAL BENCHMARKS MET

4

RESOURCES

Total state pre-K spending $336,469,116

Local match required? ....No

State spending per child enrolled $2,500

All reported spending per child enrolled* $2,500

SPENDING PER CHILD ENROLLED

PRE-K* $2,500

HDST $8,083

K–12** $12,241

0 2 4 6 8 10 12 14 16 18
$ THOUSANDS

■ State Contributions   ■ Federal Contributions
■ Local Contributions   ■ TANF Spending

* Pre-K programs may receive additional funds from federal or local sources that are not included in this figure.

**K–12 expenditures include capital spending as well as current operating expenditures.

Data are for the '07-'08 school year, unless otherwise noted.

[1] The total may contain a duplicate count of children served if a child enrolled at more than one coalition during the course of the year (e.g., a child moved location).

[2] VPK programs may choose to operate a summer program, totaling at least 300 hours of service, or a school year program, totaling at least 540 hours of service. The operating schedule and hours are determined locally, but the average number of hours per day for a 180-day, 540-hour program is 3 and the average number of hours per day for the 300-hour summer program is 7.5.

[3] Teacher qualification requirements are different for the summer and school year programs. Teachers in the summer programs are required either to be certified teachers or to have a BA in early childhood, primary or preschool education, family and consumer science, or elementary education. Teachers in the school year programs are required to have a CDA or equivalent and have completed a Department of Education course on emergent literacy.

[4] Assistant teachers do not have to meet any degree requirements, but must complete a 40-hour training for licensed child care providers.

[5] For the CDA or equivalent, the requirement is 10 clock hours per year. For the certified teacher, the requirement is 120 clock hours per 60 months.

[6] Summer programs have a maximum class size of 10 with one teacher. School year programs have one teacher for classes of up to 10 students, and must have a second staff member in classes of 11 students up to the maximum of 18 students.

[7] Public schools, Head Start, and subsidized child care programs are required to offer vision, hearing, and physical health screenings.

[8] Meals and snacks are required for full-day programs.

Georgia

PERCENT OF STATE POPULATION ENROLLED

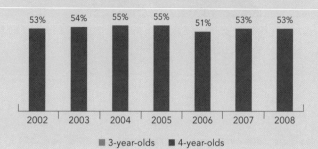

53% 54% 55% 55% 51% 53% 53%
2002 2003 2004 2005 2006 2007 2008

■ 3-year-olds ■ 4-year-olds

STATE SPENDING PER CHILD ENROLLED
(2008 DOLLARS)

$4,956 $4,933 $4,751 $4,577 $4,370 $4,354 $4,249
2002 2003 2004 2005 2006 2007 2008

Georgia became the first state to offer a universally available preschool education program for 4-year-olds in 1995. Although Georgia's Pre-K Program has operated since 1993, it was not always universally available. The program provides services through a variety of settings including public schools, Head Start programs, private child care centers, faith-based organizations, military facilities, and state colleges and universities. The Pre-K Program receives funds from the Georgia lottery. Funding for individual programs is determined by the number of students in the class, teacher credentials, and the program zone (metropolitan or non-metropolitan area).

All Georgia Pre-K programs are required to follow the Bright from the Start Pre-K Operating Guidelines and must use Georgia's Pre-K Content Standards to guide instruction. The Pre-K Content Standards are aligned with both the Georgia Performance Standards for Kindergarten and the Georgia Early Learning Standards for children from birth through age 3. On-site program monitoring assures adherence to the quality standards. Beginning in the 2008-2009 school year, teacher assistants are required to have a minimum of a CDA.

The Georgia Pre-K Child Assessment Program was implemented statewide during the 2006-2007 school year and is based on the Work Sampling System. Teachers have been trained to use the pre-K assessment to individualize instruction and to document and inform parents of children's progress. Parents receive two progress reports a year that are linked to the assessment program.

ACCESS RANKINGS		RESOURCES RANKINGS	
4-YEAR-OLDS	3-YEAR-OLDS	STATE SPENDING	ALL REPORTED SPENDING
3	None Served	15	22

GEORGIA PRE-K PROGRAM

ACCESS

Total state program enrollment 76,491

School districts that offer state program ....100% (counties)

Income requirement ....None

Hours of operation ....6.5 hours/day, 5 days/week

Operating schedule ....Academic year

Special education enrollment 9,300

Federally funded Head Start enrollment 21,923

State-funded Head Start enrollment 0

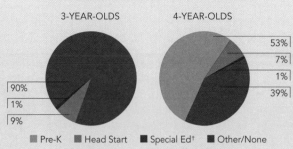

STATE PRE-K AND HEAD START ENROLLMENT AS PERCENTAGE OF TOTAL POPULATION

3-YEAR-OLDS

4-YEAR-OLDS

90%
1%
9%

53%
7%
1%
39%

■ Pre-K ■ Head Start ■ Special Ed† ■ Other/None

† This number represents children in special education who are not enrolled in state-funded pre-K or Head Start.

QUALITY STANDARDS CHECKLIST

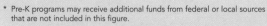

POLICY	STATE PRE-K REQUIREMENT	BENCHMARK	DOES REQUIREMENT MEET BENCHMARK?
Early learning standards	Comprehensive	Comprehensive	☑
Teacher degree	AA or Montessori diploma	BA	☐
Teacher specialized training	Degree and certification in ECE or meet Montessori requirements[1]	Specializing in pre-K	☑
Assistant teacher degree	HSD[2]	CDA or equivalent	☐
Teacher in-service	15 clock hours	At least 15 hours/year	☑
Maximum class size		20 or lower	☑
3-year-olds	NA		
4-year-olds	20		
Staff-child ratio		1:10 or better	☑
3-year-olds	NA		
4-year-olds	1:10		
Screening/referral and support services	Vision, hearing, health, dental, developmental; and support services[3]	Vision, hearing, health; and at least 1 support service	☑
Meals	Lunch	At least 1/day	☑
Monitoring	Site visits and other monitoring	Site visits	☑

TOTAL BENCHMARKS MET

8

RESOURCES

Total state pre-K spending $325,000,000

Local match required? ....No

State spending per child enrolled $4,249

All reported spending per child enrolled* $4,249

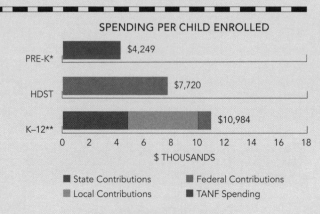

SPENDING PER CHILD ENROLLED

PRE-K* $4,249

HDST $7,720

K–12** $10,984

0 2 4 6 8 10 12 14 16 18
$ THOUSANDS

■ State Contributions   ■ Federal Contributions
■ Local Contributions   ■ TANF Spending

* Pre-K programs may receive additional funds from federal or local sources that are not included in this figure.

**K–12 expenditures include capital spending as well as current operating expenditures.

Data are for the '07-'08 school year, unless otherwise noted.

[1] Local school systems typically require that Pre-K teachers be certified.

[2] Beginning in the 2008-2009 program year, the minimum requirement for teacher assistants will be a CDA.

[3] Support services include two annual parent conferences or home visits, parent involvement activities, transition to kindergarten activities, and other locally determined support services.

Hawaii

NO PROGRAM

H awaii does not have a state-funded preschool initiative meeting the criteria set forth in this report. However, the state does offer funding for initiatives that provide some support for early childhood education.

Since the early 1980s, the Preschool Open Doors Project has provided low-income parents with subsidy payments allowing them to purchase preschool for their 4-year-olds and, on a case-by-case basis, 3-year-olds with special needs. Parents select their own program, but the subsidy is delivered directly to the chosen provider. Children are eligible for the program if their family income is below 85 percent of the state median income, with family income reassessed every 6 months. Because the Preschool Open Doors Project does not necessarily offer continuous enrollment to children once they initially qualify, this initiative is best viewed as a type of support for working families rather than as a dedicated preschool education program.

In 2002, Hawaii established the Pre-Plus Program, which supports construction of prekindergarten facilities at public school sites but does not directly fund educational services for children. Seventeen Pre-Plus facilities have been constructed but there currently are no additional funds available for further construction.

During the 2006-2007 school year, the state established a third initiative, Junior Kindergarten. This program offers educational services for children who are age eligible for kindergarten but turn 5 later than July 31, making them younger than most children in the regular kindergarten program. Children may also be enrolled in Junior Kindergarten if the results of school assessments show that they are not developmentally ready for kindergarten despite being age eligible. Depending on the child's readiness and individual program practices, children may attend kindergarten or first grade after completing a year of Junior Kindergarten.

Additionally, in July of 2008 a bill was passed to establish an early learning system known as Keiki First Steps, which is designed to offer a spectrum of early learning opportunities for children throughout the state from birth until kindergarten entry. This legislation created an Early Learning Council that will develop and administer the early learning system, establish the Keiki First Steps grant program, and promote the development of additional early learning facilities.

ACCESS RANKINGS		RESOURCES RANKINGS	
4-YEAR-OLDS	3-YEAR-OLDS	STATE SPENDING	ALL REPORTED SPENDING
No Program		No Program	

ACCESS

Total state program enrollment 0

School districts that offer state program.........................NA

Income requirement ....NA

Hours of operation ....NA

Operating schedule ....NA

Special education enrollment 1,543

Federally funded Head Start enrollment....................2,667

State-funded Head Start enrollment 0

STATE PRE-K AND HEAD START ENROLLMENT AS PERCENTAGE OF TOTAL POPULATION

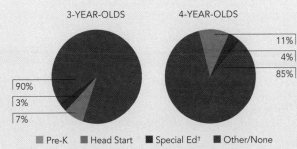

3-YEAR-OLDS   4-YEAR-OLDS

90%   11%
3%   4%
7%   85%

■ Pre-K   ■ Head Start   ■ Special Ed†   ■ Other/None

† This number represents children in special education who are not enrolled in Head Start.

QUALITY STANDARDS CHECKLIST

TOTAL BENCHMARKS MET
No Program

RESOURCES

Total state pre-K spending...$0

Local match required? ....NA

State Head Start spending..$0

State spending per child enrolled $0

All reported spending per child enrolled*......................$0

* Pre-K programs may receive additional funds from federal or local sources that are not included in this figure.

** K–12 expenditures include capital spending as well as current operating expenditures.

Data are for the '07-'08 school year, unless otherwise noted.

SPENDING PER CHILD ENROLLED

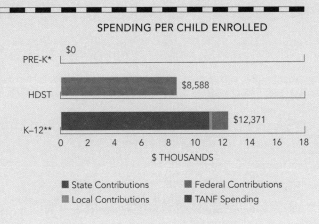

PRE-K* $0

HDST $8,588

K–12** $12,371

0   2   4   6   8   10   12   14   16   18
$ THOUSANDS

■ State Contributions   ■ Federal Contributions
■ Local Contributions   ■ TANF Spending

Idaho

NO PROGRAM

ACCESS RANKINGS	
4-YEAR-OLDS	3-YEAR-OLDS
No Program	

RESOURCES RANKINGS	
STATE SPENDING	ALL REPORTED SPENDING
No Program	

ACCESS

Total state program enrollment 0

School districts that offer state program.........................NA

Income requirement ....NA

Hours of operation ....NA

Operating schedule ....NA

Special education enrollment 2,165

Federally funded Head Start enrollment....................3,178

State-funded Head Start enrollment 191

STATE PRE-K AND HEAD START ENROLLMENT AS PERCENTAGE OF TOTAL POPULATION

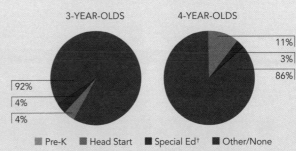

3-YEAR-OLDS

4-YEAR-OLDS

92%
4%
4%

11%
3%
86%

■ Pre-K ■ Head Start ■ Special Ed† ■ Other/None

† This number represents children in special education who are not enrolled in Head Start.

QUALITY STANDARDS CHECKLIST

TOTAL
BENCHMARKS
MET

No
Program

RESOURCES

Total state pre-K spending...$0

Local match required? ....NA

State Head Start spending................................$1,500,000

State spending per child enrolled $0

All reported spending per child enrolled*......................$0

* Pre-K programs may receive additional funds from federal or local sources that are not included in this figure.

**K–12 expenditures include capital spending as well as current operating expenditures.

Data are for the '07-'08 school year, unless otherwise noted.

SPENDING PER CHILD ENROLLED

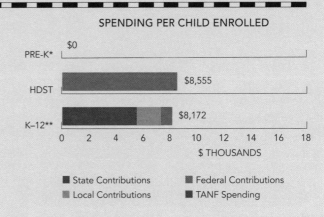

PRE-K* $0

HDST $8,555

K–12** $8,172

0   2   4   6   8   10   12   14   16   18

$ THOUSANDS

■ State Contributions   ■ Federal Contributions
■ Local Contributions   ■ TANF Spending

Illinois

PERCENT OF STATE POPULATION ENROLLED

STATE SPENDING PER CHILD ENROLLED
(2008 DOLLARS)

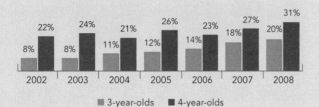

■ 3-year-olds ■ 4-year-olds

T he Prekindergarten Program for At-Risk Children, Illinois' first preschool initiative, was established in 1985 in response to calls for state education reform. Funds for the program have been provided through the state's Early Childhood Block Grant (ECBG) since 1998, and at least 11 percent of the block grant must be used to serve children age 3 and under. ECBG supports preschool education programs, provides parent training, and coordinates services for at-risk infants and toddlers.

In 2006, a new preschool initiative, Preschool for All, was established with the goal of offering access to preschool to every 3- and 4-year-old in the state. Preschool for All is available in all counties in Illinois and all public school districts and private providers are encouraged to apply for grants. Programs serving at-risk children are the first priority for new funding during the expansion, followed by programs serving families earning up to four times the federal poverty level. Criteria for at-risk status is determined by individual programs, based on needs identified by districts or agencies in their grant proposals. Among the types of risk factors considered are developmental delay, low parental education, poverty, exposure to drug or alcohol abuse in the family, and history of abuse, neglect, or family violence.

In an effort to continue moving toward the goal of providing access to all of the state's 3- and 4-year-olds whose parents wish them to attend, Illinois increased funding for the 2007-2008 program year by more than $26 million and increased enrollment by 6,622. Preschool for All is expected to be fully funded by the year 2012. At that time, programs will be allowed to use state dollars to serve children who are not at risk, and it is expected that a total of 190,000 children will be served annually.

ACCESS RANKINGS		RESOURCES RANKINGS	
4-YEAR-OLDS	3-YEAR-OLDS	STATE SPENDING	ALL REPORTED SPENDING
11	1	24	28

ILLINOIS PRESCHOOL FOR ALL

ACCESS

Total state program enrollment 91,808

School districts that offer state program ....100% (counties)

Income requirement ....None[1]

Hours of operation ....2.5 hours/day, 5 days/week

Operating schedule ....Academic year

Special education enrollment 21,580

Federally funded Head Start enrollment 34,178

State-funded Head Start enrollment 0

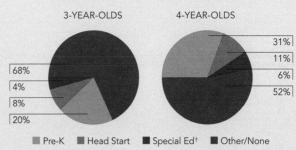

STATE PRE-K AND HEAD START ENROLLMENT
AS PERCENTAGE OF TOTAL POPULATION

3-YEAR-OLDS   4-YEAR-OLDS

68%
4%
8%
20%

31%
11%
6%
52%

■ Pre-K ■ Head Start ■ Special Ed[†] ■ Other/None

[†] This number represents children in special education who are not enrolled in Head Start but may be enrolled in state-funded pre-K.

QUALITY STANDARDS CHECKLIST

POLICY	STATE PRE-K REQUIREMENT	BENCHMARK	DOES REQUIREMENT MEET BENCHMARK?
Early learning standards	Comprehensive	Comprehensive	☑
Teacher degree	BA	BA	☑
Teacher specialized training	EC certificate[2]	Specializing in pre-K	☑
Assistant teacher degree	AA	CDA or equivalent	☑
Teacher in-service	120 clock hours/5 years	At least 15 hours/year	☑
Maximum class size		20 or lower	☑
3-year-olds	20		
4-year-olds	20		
Staff-child ratio		1:10 or better	☑
3-year-olds	1:10		
4-year-olds	1:10		
Screening/referral and support services	Vision, hearing, health, developmental; and support services[3]	Vision, hearing, health; and at least 1 support service	☑
Meals	Snack[4]	At least 1/day	☐
Monitoring	Site visits and other monitoring	Site visits	☑

TOTAL BENCHMARKS MET

9

RESOURCES

Total state pre-K spending $309,596,682

Local match required? ....No

State spending per child enrolled $3,372

All reported spending per child enrolled* $3,372

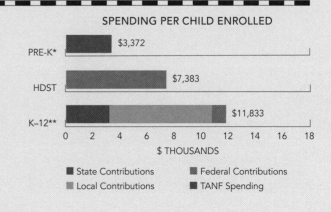

SPENDING PER CHILD ENROLLED

PRE-K* $3,372

HDST $7,383

K–12** $11,833

0 2 4 6 8 10 12 14 16 18
$ THOUSANDS

■ State Contributions   ■ Federal Contributions
■ Local Contributions   ■ TANF Spending

* Pre-K programs may receive additional funds from federal or local sources that are not included in this figure.

**K–12 expenditures include capital spending as well as current operating expenditures.

Data are for the '07-'08 school year, unless otherwise noted.

[1] Eligibility criteria are determined locally, but low-income status may be one of the risk factors considered.

[2] The early childhood certificate covers birth through age 8.

[3] Support services include education services or job training for parents, parenting support or training, parent involvement activities, referral to social services, and transition to kindergarten activities. The number of required annual parent conferences or home visits is locally determined.

[4] Children in full-day programs receive lunch and a snack.

Indiana

NO PROGRAM

ACCESS RANKINGS		RESOURCES RANKINGS	
4-YEAR-OLDS	3-YEAR-OLDS	STATE SPENDING	ALL REPORTED SPENDING
No Program		No Program	

ACCESS

Total state program enrollment 0

School districts that offer state program........................NA

Income requirement ....NA

Hours of operation ....NA

Operating schedule ....NA

Special education enrollment 10,999

Federally funded Head Start enrollment..................11,870

State-funded Head Start enrollment 0

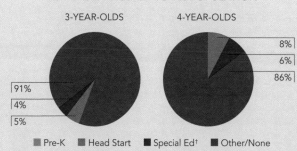

STATE PRE-K AND HEAD START ENROLLMENT AS PERCENTAGE OF TOTAL POPULATION

3-YEAR-OLDS   4-YEAR-OLDS

91%
4%
5%

8%
6%
86%

■ Pre-K   ■ Head Start   ■ Special Ed†   ■ Other/None

† This number represents children in special education who are not enrolled in Head Start.

QUALITY STANDARDS CHECKLIST

TOTAL
BENCHMARKS
MET

No
Program

RESOURCES

Total state pre-K spending...$0

Local match required? ....NA

State Head Start spending...$0

State spending per child enrolled $0

All reported spending per child enrolled* $0

* Pre-K programs may receive additional funds from federal or local sources that are not included in this figure.

**K–12 expenditures include capital spending as well as current operating expenditures.

Data are for the '07-'08 school year, unless otherwise noted.

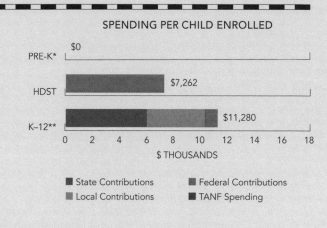

SPENDING PER CHILD ENROLLED

PRE-K* $0

HDST $7,262

K–12** $11,280

0   2   4   6   8   10   12   14   16   18
$ THOUSANDS

■ State Contributions   ■ Federal Contributions
■ Local Contributions   ■ TANF Spending

Iowa

PERCENT OF STATE POPULATION ENROLLED

STATE SPENDING PER CHILD ENROLLED
(2008 DOLLARS)

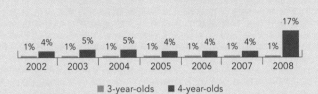

■ 3-year-olds   ■ 4-year-olds

In 1989, Iowa began to offer the prekindergarten initiative *Shared Visions*, which serves 3-, 4-, and 5-year-olds in full- or part-day programs. Through a competitive grant process, funds are distributed directly to public schools, private agencies, faith-based centers and Head Start programs. Those programs can choose to subcontract with other programs located in the same types of settings. Income is the primary risk factor used to determine eligibility, and at least 80 percent of children in each classroom must be eligible to receive free lunch. However, up to 20 percent of children can be eligible based on secondary risk factors. Secondary risk factors include developmental delay, homelessness, low birth weight, or having a parent who has a substance abuse problem or is incarcerated.

Each grantee of the *Shared Visions* program decides how to tailor services to meet local needs such as determining operating schedules and how sliding payment scales will be used for children from over-income families. The *Shared Visions* initiative was flat funded from 1995 until 2007, leading to service cuts or shorter program days for some grantees as well causing some grantees to increase their use of local funds. However, for the first time in more than a decade, in fiscal year 2008 state funding levels increased for Iowa's *Shared Visions*, providing a 2 percent increase overall.

In the 2007-2008 program year, the state started an initiative designed to be available to all 4-year-old children known as the Statewide Voluntary Preschool Program (SVPP). The program is located in 18 percent of Iowa's school districts and serves more than 5,000 4-year-old children for a minimum of 10 hours per week. The Preschool Program only provides funding for 4-year-olds although some 3- and 5-year-old children may also be enrolled in the program. To be eligible for the Preschool Program, children must be 4 years old and live in Iowa although they do not have to be a resident of the school district. A sliding payment scale may apply to children not meeting free and reduced-price lunch qualifications; however, this is determined locally. In fiscal year 2008, total spending was $14,670,000 coming from the general revenue fund. Public schools receive Preschool Program funding directly from the state but may subcontract with Head Start agencies, private child care, and faith-based centers.

The first two pages of this state profile document Iowa's overall contributions and commitment to state prekindergarten, including state spending and enrollment for both *Shared Visions* and the Statewide Voluntary Preschool Program. The third page focuses exclusively on the *Shared Visions* and the final page presents specific details about the Statewide Voluntary Preschool Program.

STATE OVERVIEW

Total state program enrollment 7,367

Total state spending $22,391,481

State spending per child enrolled $3,039

All reported spending per child enrolled* $4,932

STATE PRE-K AND HEAD START ENROLLMENT AS PERCENTAGE OF TOTAL POPULATION

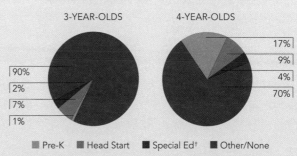

3-YEAR-OLDS

90%
2%
7%
1%

4-YEAR-OLDS

17%
9%
4%
70%

■ Pre-K   ■ Head Start   ■ Special Ed†   ■ Other/None

† This number represents children in special education who are not enrolled in Head Start but may be enrolled in state-funded pre-K.

SPENDING PER CHILD ENROLLED

IA PGMS* $4,932

HDST $7,805

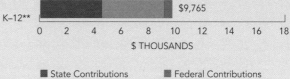

K–12** $9,765

0   2   4   6   8   10   12   14   16   18

$ THOUSANDS

■ State Contributions   ■ Federal Contributions
■ Local Contributions   ■ TANF Spending

* Pre-K programs may receive additional funds from federal or local sources that are not included in this figure.

** K–12 expenditures include capital spending as well as current operating expenditures.

Data are for the '07-'08 school year, unless otherwise noted.

ACCESS RANKINGS	
4-YEAR-OLDS	3-YEAR-OLDS
20	20

RESOURCES RANKINGS	
STATE SPENDING	ALL REPORTED SPENDING
29	18

IOWA SHARED VISIONS

ACCESS

Total state program enrollment 2,242

School districts that offer state program ....10%[1]

Income requirement ....80% of children must
be below 130% FPL

Hours of operation ....Determined locally[2]

Operating schedule ....Determined locally[2]

Special education enrollment 3,339

Federally funded Head Start enrollment...........................5,982

State-funded Head Start enrollment 0

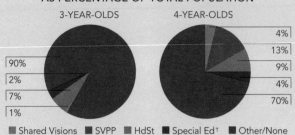

STATE PRE-K AND HEAD START ENROLLMENT AS PERCENTAGE OF TOTAL POPULATION

3-YEAR-OLDS
90%
2%
7%
1%

4-YEAR-OLDS
4%
13%
9%
4%
70%

■ Shared Visions ■ SVPP ■ HdSt ■ Special Ed[†] ■ Other/None

[†] This number represents children in special education who are not enrolled in Head Start but may be enrolled in state-funded pre-K.

QUALITY STANDARDS CHECKLIST

POLICY	STATE PRE-K REQUIREMENT	BENCHMARK	DOES REQUIREMENT MEET BENCHMARK?
Early learning standards	Comprehensive	Comprehensive	☑
Teacher degree	BA (public); CDA (nonpublic)[3]	BA	☐
Teacher specialized training	EC teaching endorsement (public),[4] Meets CDA requirements (nonpublic)	Specializing in pre-K	☑
Assistant teacher degree	HSD (public and nonpublic)[5]	CDA or equivalent	☐
Teacher in-service	6 credit hours/5 years (public); None (nonpublic)[5]	At least 15 hours/year	☐
Maximum class size		20 or lower	☑
3-year-olds	20		
4-year-olds	20		
Staff-child ratio		1:10 or better	☑
3-year-olds	1:8		
4-year-olds	1:8		
Screening/referral and support services	Vision, hearing, health, dental, developmental; and support services[6]	Vision, hearing, health; and at least 1 support service	☑
Meals	Lunch and snack[7]	At least 1/day	☑
Monitoring	Other monitoring[8]	Site visits	☐

TOTAL BENCHMARKS MET

6

RESOURCES

Total state pre-K spending $7,721,481

Local match required?...............Yes, 20% of total grant amount[9]

State spending per child enrolled $3,444

All reported spending per child enrolled* $9,664

* Pre-K programs may receive additional funds from federal or local sources that are not included in this figure.

**K–12 expenditures include capital spending as well as current operating expenditures.

Data are for the '07-'08 school year, unless otherwise noted.

SPENDING PER CHILD ENROLLED

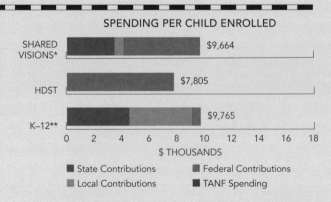

SHARED VISIONS* $9,664

HDST $7,805

K–12** $9,765

0 2 4 6 8 10 12 14 16 18
$ THOUSANDS

■ State Contributions ■ Federal Contributions
■ Local Contributions ■ TANF Spending

[1] In addition, 36 Shared Visions programs are offered by Head Start grantees, and 14 are offered in child care centers.

[2] Programs operate an average of 6.5 hours per day, 4.7 days per week, and generally operate during the academic year.

[3] Teachers in nonpublic settings follow NAEYC standards, which require a minimum of a CDA.

[4] Required endorsements cover children from birth to age 5, or from birth to age 8, with or without special education.

[5] Teachers employed in school district programs must renew their license every 5 years, including 6 credit hours of training. There is no specific requirement for the amount of in-service training for the remaining grantees, although most do provide at least 15 clock hours per year.

[6] Although Shared Visions does not have specific requirements for screening and referral, applicants are required to address the types of screening and referral that will be provided. All Shared Visions programs provide screening and referral for vision, hearing, and health. The number of required parent conferences is not specified in state regulations. Additional support services include parenting support or training, parent involvement activities, health services for children, information about nutrition, and referral to social services.

[7] Applicants for Shared Visions funding are required through their grant applications to address meals and meet the requirements of NAEYC accreditation. The specific meals offered depend on the hours of operation, but are required by NAEYC criteria.

[8] Monitoring information is collected through periodic program evaluation by an outside agency.

[9] While the local match requirement is 20 percent, the sources are determined locally and local contributions have exceeded the required amount in recent years.

IOWA STATEWIDE VOLUNTARY PRESCHOOL PROGRAM

ACCESS

Total state program enrollment 5,125

School districts that offer state program ....18%[1]

Income requirement ....None

Hours of operation ....Determined locally[2]

Operating schedule ....Academic year

Special education enrollment 3,339

Federally funded Head Start enrollment 5,982

State-funded Head Start enrollment 0

STATE PRE-K AND HEAD START ENROLLMENT AS PERCENTAGE OF TOTAL POPULATION

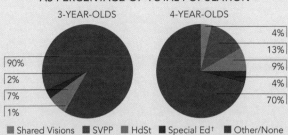

3-YEAR-OLDS
- 90%
- 2%
- 7%
- 1%

4-YEAR-OLDS
- 4%
- 13%
- 9%
- 4%
- 70%

■ Shared Visions ■ SVPP ■ HdSt ■ Special Ed† ■ Other/None

† This number represents children in special education who are not enrolled in Head Start but may be enrolled in state-funded pre-K.

QUALITY STANDARDS CHECKLIST

POLICY	STATE PRE-K REQUIREMENT	BENCHMARK	DOES REQUIREMENT MEET BENCHMARK?
Early learning standards	Comprehensive	Comprehensive	☑
Teacher degree	BA (public and nonpublic)	BA	☑
Teacher specialized training	EC teaching endorsement[3]	Specializing in pre-K	☑
Assistant teacher degree	CDA or Iowa Para-educator certificate (public and nonpublic)[4]	CDA or equivalent	☐
Teacher in-service	6 credit hours/5 years	At least 15 hours/year	☑
Maximum class size		20 or lower	☑
3-year-olds	20		
4-year-olds	20		
Staff-child ratio		1:10 or better	☑
3-year-olds	1:10		
4-year-olds	1:10		
Screening/referral and support services	Vision, hearing, health, developmental; and support services[5]	Vision, hearing, health; and at least 1 support service	☑
Meals	Snack[6]	At least 1/day	☐
Monitoring	None[7]	Site visits	☐

TOTAL BENCHMARKS MET

7

RESOURCES

Total state pre-K spending ....$14,670,000[8]

Local match required? ....No

State spending per child enrolled $2,862

All reported spending per child enrolled* $2,862

SPENDING PER CHILD ENROLLED

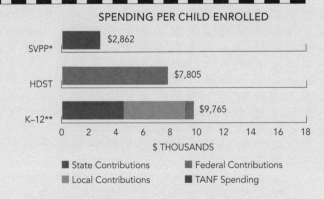

- SVPP* $2,862
- HDST $7,805
- K–12** $9,765

$ THOUSANDS (0 2 4 6 8 10 12 14 16 18)

■ State Contributions ■ Federal Contributions
■ Local Contributions ■ TANF Spending

* Pre-K programs may receive additional funds from federal or local sources that are not included in this figure.

** K–12 expenditures include capital spending as well as current operating expenditures.

Data are for the '07-'08 school year, unless otherwise noted.

---

1 Two of the school districts created a consortium including 1 or 2 additional districts so while the Department of Education funded 64 districts, with the consortium there are 67 districts.

2 A minimum of 10 hours per week, 360 hours per year must be provided and funded. Most programs operate an average of 13 hours or 4 days per week.

3 Required endorsements cover children from birth to age 5, or from birth to age 8, with or without special education.

4 Assistant teachers must have either a CDA or an Iowa Para-educator certificate. The certificate requires 90 hours of generalized education courses plus 45 hours of ECE specific training.

5 Support services include two parent conferences, one home visit and one family night, as well as parenting support or training, parent involvement activities, health services for children, and referral for social services.

6 According to Iowa program standards additional meals must be provided if the program is longer than 10 hours per week.

7 Site visits will be conducted once every 5 years beginning in the 2008-2009 school year starting with districts awarded in the 2007-2008 school year.

8 This is the total spending allocation and may not reflect the final spending amount for 2007-2008.

Kansas

PERCENT OF STATE POPULATION ENROLLED

STATE SPENDING PER CHILD ENROLLED
(2008 DOLLARS)

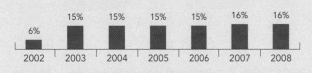

6% 2002
15% 2003
15% 2004
15% 2005
15% 2006
16% 2007
16% 2008

■ 3-year-olds   ■ 4-year-olds

$2,688 2002
$2,221 2003
$2,163 2004
$2,123 2005
$2,807 2006
$2,749 2007
$2,843 2008

I n 1998, Kansas established its At-Risk Four-Year-Old Children Preschool Program, which operates exclusively in public schools. Children are eligible for the program if they meet one of the following eight criteria: academic delay based upon validated assessment, developmental delay, English Language Learner status, migrant status, free lunch eligibility, having a parent lacking a high school diploma or GED, having a single parent, or referral from the Social and Rehabilitative Services agency. Local school districts receive a per-child allocation of state funds based upon the September 20 state enrollment count.

Kansas increased its requirements for the At-Risk Four-Year-Old Children Preschool Program for the 2007-2008 school year. For the first time, class size was limited to 20 children, with a staff to child ratio of 1:10 and teachers and assistant teachers were required to have at least 15 hours of in-service training. Kansas also implemented its Early Learning Standards during this school year. Staff from many state and local agencies and organizations serving children from birth to third grade and their families worked together to develop these early learning standards as well as core competencies for staff.

Kansas began a small pilot of a prekindergarten program during the 2006-2007 school year. This initiative expanded in 2007-2008 to serve 1,500 4-year-olds in 14 of 105 counties in the state.

Kansas' Parents as Teachers initiative is a separate program that serves children from birth to age 3 and their families. Agencies at the state and local levels collaborate to meet the needs of the children and families served in the program.

ACCESS RANKINGS		RESOURCES RANKINGS	
4-YEAR-OLDS	3-YEAR-OLDS	STATE SPENDING	ALL REPORTED SPENDING
21	None Served	31	34

KANSAS AT-RISK FOUR-YEAR-OLD CHILDREN PRESCHOOL PROGRAM

ACCESS

Total state program enrollment 6,281

School districts that offer state program 56%

Income requirement ....130% FPL[1]

Hours of operation ....At least 2.5 hours/day,
4 or 5 days/week

Operating schedule ....Academic year

Special education enrollment 5,716

Federally funded Head Start enrollment 6,503

State-funded Head Start enrollment 0

STATE PRE-K AND HEAD START ENROLLMENT AS PERCENTAGE OF TOTAL POPULATION

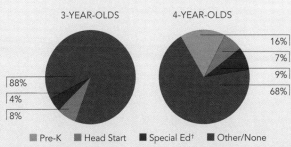

3-YEAR-OLDS

4-YEAR-OLDS

88%
4%
8%

16%
7%
9%
68%

■ Pre-K ■ Head Start ■ Special Ed[†] ■ Other/None

[†] This number represents children in special education who are not enrolled in Head Start but may be enrolled in state-funded pre-K.

QUALITY STANDARDS CHECKLIST

POLICY	STATE PRE-K REQUIREMENT	BENCHMARK	DOES REQUIREMENT MEET BENCHMARK?
Early learning standards	Comprehensive[2]	Comprehensive	☑
Teacher degree	BA[3]	BA	☑
Teacher specialized training	EE license, ECE license, ECE SpEd license, EC Unified (B–K, B–3rd grade) license, or EE license ECE endorsement[3]	Specializing in pre-K	☐
Assistant teacher degree	CDA	CDA or equivalent	☑
Teacher in-service	15 clock hours[4]	At least 15 hours/year	☑
Maximum class size		20 or lower	☑
3-year-olds	NA		
4-year-olds	20[5]		
Staff-child ratio		1:10 or better	☑
3-year-olds	NA		
4-year-olds	1:10[5]		
Screening/referral and support services	Vision, hearing, health, dental, developmental; and support services[6]	Vision, hearing, health; and at least 1 support service	☑
Meals	Snack	At least 1/day	☐
Monitoring	Other monitoring	Site visits	☐

TOTAL BENCHMARKS MET

7

RESOURCES

Total state pre-K spending $17,857,511

Local match required? ....No

State spending per child enrolled $2,843

All reported spending per child enrolled* $2,843

SPENDING PER CHILD ENROLLED

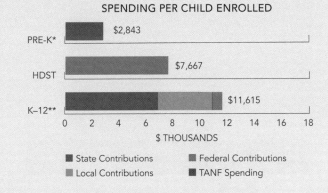

PRE-K* $2,843

HDST $7,667

K–12** $11,615

0 2 4 6 8 10 12 14 16 18
$ THOUSANDS

■ State Contributions ■ Federal Contributions
■ Local Contributions ■ TANF Spending

* Pre-K programs may receive additional funds from federal or local sources that are not included in this figure.

** K–12 expenditures include capital spending as well as current operating expenditures.

Data are for the '07-'08 school year, unless otherwise noted.

[1] Eligibility for free lunch is one of eight risk factors used to determine eligibility for this program. Every child must have at least one risk factor.

[2] The state adopted comprehensive early learning standards. Training on the Kansas Early Learning Standards occurred during the 2007-2008 school year.

[3] Teachers must have a current license. An early childhood license is recommended.

[4] Beginning with the 2007-2008 school year, all teachers are required to have 15 clock hours of professional development each year.

[5] Beginning with the 2007-2008 school year, a class size of 20 children and a staff-child ratio of 1:10 is required.

[6] Support services include two annual parent conferences or home visits, parenting support or training, referral to social services, and transition to kindergarten activities.

Kentucky

PERCENT OF STATE POPULATION ENROLLED

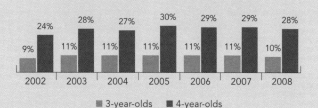

	2002	2003	2004	2005	2006	2007	2008
3-year-olds	9%	11%	11%	11%	11%	11%	10%
4-year-olds	24%	28%	27%	30%	29%	29%	28%

■ 3-year-olds ■ 4-year-olds

STATE SPENDING PER CHILD ENROLLED
(2008 DOLLARS)

2002	2003	2004	2005	2006	2007	2008
$3,486	$3,204	$2,766	$2,823	$2,635	$3,679	$3,497

In response to the Kentucky Education Reform Act of 1990, the Kentucky Preschool Program was established. All of the state's 4-year-olds and 3-year-olds with disabilities are eligible to participate in the program. Children who do not meet these eligibility requirements may also participate, but are funded by the district or tuition rather than the state. Eligibility was extended to additional children beginning with the 2006-2007 school year when income eligibility was raised from 130 percent of the federal poverty level (FPL) to 150 percent of FPL.

Funds for the Kentucky Preschool Program are allocated to local school districts through a school funding formula. School districts may contract with private child care centers, Head Start, and special education providers to offer preschool. In 2006-2007, Kentucky increased its biennium budget for state preschool education by $23.5 million, leading to notable increases in per child spending.

In the 2006-2007 school year, the Kentucky Department of Education implemented a process to identify high-quality state-funded preschool classrooms, which are known as Classrooms of Excellence. Preschool teachers must complete a rigorous application process to qualify. This process includes intensive self-study, implementation of the early childhood standards, early childhood certification, and regional or national accreditation.

The Prichard Committee, with funding from Pre-K Now, created the Strong Start initiative in Kentucky during the 2008-2009 school year. This program aims to create public/private partnerships to make high-quality preschool available to all 3- and 4-year-olds from families with incomes up to 200 percent FPL.

Kentucky also passed the Kentucky Student Intervention, the state's version of Response to Intervention, which includes preschool. This new regulation requires programs to implement relevant, research-based instruction and interventions by qualified personnel.

ACCESS RANKINGS		RESOURCES RANKINGS	
4-YEAR-OLDS	3-YEAR-OLDS	STATE SPENDING	ALL REPORTED SPENDING
13	6	23	19

KENTUCKY PRESCHOOL PROGRAM

ACCESS

Total state program enrollment ....21,485[1]

School districts that offer state program 100%

Income requirement ....150% FPL

Hours of operation ....2.5 hours/day, + meal time, 4 or 5 days/week

Operating schedule ....Academic year

Special education enrollment ....12,009[2]

Federally funded Head Start enrollment.........................14,774

State-funded Head Start enrollment 0

STATE PRE-K AND HEAD START ENROLLMENT AS PERCENTAGE OF TOTAL POPULATION

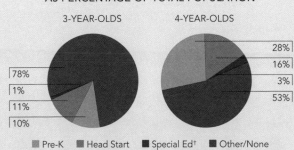

3-YEAR-OLDS: 78%, 1%, 11%, 10%

4-YEAR-OLDS: 28%, 16%, 3%, 53%

■ Pre-K ■ Head Start ■ Special Ed[†] ■ Other/None

[†] This number represents children in special education who are not enrolled in state-funded pre-K or Head Start.

QUALITY STANDARDS CHECKLIST

POLICY	STATE PRE-K REQUIREMENT	BENCHMARK	DOES REQUIREMENT MEET BENCHMARK?
Early learning standards	Comprehensive	Comprehensive	☑
Teacher degree	BA[3]	BA	☑
Teacher specialized training	Interdisciplinary ECE - Birth to K	Specializing in pre-K	☑
Assistant teacher degree	HSD (public); None (nonpublic)[4]	CDA or equivalent	☐
Teacher in-service	28 clock hours	At least 15 hours/year	☑
Maximum class size		20 or lower	☑
3-year-olds	20		
4-year-olds	20		
Staff-child ratio		1:10 or better	☑
3-year-olds	1:10		
4-year-olds	1:10		
Screening/referral and support services	Vision, hearing, health, developmental; and support services[5]	Vision, hearing, health; and at least 1 support service	☑
Meals	Breakfast or lunch[6]	At least 1/day	☑
Monitoring	Other monitoring	Site visits	☐

TOTAL BENCHMARKS MET

8

RESOURCES

Total state pre-K spending $75,127,000

Local match required? ....No

State spending per child enrolled $3,497

All reported spending per child enrolled* $4,860

SPENDING PER CHILD ENROLLED

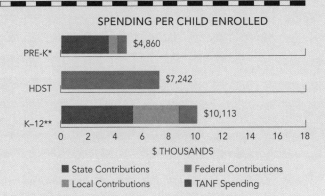

PRE-K*: $4,860

HDST: $7,242

K–12**: $10,113

$ THOUSANDS

■ State Contributions ■ Federal Contributions
■ Local Contributions ■ TANF Spending

* Pre-K programs may receive additional funds from federal or local sources that are not included in this figure.

**K–12 expenditures include capital spending as well as current operating expenditures.

Data are for the '07-'08 school year, unless otherwise noted.

[1] This total includes a supplemental count of 1,136 3-year-olds who received preschool special education services after reaching their third birthday later than December 1. An additional 2,766 children who were not eligible for state funding were served using district funds or tuition; they are not counted here.

[2] Because the state pre-K program is interrelated with the state special education program, it is not possible to provide a unique special education enrollment count for Kentucky. The estimates for special education enrollment include some children also counted in the totals for state pre-K.

[3] Teachers hired as lead teachers before 2004-2005 can hold a CDA or AA in child development. These teachers are allowed to remain in their current positions but may not transfer to other districts.

[4] Beginning with the 2008-2009 school year, newly hired assistant teachers in nonpublic settings will be required to have a HSD or GED.

[5] Support services include two annual parent conferences or home visits, education services or job training for parents, parenting support or training, parent involvement activities, health services for parents and children, information about nutrition, referral to social services, and transition to kindergarten activities.

[6] Programs must offer at least one meal. Additional meals and/or snacks are determined locally.

Louisiana

PERCENT OF STATE POPULATION ENROLLED

STATE SPENDING PER CHILD ENROLLED
(2008 DOLLARS)

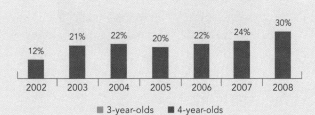

■ 3-year-olds ■ 4-year-olds

Louisiana currently operates three state-funded preschool initiatives. The state first offered prekindergarten in 1988 through the Model Early Childhood program. In 1993, when the state discontinued annual appropriations to the initiative, local school districts began using the 8(g) Student Enhancement Block Grant program to provide preschool for at-risk children. All Louisiana school districts currently offer preschool services to at-risk 4-year-olds through the 8(g) Student Enhancement Block Grant program. To be eligible to participate, children must be considered at risk of being "insufficiently ready for the regular school program," with priority given to children from low-income families.

The Cecil J. Picard LA4 Early Childhood program (formerly LA4 and Starting Points) started in 2001. This program offers up to 6 hours of regular instruction and up to 4 hours of before- and after-school programming per day. The program is available in 67 out of 71 Louisiana school districts (plus 12 charter schools) and is funded entirely by state dollars. The program serves 4-year-olds who qualify for free or reduced-price lunch, but 4-year-olds from higher income families are also eligible to participate through local funds or tuition.

The Nonpublic Schools Early Childhood Development Program (NSECD) was established in 2001 to provide tuition reimbursement to families with incomes below 200 percent of the federal poverty level who send their 4-year-olds to state-approved private preschools. These programs must offer at least a 6-hour instructional day and up to 4 hours of before- and after-school services each day.

In 2008, legislation was passed mandating access for all 4-year-olds, regardless of income, by the 2013-2014 academic year. School districts will also be required to allocate a minimum of 10 percent of new funding after the 2009-2010 academic year to provide programs in diverse delivery settings. In addition to the three initiatives profiled in this report, Louisiana used approximately $23 million in Title I funding to support preschool services for more than 7,000 students.

In order to document the contributions Louisiana makes to prekindergarten through its three separate initiatives, we first present summary information reflecting the state's overall commitment to prekindergarten. Enrollment and state spending for the 8(g), Cecil J. Picard LA4 Early Childhood, and NSECD programs are taken into account. Next, we present specific details about each initiative. The third page of this profile focuses exclusively on the 8(g) program; the fourth page focuses exclusively on the Cecil J. Picard LA4 Early Childhood program; and the final page focuses exclusively on the NSECD program.

STATE OVERVIEW

Total state program enrollment 17,788

Total state spending $104,674,104

State spending per child enrolled $5,885

All reported spending per child enrolled $5,997

STATE PRE-K AND HEAD START ENROLLMENT AS PERCENTAGE OF TOTAL POPULATION

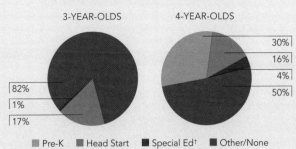

3-YEAR-OLDS

82%
1%
17%

4-YEAR-OLDS

30%
16%
4%
50%

■ Pre-K   ■ Head Start   ■ Special Ed†   ■ Other/None

† This number represents children in special education who are not enrolled in Head Start but may be enrolled in state-funded pre-K.

SPENDING PER CHILD ENROLLED

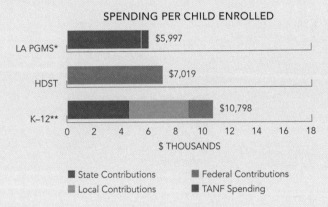

LA PGMS* $5,997

HDST $7,019

K–12** $10,798

0   2   4   6   8   10   12   14   16   18
$ THOUSANDS

■ State Contributions   ■ Federal Contributions
■ Local Contributions   ■ TANF Spending

* Pre-K programs may receive additional funds from federal or local sources that are not included in this figure.

** K–12 expenditures include capital spending as well as current operating expenditures.

Data are for the '07-'08 school year, unless otherwise noted.

ACCESS RANKINGS	
4-YEAR-OLDS	3-YEAR-OLDS
12	None Served

RESOURCES RANKINGS	
STATE SPENDING	ALL REPORTED SPENDING
9	**15**

LOUISIANA 8(g) STUDENT ENHANCEMENT BLOCK GRANT PROGRAM

ACCESS

Total state program enrollment 3,065

School districts that offer state program 100%

Income requirement ....None[1]

Hours of operation...........................6 hours/day, 5 days/week[2]

Operating schedule ....Academic year

Special education enrollment 5,031

Federally funded Head Start enrollment 20,202

State-funded Head Start enrollment 0

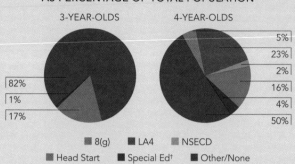

STATE PRE-K AND HEAD START ENROLLMENT AS PERCENTAGE OF TOTAL POPULATION

3-YEAR-OLDS

82%
1%
17%

4-YEAR-OLDS

5%
23%
2%
16%
4%
50%

■ 8(g) ■ LA4 ■ NSECD
■ Head Start ■ Special Ed† ■ Other/None

† This number represents children in special education who are not enrolled in Head Start but may be enrolled in state-funded pre-K.

QUALITY STANDARDS CHECKLIST

POLICY	STATE PRE-K REQUIREMENT	BENCHMARK	DOES REQUIREMENT MEET BENCHMARK?
Early learning standards	Comprehensive	Comprehensive	☑
Teacher degree	BA	BA	☑
Teacher specialized training	Certification in Nursery, K, Pre-K–3, or Early Intervention	Specializing in pre-K	☐
Assistant teacher degree	Determined locally	CDA or equivalent	☐
Teacher in-service	150 clock hours/5 years	At least 15 hours/year	☑
Maximum class size		20 or lower	☑
3-year-olds	NA		
4-year-olds	20		
Staff-child ratio		1:10 or better	☑
3-year-olds	NA		
4-year-olds	1:10		
Screening/referral and support services	Developmental screening;[3] and support services[4]	Vision, hearing, health; and at least 1 support service	☐
Meals	Breakfast, lunch and snack	At least 1/day	☑
Monitoring	Site visits and other monitoring	Site visits	☑

TOTAL BENCHMARKS MET

7

RESOURCES

Total state pre-K spending $12,674,104

Local match required? ....No

State spending per child enrolled $4,135

All reported spending per child enrolled* $4,135

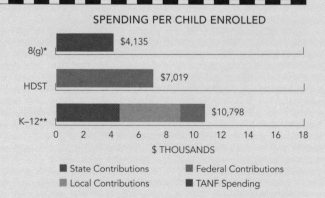

SPENDING PER CHILD ENROLLED

8(g)* — $4,135

HDST — $7,019

K–12** — $10,798

0 2 4 6 8 10 12 14 16 18
$ THOUSANDS

■ State Contributions ■ Federal Contributions
■ Local Contributions ■ TANF Spending

---

* Pre-K programs may receive additional funds from federal or local sources that are not included in this figure.

** K–12 expenditures include capital spending as well as current operating expenditures.

Data are for the '07-'08 school year, unless otherwise noted.

---

1 The state does not set specific income eligibility criteria but stipulates that priority be given to children from low-income families.

2 Programs must offer at least 63,720 minutes of instructional time per year. The 8(g) program funds a 6-hour instructional day, 5 days per week, but not wrap-around/extended-day services. However, these services may be provided through other funding sources to children served in 8(g)-funded classrooms. Two districts operated 4 days/week.

3 Developmental screening is conducted to determine which children are potentially eligible and to plan an appropriate program. Vision, hearing, dental, and general physical health screening is determined at the local level. The 8(g) program follows the referral process and policies established by the state Board of Elementary and Secondary Education.

4 Support services include parenting support or training, parent involvement activities, health services for children, information about nutrition, referral to social services, and transition to kindergarten activities. The number of required annual parent conferences or home visits is determined locally.

CECIL J. PICARD LA4 EARLY CHILDHOOD PROGRAM

ACCESS

Total state program enrollment ....13,668[1]

School districts that offer state program 94%

Income requirement ....185% FPL

Hours of operation............................6 hours/day, 5 days/week[2]

Operating schedule ....Academic year

Special education enrollment 5,031

Federally funded Head Start enrollment........................20,202

State-funded Head Start enrollment 0

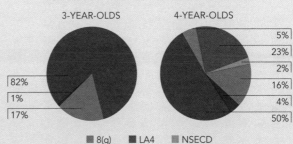

STATE PRE-K AND HEAD START ENROLLMENT AS PERCENTAGE OF TOTAL POPULATION

3-YEAR-OLDS

82%
1%
17%

4-YEAR-OLDS

5%
23%
2%
16%
4%
50%

■ 8(g) ■ LA4 ■ NSECD
■ Head Start ■ Special Ed[†] ■ Other/None

† This number represents children in special education who are not enrolled in Head Start but may be enrolled in state-funded pre-K.

QUALITY STANDARDS CHECKLIST

POLICY	STATE PRE-K REQUIREMENT	BENCHMARK	DOES REQUIREMENT MEET BENCHMARK?
Early learning standards	Comprehensive	Comprehensive	☑
Teacher degree	BA	BA	☑
Teacher specialized training	Certification in Nursery, K, Pre-K, Pre-K–3, or Early Intervention[3]	Specializing in pre-K	☐
Assistant teacher degree	HSD	CDA or equivalent	☐
Teacher in-service	18 clock hours	At least 15 hours/year	☑
Maximum class size		20 or lower	☑
3-year-olds	NA		
4-year-olds	20		
Staff-child ratio		1:10 or better	☑
3-year-olds	NA		
4-year-olds	1:10		
Screening/referral and support services	Vision, hearing, health, developmental; and support services[4]	Vision, hearing, health; and at least 1 support service	☑
Meals	Lunch and snack	At least 1/day	☑
Monitoring	Site visits and other monitoring	Site visits	☑

TOTAL BENCHMARKS MET

8

RESOURCES

Total state pre-K spending $83,500,000

Local match required? ....No

State spending per child enrolled $6,109

All reported spending per child enrolled* $6,255

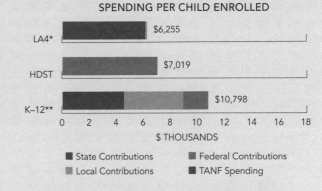

SPENDING PER CHILD ENROLLED

LA4* $6,255

HDST $7,019

K–12** $10,798

0 2 4 6 8 10 12 14 16 18
$ THOUSANDS

■ State Contributions ■ Federal Contributions
■ Local Contributions ■ TANF Spending

* Pre-K programs may receive additional funds from federal or local sources that are not included in this figure.

**K–12 expenditures include capital spending as well as current operating expenditures.

Data are for the '07-'08 school year, unless otherwise noted.

---

[1] The state-funded enrollment total does not include children whose before- and after-school enrichment services were funded by LA4. The total also does not include 438 tuition-paying students from families with incomes above the income requirement.

[2] LA4 funds also supported 4 hours of before- and after-school enrichment for 1,874 children.

[3] Accepted certifications include: Nursery, Kindergarten, Non-categorical Pre-K, Pre-K–3, or Early Intervention. Teachers may also qualify with any of the

following: Elementary certificate and an Out-of-Field Authorization to Teach, a BA and a Temporary Employment Permit, or an Out-of-State Provisional Certificate. Teachers qualifying under these conditions must be working toward obtaining a Louisiana teaching certificate specified in program requirements.

[4] Support services include two parent conferences, education services or job training for parents, parenting support or training, parent involvement activities, health services for children, information about nutrition, referral to social services, GED training, and literacy training.

LOUISIANA NONPUBLIC SCHOOLS EARLY CHILDHOOD DEVELOPMENT PROGRAM

ACCESS

Total state program enrollment ....1,055[1]

School districts that offer state program ....100% (parishes)

Income requirement ....200% FPL

Hours of operation..........................10 hours/day, 5 days/week

Operating schedule ....Academic year[2]

Special education enrollment 5,031

Federally funded Head Start enrollment........................20,202

State-funded Head Start enrollment 0

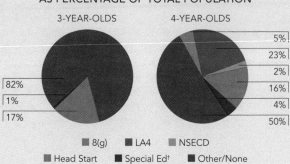

STATE PRE-K AND HEAD START ENROLLMENT AS PERCENTAGE OF TOTAL POPULATION

3-YEAR-OLDS
- 82%
- 1%
- 17%

4-YEAR-OLDS
- 5%
- 23%
- 2%
- 16%
- 4%
- 50%

■ 8(g) ■ LA4 ■ NSECD
■ Head Start ■ Special Ed† ■ Other/None

† This number represents children in special education who are not enrolled in Head Start but may be enrolled in state-funded pre-K.

QUALITY STANDARDS CHECKLIST

POLICY	STATE PRE-K REQUIREMENT	BENCHMARK	DOES REQUIREMENT MEET BENCHMARK?
Early learning standards	Comprehensive	Comprehensive	☑
Teacher degree	BA	BA	☑
Teacher specialized training	Pre-K–3, Pre-K, Early Interventionist, N, K, or Noncategorical Preschool Handicapped Certification[3]	Specializing in pre-K	☐
Assistant teacher degree	CDA[4]	CDA or equivalent	☑
Teacher in-service	18 clock hours	At least 15 hours/year	☑
Maximum class size		20 or lower	☑
3-year-olds	NA		
4-year-olds	20		
Staff-child ratio		1:10 or better	☑
3-year-olds	NA		
4-year-olds	1:10		
Screening/referral and support services	Vision, hearing, health; and support services[5]	Vision, hearing, health; and at least 1 support service	☑
Meals	Breakfast, lunch and snack	At least 1/day	☑
Monitoring	Site visits and other monitoring	Site visits	☑

TOTAL BENCHMARKS MET

9

RESOURCES

Total state pre-K spending ....$8,500,000[6]

Local match required? ....No

State spending per child enrolled ....$8,057[7]

All reported spending per child enrolled* ....$8,057[7]

SPENDING PER CHILD ENROLLED

NSECD*	$8,057
HDST	$7,019
K–12**	$10,798

0 2 4 6 8 10 12 14 16 18
$ THOUSANDS

■ State Contributions ■ Federal Contributions
■ Local Contributions ■ TANF Spending

* Pre-K programs may receive additional funds from federal or local sources that are not included in this figure.

** K–12 expenditures include capital spending as well as current operating expenditures.

Data are for the '07-'08 school year, unless otherwise noted.

[1] This is the average enrollment throughout the school year. A total of 1,114 4-year-olds were served during the year.

[2] There is also an optional summer program when the budget permits.

[3] Effective with the 2005-2006 program year, teachers who do not hold early childhood-level certification must enroll in courses required to add the Pre-K–3 or Early Interventionist certification. Teachers must be enrolled by January 2008. Incumbent teachers must complete their early childhood certification within three years and new teachers must complete the certification within three years of their hire date.

[4] Beginning with the 2007-2008 school year, only assistant teachers with at least a CDA are hired. Incumbent assistant teachers must enroll in a CDA program and maintain enrollment until completion of the program.

[5] Developmental and dental screening and referrals are determined locally. Support services include two parent conferences, parenting support or training, parent involvement activities, health services for children, referral to social services, transition to kindergarten activities, and social/emotional support services.

[6] This funding total consists of federal TANF funds that the state has chosen to direct toward prekindergarten. There are no additional state funds.

[7] This figure is based on the state's use of federal TANF funds.

Maine

PERCENT OF STATE POPULATION ENROLLED

STATE SPENDING PER CHILD ENROLLED
(2008 DOLLARS)

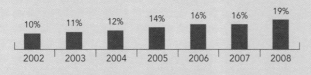

2002	2003	2004	2005	2006	2007	2008
10%	11%	12%	14%	16%	16%	19%

■ 3-year-olds   ■ 4-year-olds

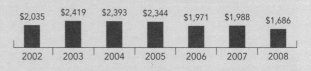

2002	2003	2004	2005	2006	2007	2008
$2,035	$2,419	$2,393	$2,344	$1,971	$1,988	$1,686

In 1983, Maine's Two-Year Kindergarten initiative was established to support public preschool education programs for 4-year-olds by allocating resources to districts through the school funding formula. Effective in 2007, public programs for 4-year-olds received a distinct definition as a Public Preschool Program.

While participation is optional, school districts choosing to provide public pre-K must receive approval from the Department of Education, which includes a planning process that incorporates collaboration with local providers. When a minimum of 10 hours a week of programming is offered, districts are eligible to receive a full per-pupil subsidy. Maine also provides an additional "weighted" subsidy to supplement the regular per-pupil allocation for grades pre-K–2.

Twenty-four percent of elementary schools across the state chose to offer public preschool programs in 2007-2008, and the Department of Education actively encourages more districts to do so. The majority of preschool education programs operate in public schools but districts can choose to collaborate with Head Start or contract private child care centers or family child care homes to provide pre-K services. In the 2007-2008 school year, 7 percent of children enrolled in the initiative were located in partnership programs with a community agency, most often a local Head Start program.

Effective for the 2007-2008 academic year, teachers in the Public Preschool Program initiative are required to have the Birth–Five teaching endorsement. Beginning in 2008-2009, all schools are required to offer transportation for the Public Preschool Program.

In addition to providing funds for the Public Preschool Program, Maine also provided $3,937,668 as a supplement to the federal Head Start program during fiscal year 2008.

ACCESS RANKINGS		RESOURCES RANKINGS	
4-YEAR-OLDS	3-YEAR-OLDS	STATE SPENDING	ALL REPORTED SPENDING
18	None Served	38	31

MAINE PUBLIC PRESCHOOL PROGRAM

ACCESS

Total state program enrollment 2,675

School districts that offer state program ....24% (public elementary schools)

Income requirement ....None

Hours of operation ....Determined locally[1]

Operating schedule ....Academic year[1]

Special education enrollment 2,399

Federally funded Head Start enrollment 3,211

State-funded Head Start enrollment ....355[2]

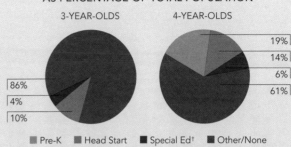

STATE PRE-K AND HEAD START ENROLLMENT AS PERCENTAGE OF TOTAL POPULATION

3-YEAR-OLDS 86%, 4%, 10%

4-YEAR-OLDS 19%, 14%, 6%, 61%

■ Pre-K ■ Head Start ■ Special Ed[†] ■ Other/None

[†] This number represents children in special education who are not enrolled in Head Start, but includes children who are enrolled in state-funded pre-K.

QUALITY STANDARDS CHECKLIST

POLICY	STATE PRE-K REQUIREMENT	BENCHMARK	DOES REQUIREMENT MEET BENCHMARK?
Early learning standards	Comprehensive	Comprehensive	☑
Teacher degree	BA	BA	☑
Teacher specialized training	EC birth–5 endorsement[3]	Specializing in pre-K	☑
Assistant teacher degree	Ed Tech II (30 credit hours)	CDA or equivalent	☑
Teacher in-service	90 clock hours/5 years	At least 15 hours/year	☑
Maximum class size		20 or lower	☐
3-year-olds	NA		
4-year-olds	No limit		
Staff-child ratio		1:10 or better	☐
3-year-olds	NA		
4-year-olds	1:15		
Screening/referral and support services	Vision, hearing, developmental[4]	Vision, hearing, health; and at least 1 support service	☐
Meals	None[5]	At least 1/day	☐
Monitoring	Other monitoring	Site visits	☐

TOTAL BENCHMARKS MET

5

RESOURCES

Total state pre-K spending ....$4,510,608[6]

Local match required? ......Yes, tied to school funding formula

State Head Start spending $3,937,668

State spending per child enrolled $1,686

All reported spending per child enrolled* $3,281

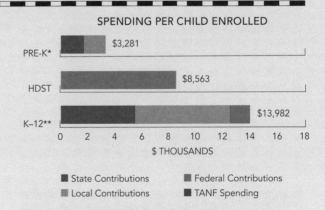

SPENDING PER CHILD ENROLLED

PRE-K* $3,281

HDST $8,563

K–12** $13,982

0 2 4 6 8 10 12 14 16 18

$ THOUSANDS

■ State Contributions ■ Federal Contributions
■ Local Contributions ■ TANF Spending

* Pre-K programs may receive additional funds from federal or local sources that are not included in this figure.

** K–12 expenditures include capital spending as well as current operating expenditures.

Data are for the '07-'08 school year, unless otherwise noted.

---

[1] Programs must operate a minimum of 10 hours per week to receive a per-pupil subsidy through the school funding formula. Some districts provide a full school day program five days a week, some provide a part-day program and operate four half days with the fifth day used for home visits and teacher planning, and some offer the program within a longer child care day. Programs operating within a child care setting may offer services on a year-round basis.

[2] This figure is based on the federal PIR total of non-ACF-funded enrollment and the proportion of all enrollees who were ages 3 or 4.

[3] Beginning with the 2007-2008 school year, teachers must have the state's new Birth–Five endorsement.

[4] A minimum of one annual parent conference or home visit is required. Programs are required to provide some comprehensive services, but specific services are determined locally.

[5] While not required, most programs offer a snack and others offer either breakfast or lunch. Programs that partner with Head Start must follow Head Start requirements for meals.

[6] In addition to Public Preschool Program funding, a total of $24,103,395 in weighted funds were available for pre-K through grade 2, including a state share of $12,387,759. It is not possible to estimate the amount used to serve 4-year-olds.

Maryland

PERCENT OF STATE POPULATION ENROLLED

STATE SPENDING PER CHILD ENROLLED
(2008 DOLLARS)

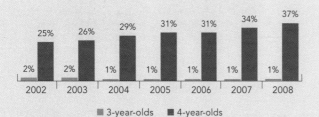

■ 3-year-olds ■ 4-year-olds

Maryland has been providing preschool for at-risk 4-year-olds since 1980. The Extended Elementary Education Program (EEEP) began as a pilot program in Baltimore City and in Prince George's County. Eventually, it expanded to all jurisdictions of Maryland, serving 25 percent of all 4-year-olds in 2002. As part of a school finance reform law in 2002, the state required that all local boards of education expand the prekindergarten services to all "economically disadvantaged" 4-year-olds by the 2007-2008 school year. The state's prekindergarten regulations were revised to reflect the new statute and to maintain a high-quality program to address the school readiness needs of low-income, special education students and English Language Learners. In an effort to serve all 4-year-olds with economically disadvantaged backgrounds by the 2007-2008 school year, the state significantly increased funding to school districts.

The state's school finance reform law also redefined the funding for prekindergarten. The local school systems received dedicated EEEP funds until 2007, which served as a state subsidy to the local school systems' general education funds. Starting in 2007-2008, all prekindergarten programs are strictly funded with state aid and local education dollars. Maryland includes costs for prekindergarten in the cost estimates of state aid for K–12 education and accounts for weighted costs for low-income and special education students as well as English Language Learners.

In late 2007, the Task Force on Universal Preschool Education submitted a report to the governor to expand prekindergarten to all 4-year-olds in Maryland. While parts of the task force recommendations are being implemented, major funding support for the program is stalled due to the state's budgetary constraints.

In addition, Maryland has created early learning centers of excellence in especially impacted school districts, called Judy Center Partnerships. Judy Center Partnerships collaborate with selected schools with early care and education centers to serve children from birth to age 5, in order to continually enhance the learning opportunities of young children. More than 8,000 children are currently enrolled in 24 Judy Center Partnerships.

In addition, Maryland provides funds to supplement the federal Head Start program, which are used to support extended-year and extended-day services as well as quality improvement. In the 2007-2008 program year, the state dedicated $3 million, which, along with federal CCDF money, provided funds for 1,508 additional Head Start slots.

ACCESS RANKINGS		RESOURCES RANKINGS	
4-YEAR-OLDS	3-YEAR-OLDS	STATE SPENDING	ALL REPORTED SPENDING
9	19	19	3

MARYLAND PREKINDERGARTEN PROGRAM

ACCESS

Total state program enrollment ....27,719[1]

School districts that offer state program 100%

Income requirement ....185% FPL

Hours of operation...........................2.5 hours/day (part-day) or
6.5 hours/day (full-day); 5 days/week

Operating schedule ....Academic year

Special education enrollment 6,984

Federally funded Head Start enrollment 9,200

State-funded Head Start enrollment 1,508

STATE PRE-K AND HEAD START ENROLLMENT AS PERCENTAGE OF TOTAL POPULATION

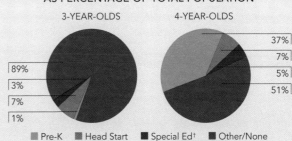

3-YEAR-OLDS

89%
3%
7%
1%

4-YEAR-OLDS

37%
7%
5%
51%

■ Pre-K   ■ Head Start   ■ Special Ed†   ■ Other/None

† This number represents children in special education who are not enrolled in Head Start but may be enrolled in state-funded pre-K.

QUALITY STANDARDS CHECKLIST

POLICY	STATE PRE-K REQUIREMENT	BENCHMARK	DOES REQUIREMENT MEET BENCHMARK?
Early learning standards	Comprehensive	Comprehensive	☑
Teacher degree	BA[2]	BA	☑
Teacher specialized training	N–3 certification[2]	Specializing in pre-K	☑
Assistant teacher degree	HSD	CDA or equivalent	☐
Teacher in-service	6 credit hours/5 years	At least 15 hours/year	☑
Maximum class size		20 or lower	☑
3-year-olds	NA[3]		
4-year-olds	20		
Staff-child ratio		1:10 or better	☑
3-year-olds	NA[3]		
4-year-olds	1:10		
Screening/referral and support services	Vision, hearing, health, immunization, lead screening; and support services[4]	Vision, hearing, health; and at least 1 support service	☑
Meals	At least 1 meal[5]	At least 1/day	☑
Monitoring	Site visits and other monitoring[6]	Site visits	☑

TOTAL BENCHMARKS MET

9

RESOURCES

Total state pre-K spending ....$104,509,466[7]

Local match required? ....No

State Head Start spending ....$3,000,000[8]

State spending per child enrolled $3,770

All reported spending per child enrolled* $8,558

SPENDING PER CHILD ENROLLED

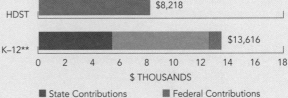

PRE-K* $8,558

HDST $8,218

K–12** $13,616

0   2   4   6   8   10   12   14   16   18

$ THOUSANDS

■ State Contributions   ■ Federal Contributions
■ Local Contributions   ■ TANF Spending

* Pre-K programs may receive additional funds from federal or local sources that are not included in this figure.

**K–12 expenditures include capital spending as well as current operating expenditures.

Data are for the '07-'08 school year, unless otherwise noted.

[1] The enrollment total includes 3- and 4-year-olds participating in Judy Center Partnerships.

[2] Teachers in public schools are required to have a degree in ECE and teachers in nonpublic schools are required to have a degree plus an ECE certification.

[3] By policy, 3-year-olds are not eligible, but state child care regulations require a maximum class size of 20 and a staff to child ratio of 1:10 for 3- and 4-year-olds.

[4] Vision and health screening and referral are the responsibility of the school health services program in conjunction with the health department under Title I, which applies to all children enrolled. Support services include two annual parent conferences or home visits, parenting support or training, parent involvement activities (as specified by NCLB), health services for children, transition to kindergarten activities, and other locally determined services.

[5] Children in full-day programs are offered breakfast and lunch. In half-day programs, children are offered either breakfast or lunch.

[6] Starting in the 2007-2008 program year, the Maryland State Department of Education required bi-annual visits to randomly selected prekindergarten locations, eventually visiting all programs, to monitor compliance with regulations of the initiative.

[7] The mandate to provide services also requires local spending as necessary to serve enrolled children.

[8] State Head Start funds were used for additional slots, professional development, parent education, mental health services, expanded transitional services, and literacy projects. In addition, funds were devoted to summer care, extended-day, or extended-year services.

Massachusetts

PERCENT OF STATE POPULATION ENROLLED

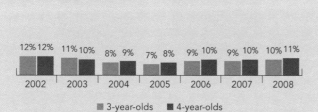

12% 12% 11% 10% 8% 9% 7% 8% 9% 10% 9% 10% 10% 11%
2002 2003 2004 2005 2006 2007 2008

■ 3-year-olds ■ 4-year-olds

STATE SPENDING PER CHILD ENROLLED
(2008 DOLLARS)

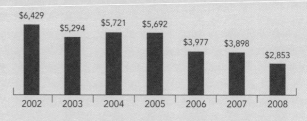

$6,429 $5,294 $5,721 $5,692 $3,977 $3,898 $2,853
2002 2003 2004 2005 2006 2007 2008

The Massachusetts Department of Early Education and Care (EEC) was established in July 2006 with a strategic focus on improving the access, quality, and affordability of preschool education in the state. At that time, Massachusetts launched a Universal Pre-kindergarten (UPK) initiative and also changed the name of its existing prekindergarten initiative from Community Partnerships for Children (CPC) to Preschool Direct, which was again renamed Preschool Scholarships in fiscal year 2008. Children are eligible to participate in Preschool Scholarships and UPK from age 2 years, 9 months until they reach the locally determined kindergarten eligibility age.

Established by the Massachusetts School Improvement Act of 1985, the CPC initiative was responsible for coordinating the planning and delivery of services offered by all early care and education programs within a funded community. By 1996, it focused on serving 3-and 4-year-old children with working parents. As Preschool Scholarships, the program continues to expand and coordinate preschool services based on community needs and resources. Funds are distributed to eligible local preschool providers, including private child care centers, public schools, Head Start agencies, and family child care homes that comply with the Early Childhood Program Standards and the Guidelines for Preschool Learning Experiences. Children from families with incomes up to 100 percent of SMI are eligible to enroll in Preschool Scholarships but priority is given to children from families at or below 50 percent of SMI. Most families do pay some tuition, based on the program's sliding scale. Children are exempt from these fees if they are in foster care, are homeless, or have other risk factors.

Massachusetts' Universal Pre-Kindergarten initiative began when the Commonwealth funded the program with $4.7 million in fiscal year 2007. Grants are awarded to public school prekindergarten programs, family child care providers, Head Start agencies, and private child care centers across 95 cities and towns. While all children are eligible for UPK funding at participating programs, additional funding is provided for children from families with incomes at or below 85 percent of SMI. Programs receiving UPK funding are required to operate or provide access to full-day, full-year services, follow specific standards for child assessment, and use the Early Childhood Program Standards and the Guidelines for Preschool Learning Experiences. In fiscal year 2008, Massachusetts increased spending for UPK to $7.1 million to serve additional children, and further increased funding in fiscal year 2009 to $12.1 million, with an emphasis on targeting at-risk communities.

Massachusetts also supplements federal funding for Head Start as a separate initiative. The state provided $9 million for teacher salary enhancement, program expansion, and to serve approximately 200 additional Head Start children in 2007-2008. This profile focuses on Preschool Scholarships and UPK, which are reported together because both programs have similar requirements and standards.

ACCESS RANKINGS		RESOURCES RANKINGS	
4-YEAR-OLDS	3-YEAR-OLDS	STATE SPENDING	ALL REPORTED SPENDING
27	5	30	25

MASSACHUSETTS UNIVERSAL PRE-KINDERGARTEN AND PRESCHOOL SCHOLARSHIPS

ACCESS

Total state program enrollment 19,257

School districts that offer state program ....96% (towns)

Income requirement..........................100% SMI with priority at
or below 50% SMI (Preschool
Scholarships); None (UPK)[1]

Hours of operation ....Determined locally[2]

Operating schedule ....Determined locally[2]

Special education enrollment 9,572

Federally funded Head Start enrollment 11,144

State-funded Head Start enrollment ....203[3]

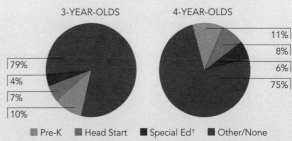

STATE PRE-K AND HEAD START ENROLLMENT AS PERCENTAGE OF TOTAL POPULATION

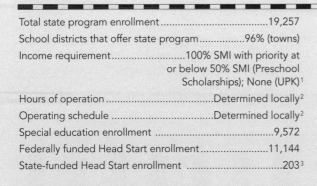

3-YEAR-OLDS
79%
4%
7%
10%

4-YEAR-OLDS
11%
8%
6%
75%

■ Pre-K   ■ Head Start   ■ Special Ed[†]   ■ Other/None

[†] This number represents children in special education who are not enrolled in Head Start, but includes children who are enrolled in state-funded pre-K.

QUALITY STANDARDS CHECKLIST

POLICY	STATE PRE-K REQUIREMENT	BENCHMARK	DOES REQUIREMENT MEET BENCHMARK?
Early learning standards	Comprehensive	Comprehensive	☑
Teacher degree	BA (public); None (nonpublic)[4]	BA	☐
Teacher specialized training	EC teacher of student with and without disabilities, Pre-K–2 (public); 3 credits (nonpublic)[4]	Specializing in pre-K	☐
Assistant teacher degree	HSD (public); None (nonpublic)[5]	CDA or equivalent	☐
Teacher in-service	20 clock hours	At least 15 hours/year	☑
Maximum class size		20 or lower	☑
3-year-olds	20		
4-year-olds	20		
Staff-child ratio		1:10 or better	☑
3-year-olds	1:10		
4-year-olds	1:10		
Screening/referral and support services	Vision, hearing, health; and support services[6]	Vision, hearing, health; and at least 1 support service	☑
Meals	Depend on length of program day[7]	At least 1/day	☐
Monitoring	Other monitoring[8]	Site visits	☐

TOTAL BENCHMARKS MET

5

RESOURCES

Total state pre-K spending ....$54,940,492[9]

Local match required? ....No

State Head Start spending $9,000,000

State spending per child enrolled $2,853

All reported spending per child enrolled* $3,811

* Pre-K programs may receive additional funds from federal or local sources that are not included in this figure.

**K–12 expenditures include capital spending as well as current operating expenditures.

Data are for the '07-'08 school year, unless otherwise noted.

SPENDING PER CHILD ENROLLED

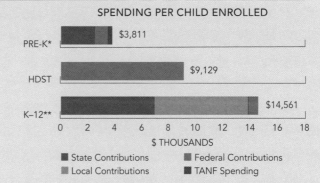

PRE-K* $3,811

HDST $9,129

K–12** $14,561

0   2   4   6   8   10   12   14   16   18

$ THOUSANDS

■ State Contributions   ■ Federal Contributions
■ Local Contributions   ■ TANF Spending

[1] UPK quality grants provide universal funding for all children enrolled in addition to higher levels of funding for children in families with incomes at or below 85 percent SMI.

[2] Preschool Scholarships programs operate 2.5 to 10 hours per day, 2 to 5 days per week, 9 to 12 months per year, depending on families' needs and preferences. At least one-third of children served statewide must be served in full-day, full-year programs. UPK quality grantees are required to provide or facilitate access to full-day and full-year programs.

[3] This is the number of children reported as non-ACF-funded in the federal PIR.

[4] Entry level public school teachers must also have an early childhood certification. Nonpublic school teachers must be certified by the Department of Early Education and Care. Teachers must either be 21 years old or have a high school diploma, and must complete a 3-credit college course in child growth and development. All classrooms funded through the UPK quality program must be accredited by NAEYC, NEASC or NAFCC, which encompass their own educational requirements.

[5] Assistant teachers in nonpublic settings must complete a 3-credit child development course and be at least 18 years old. A CDA may be substituted for these requirements.

[6] Preschool Scholarships require programs to have a plan for referring families to dental, vision, and hearing screenings; public school preschool screening; mental health, educational, and medical services. Programs are not required to provide them directly. However, all LEAs are required to provide screenings under "child find" and evaluations upon referral for all 3-, 4-, and 5-year-olds. Required support services include two annual parent conferences or home visits, and additional support services are determined locally.

[7] Programs operating fewer than 4 hours per day must provide snacks, and programs operating between 4 and 9 hours must provide a regularly scheduled meal in addition to a snack. Programs operating more than 9 hours must provide two meals and two snacks.

[8] Some UPK classrooms received site visits during 2007-2008, but Preschool Scholarships classrooms did not receive site visits during 2007-2008. Other monitoring includes regular monitoring of fiscal and programmatic practices at the lead agency level. Both Preschool Scholarship funds and UPK Quality grants go through an extensive annual grant review application process.

[9] This figure includes $6,886,933 in TANF funds.

Michigan

PERCENT OF STATE POPULATION ENROLLED	STATE SPENDING PER CHILD ENROLLED (2008 DOLLARS)

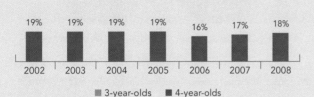

■ 3-year-olds ■ 4-year-olds

I n 1985, Michigan began offering preschool education programs to at-risk 4-year-olds through the Michigan School Readiness Program (MSRP). At least 50 percent of the children enrolled in MSRP must come from families with an income under 250 percent of the federal poverty level. Children under the income threshold must additionally have at least one of 24 other risk factors for educational disadvantage. Children above the income threshold must have at least two of these risk factors.

Funding for MSRP is based on a school funding formula that calculates the level of need in each district. Public school districts receive funding directly and may subcontract with other local providers. Beginning in 2003-2004, public school districts can also use some MSRP funds for parent involvement and education programs. MSRP awards competitive grants to Head Start agencies, private child care centers, and mental health and social service agencies to provide preschool programs. During the 2006-2007 and 2007-2008 school years, there was an increase in the number of children served in full-day programs, resulting in a decrease in the total number of children that could have been served given the level of funding for MSRP.

The Early Childhood Investment Corporation (ECIC) was recently established by the state to integrate Michigan's system of early childhood education and related family services. ECIC plans to establish standards and guidelines for early childhood development activities with the goal of promoting a high-quality statewide system. Recent early childhood proposals include increasing funding for MSRP and allocating funds for programs serving children prior to birth through age 3. Increasing MSRP funding would enable the state to tie the pre-K reimbursement rate to that of K–12, ultimately resulting in increases in pre-K funding as K–12 funding increases.

ACCESS RANKINGS		RESOURCES RANKINGS	
4-YEAR-OLDS	3-YEAR-OLDS	STATE SPENDING	ALL REPORTED SPENDING
19	None Served	16	23

MICHIGAN SCHOOL READINESS PROGRAM

ACCESS

Total state program enrollment ....23,134[1]

School districts that offer state program 81%

Income requirement ....50% of children must
be below 250% FPL[2]

Hours of operation ....At least 2.5 hours/day (half-day),
6-7 hours/day (full-day), 4 days/week

Operating schedule..30 weeks/year

Special education enrollment 13,549

Federally funded Head Start enrollment.........................32,828

State-funded Head Start enrollment 0

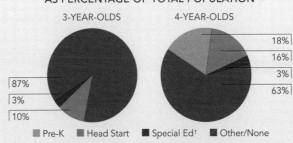

STATE PRE-K AND HEAD START ENROLLMENT AS PERCENTAGE OF TOTAL POPULATION

3-YEAR-OLDS: 87%, 3%, 10%

4-YEAR-OLDS: 18%, 16%, 3%, 63%

■ Pre-K ■ Head Start ■ Special Ed† ■ Other/None

† This number represents children in special education
who are not enrolled in state-funded pre-K or Head Start.

QUALITY STANDARDS CHECKLIST

POLICY	STATE PRE-K REQUIREMENT	BENCHMARK	DOES REQUIREMENT MEET BENCHMARK?
Early learning standards	Comprehensive	Comprehensive	☑
Teacher degree	BA[3]	BA	☑
Teacher specialized training	EE teaching certificate + ECE endorsement (public); EE teaching certificate + either ECE endorsement or CDA, or BA in CD (nonpublic)	Specializing in pre-K	☑
Assistant teacher degree	CDA or equivalent[4]	CDA or equivalent	☑
Teacher in-service	6 credit hours per 5 years[5]	At least 15 hours/year	☑
Maximum class size		20 or lower	☑
3-year-olds	NA		
4-year-olds	18		
Staff-child ratio		1:10 or better	☑
3-year-olds	NA		
4-year-olds	1:8[6]		
Screening/referral and support services	Vision, hearing, health; and support services[7]	Vision, hearing, health; and at least 1 support service	☑
Meals	Snack[8]	At least 1/day	☐
Monitoring	Other monitoring[9]	Site visits	☐

TOTAL BENCHMARKS MET

8

RESOURCES

Total state pre-K spending $97,850,000

Local match required?...Yes[10]

State spending per child enrolled $4,230

All reported spending per child enrolled* $4,230

* Pre-K programs may receive additional funds from federal or local sources
that are not included in this figure.

** K–12 expenditures include capital spending as well as current operating
expenditures.

Data are for the '07-'08 school year, unless otherwise noted.

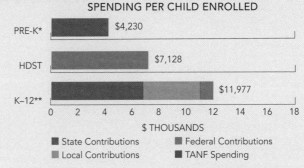

SPENDING PER CHILD ENROLLED

PRE-K*: $4,230

HDST: $7,128

K–12**: $11,977

0 2 4 6 8 10 12 14 16 18
$ THOUSANDS

■ State Contributions   ■ Federal Contributions
■ Local Contributions   ■ TANF Spending

1. This is the number of children planned to be served. Some children were served
in full-day programs which use two half-day slots. They are only counted once
in the enrollment.

2. The income requirement increased to 300 percent FPL beginning with the
2008-2009 school year.

3. The minimum teacher degree requirement in nonpublic settings changed from
an AA plus a CDA in 2004-2005 to a BA in 2005-2006. Programs who cannot find
a person who meets these requirements are considered "out of compliance."

4. Assistant teachers are given two years to meet this requirement but must have
one course in child development to start working. An associate degree in early
childhood education/child development or equivalent training approved by the
State Board of Education is also permissible.

5. All classroom staff must have 12 clock hours of in-service professional development
per year, not including CPR, first aid, and blood pathogen training. Certified
teachers need 6 credit hours of professional development every five years to
renew their certificates.

6. A qualified teacher and associate teacher must be present in classes of 9-16
children. If more than 16 children are in a class, a third adult must be present.

7. Programs must assure that children have a health screening, including vision and
hearing, and have a medical form on file for each child regarding vision, hearing,
health, and dental screenings. Screenings are often provided by the local health
department. Programs are required to make referrals. Support services include four
parent conferences or home visits, parent involvement activities, health services for
children, referral to social services, and transition to kindergarten activities.

8. Part-day programs must provide at least a snack. They are encouraged to provide
breakfast or lunch in lieu of or in addition to a snack, and to extend the day to 3
hours if providing a full meal. School-day programs must provide lunch and two
snacks or breakfast, lunch and one snack.

9. The MSRP office protocol includes site visits to programs, but the visits are not
written into state policy requirements. State administrators estimate that site
visits occur for competitive grantee agencies once during each 3-year funding
cycle. Site visits for school district programs are more limited.

10. There is not a monetary local match, but programs are not allowed to charge for
space so local funds are used for program space.

79

Minnesota

PERCENT OF STATE POPULATION ENROLLED

2002	2003	2004	2005	2006	2007	2008
1% 2%	1% 2%	1% 2%	1% 2%	1% 2%	1% 2%	1% 2%

■ 3-year-olds   ■ 4-year-olds

STATE SPENDING PER CHILD ENROLLED
(2008 DOLLARS)

2002	2003	2004	2005	2006	2007	2008
$9,324	$8,607	$8,569	$8,134	$7,916	$7,679	$8,310

Minnesota allocates funds to provide additional Head Start and Early Head Start enrollment opportunities for children from birth to age 5. Agencies currently receiving federal Head Start grants are eligible for this funding and may choose to partner with other agencies including public schools, private child care centers, and family child care homes. Service providers receiving state funds are required to follow the federal Head Start Performance Standards. Program staff receive training and technical assistance on the use of the state's early learning standards, the Early Childhood Indicators of Progress.

The School Readiness Program is another state pre-K initiative, which is offered through school districts, subcontracted charter schools, and community-based organizations. The initiative's aim is to promote kindergarten readiness through prekindergarten, services for children with disabilities, and home visits. School districts can decide which services to offer. Programs are required to assess children's cognitive skills upon entering and leaving the program, ensure that appropriate screenings and referrals occur, provide research-based program content, encourage parent involvement, and coordinate with other local programs. As program enrollment and funding data for center-based preschool education services are not tracked at the state level, the School Readiness Program is not the focus of data in this profile.

Beginning with the 2007-2008 school year, additional services for Minnesota's children and their families are available through new initiatives using a mixture of public and private funding. This funding enables low-income families to have the opportunity to purchase high-quality early care and education services for their 3- and 4-year-olds.

ACCESS RANKINGS		RESOURCES RANKINGS	
4-YEAR-OLDS	**3-YEAR-OLDS**	**STATE SPENDING**	**ALL REPORTED SPENDING**
38	21	3	5

MINNESOTA HEAD START

ACCESS

Total state program enrollment ....2,349[1]

School districts that offer state program ....100% (counties)

Income requirement ....90% of children must be at or
below 100% FPL or receiving TANF

Hours of operation ....At least 3.5 hours/day, 4 days/week[2]

Operating schedule ....At least 32 weeks/year[2]

Special education enrollment 8,236

Federally funded Head Start enrollment 9,475

State-funded Head Start enrollment ....1,866[3]

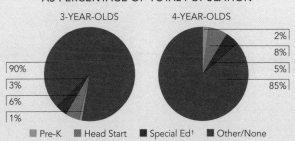

STATE PRE-K AND HEAD START ENROLLMENT AS PERCENTAGE OF TOTAL POPULATION

3-YEAR-OLDS

4-YEAR-OLDS

2%
8%
5%
85%

90%
3%
6%
1%

■ Pre-K ■ Head Start ■ Special Ed† ■ Other/None

† This number represents children in special education
who are not enrolled in state-funded pre-K or Head Start.

QUALITY STANDARDS CHECKLIST

POLICY	STATE PRE-K REQUIREMENT	BENCHMARK	DOES REQUIREMENT MEET BENCHMARK?
Early learning standards	Comprehensive	Comprehensive	☑
Teacher degree	BA (public); CDA (nonpublic)[4]	BA	☐
Teacher specialized training	License or certification in EC (public); Meets CDA requirements (nonpublic)	Specializing in pre-K	☑
Assistant teacher degree	Meet child care regs.[5]	CDA or equivalent	☑
Teacher in-service	15 clock hours[6]	At least 15 hours/year	☐
Maximum class size		20 or lower	☑
3-year-olds	17		
4-year-olds	20		
Staff-child ratio		1:10 or better	☑
3-year-olds	2:17		
4-year-olds	1:10		
Screening/referral and support services	Vision, hearing, health, dental, developmental; and support services[7]	Vision, hearing, health; and at least 1 support service	☑
Meals	Lunch and/or breakfast[8]	At least 1/day	☑
Monitoring	Site visits and other monitoring	Site visits	☑

TOTAL BENCHMARKS MET

8

RESOURCES

Total state pre-K spending ....$19,520,751[9]

Local match required? ....No

State Head Start spending ....$19,520,751[9]

State spending per child enrolled $8,310

All reported spending per child enrolled* $8,310

* Pre-K programs may receive additional funds from federal or local sources
that are not included in this figure.

** K–12 expenditures include capital spending as well as current operating
expenditures.

Data are for the '07-'08 school year, unless otherwise noted.

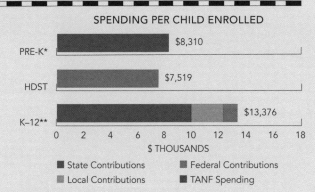

SPENDING PER CHILD ENROLLED

PRE-K* — $8,310

HDST — $7,519

K–12** — $13,376

0 2 4 6 8 10 12 14 16 18
$ THOUSANDS

■ State Contributions　　■ Federal Contributions
■ Local Contributions　　■ TANF Spending

---

1. This is the number of funded slots and includes an estimated 376 children under age 3 and an estimated 107 5-year-olds.

2. Schedules are determined locally but must be in compliance with federal Head Start regulations. Programs must operate at least 3.5 hours per day, 4 days per week, and 32 weeks per year.

3. This is an estimate of the total number of 3- and 4-year-olds served in state-funded Head Start.

4. The Head Start reauthorization that went into effect in December 2007 requires that by 2011 all teachers must have at least an AA degree and 50 percent must have at least a BA related to teaching preschool children. Currently, about 80 percent in Minnesota Head Start programs have at least an AA and 60 percent have at least a BA in ECE or a related field. In a public school, teacher union rules require that teachers have at least a bachelor's degree.

5. Assistant teachers in settings subject to child care regulations must work under the supervision of a teacher, be at least 18 years old, and meet one of nine

combined credential, educational, and experience requirements, such as a high school diploma, 12 quarter units in early childhood or a related field, and 2,080 hours of experience. Federal Head Start requires that by 2013 all assistant teachers have a CDA or be enrolled in a program to receive a CDA, AA, or BA within two years.

6. As of December 2007, the Head Start reauthorization required 15 clock hours of professional development per year.

7. Programs are also required to provide screenings and referrals for nutrition, social emotional, and behavioral issues. Support services include two annual parent conferences or home visits, education services or job training for parents, parenting support or training, parent involvement activities, health services for parents and children, information about nutrition, referral to social services, and transition to kindergarten activities.

8. Federal Head Start Performance Standards require part-day programs to provide children with at least one-third of their daily nutritional needs (breakfast or lunch), and full-day programs to provide one-half to two-thirds of daily nutritional needs.

9. All spending through this initiative is directed toward Head Start programs.

Mississippi

NO PROGRAM

ACCESS RANKINGS		RESOURCES RANKINGS	
4-YEAR-OLDS	3-YEAR-OLDS	STATE SPENDING	ALL REPORTED SPENDING
No Program		No Program	

THE STATE OF PRESCHOOL 2008 - STATE PRESCHOOL YEARBOOK - NATIONAL INSTITUTE FOR EARLY EDUCATION RESEARCH - WWW.NIEER.ORG

ACCESS

Total state program enrollment 0

School districts that offer state program.........................NA

Income requirement ....NA

Hours of operation ....NA

Operating schedule ....NA

Special education enrollment 3,908

Federally funded Head Start enrollment.................25,352

State-funded Head Start enrollment 0

STATE PRE-K AND HEAD START ENROLLMENT AS PERCENTAGE OF TOTAL POPULATION

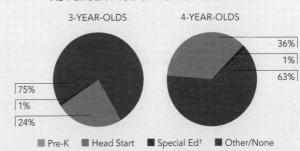

3-YEAR-OLDS

75%
1%
24%

4-YEAR-OLDS

36%
1%
63%

■ Pre-K   ■ Head Start   ■ Special Ed†   ■ Other/None

† This number represents children in special education
who are not enrolled in Head Start.

QUALITY STANDARDS CHECKLIST

TOTAL
BENCHMARKS
MET

No
Program

RESOURCES

Total state pre-K spending...$0

Local match required? ....NA

State Head Start spending...$0

State spending per child enrolled $0

All reported spending per child enrolled*......................$0

* Pre-K programs may receive additional funds from federal or local sources
that are not included in this figure.

** K–12 expenditures include capital spending as well as current operating
expenditures.

Data are for the '07-'08 school year, unless otherwise noted.

SPENDING PER CHILD ENROLLED

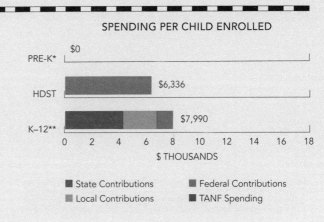

PRE-K* $0

HDST $6,336

K–12** $7,990

0   2   4   6   8   10   12   14   16   18
$ THOUSANDS

■ State Contributions   ■ Federal Contributions
■ Local Contributions   ■ TANF Spending

Missouri

PERCENT OF STATE POPULATION ENROLLED

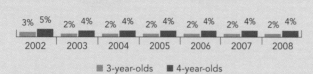

■ 3-year-olds ■ 4-year-olds

STATE SPENDING PER CHILD ENROLLED
(2008 DOLLARS)

S ince 1998, Missouri has used gaming revenues to fund the Missouri Preschool Project (MPP). With funds distributed through the Early Childhood Development Education and Care Fund, the state-funded program serves 3- and 4-year-olds in programs operating in public schools, private child care centers, and nonprofit agencies.

Funds are awarded through a competitive grant process, with priority given to programs serving children with special needs or from low-income families. With the goal of providing access to all families regardless of income, local programs offer sliding payment scales based on criteria such as free or reduced-price lunch eligibility.

All teachers who were hired after July 1, 2005, regardless of setting, must have a bachelor's degree and specialization in early childhood. New grantees must meet this teacher education requirement in order to receive state funding. Grantees must also set aside at least 10 percent of their MPP funding to provide professional development for teachers who are working within the same community for other licensed programs.

For the 2008-2009 school year, assistant teachers in public and nonpublic settings will be required to have completed 60 college hours and have experience working in a program with young children and their families. Previously they were required to have a high school vocational certificate in early childhood care and education and a high school diploma to be certified to teach.

ACCESS RANKINGS		RESOURCES RANKINGS	
4-YEAR-OLDS	3-YEAR-OLDS	STATE SPENDING	ALL REPORTED SPENDING
35	18	33	35

MISSOURI PRESCHOOL PROJECT

ACCESS

Total state program enrollment 4,640

School districts that offer state program 31%

Income requirement ....None[1]

Hours of operation ....3 hours/day (half-day),
6.5 hours/day (full day); 5 days/week[2]

Operating schedule ....Determined locally[2]

Special education enrollment 8,963

Federally funded Head Start enrollment........................14,746

State-funded Head Start enrollment 0

STATE PRE-K AND HEAD START ENROLLMENT AS PERCENTAGE OF TOTAL POPULATION

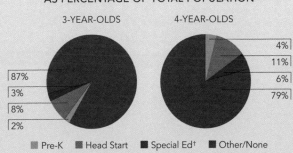

3-YEAR-OLDS: 87%, 3%, 8%, 2%

4-YEAR-OLDS: 4%, 11%, 6%, 79%

■ Pre-K   ■ Head Start   ■ Special Ed[†]   ■ Other/None

[†] This number represents children in special education who are not enrolled in state-funded pre-K or Head Start.

QUALITY STANDARDS CHECKLIST

POLICY	STATE PRE-K REQUIREMENT	BENCHMARK	DOES REQUIREMENT MEET BENCHMARK?
Early learning standards	Comprehensive	Comprehensive	☑
Teacher degree	BA	BA	☑
Teacher specialized training	EC or ECSE birth to third grade certification, or 4-year CD degree	Specializing in pre-K	☑
Assistant teacher degree	HSD + voc. cert. in ECE[3]	CDA or equivalent	☐
Teacher in-service	22 clock hours	At least 15 hours/year	☑
Maximum class size		20 or lower	☑
3-year-olds	20		
4-year-olds	20		
Staff-child ratio		1:10 or better	☑
3-year-olds	1:10		
4-year-olds	1:10		
Screening/referral and support services	None	Vision, hearing, health; and at least 1 support service	☐
Meals	Depend on length of program day[4]	At least 1/day	☐
Monitoring	Site visits and other monitoring	Site visits	☑

TOTAL BENCHMARKS MET

7

RESOURCES

Total state pre-K spending $12,794,517

Local match required?...No

State spending per child enrolled $2,757

All reported spending per child enrolled* $2,757

SPENDING PER CHILD ENROLLED

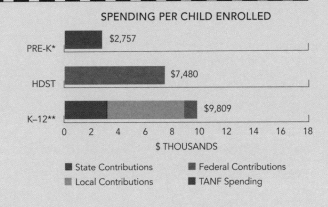

PRE-K*: $2,757

HDST: $7,480

K–12**: $9,809

■ State Contributions   ■ Federal Contributions
■ Local Contributions   ■ TANF Spending

* Pre-K programs may receive additional funds from federal or local sources that are not included in this figure.

** K–12 expenditures include capital spending as well as current operating expenditures.

Data are for the '07-'08 school year, unless otherwise noted.

[1] Programs are funded through a competitive process and receive extra points for serving children with special needs or from low-income families.

[2] Programs apply as either a full-day or half-day program. Programs awarded in 1998-1999 had the option of operating 4 days per week with the fifth day for home visiting, but this practice is being phased out. Programs are required to operate for a minimum of nine months, but may choose to operate year-round.

[3] For the 2008-2009 school year, the minimum degree requirement for assistant teachers will be a CDA

[4] A 3-hour program must serve a snack and may serve a meal. Programs longer than 3 hours must serve at least one meal and one snack.

Montana

NO PROGRAM

ACCESS RANKINGS		RESOURCES RANKINGS	
4-YEAR-OLDS	3-YEAR-OLDS	STATE SPENDING	ALL REPORTED SPENDING
No Program		No Program	

ACCESS

Total state program enrollment 0

School districts that offer state program.........................NA

Income requirement ....NA

Hours of operation ....NA

Operating schedule ....NA

Special education enrollment 1,052

Federally funded Head Start enrollment...................3,918

State-funded Head Start enrollment 0

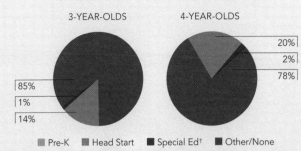

STATE PRE-K AND HEAD START ENROLLMENT
AS PERCENTAGE OF TOTAL POPULATION

3-YEAR-OLDS   4-YEAR-OLDS

85%   20%
1%   2%
14%   78%

■ Pre-K   ■ Head Start   ■ Special Ed†   ■ Other/None

† This number represents children in special education
who are not enrolled in Head Start.

QUALITY STANDARDS CHECKLIST

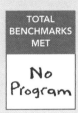

TOTAL
BENCHMARKS
MET

No
Program

RESOURCES

Total state pre-K spending...$0

Local match required? ....NA

State Head Start spending...$0

State spending per child enrolled $0

All reported spending per child enrolled*......................$0

* Pre-K programs may receive additional funds from federal or local sources
that are not included in this figure.

** K–12 expenditures include capital spending as well as current operating
expenditures.

Data are for the '07-'08 school year, unless otherwise noted.

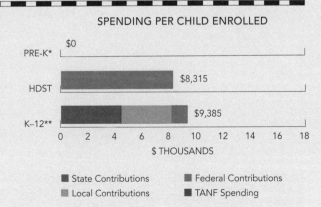

SPENDING PER CHILD ENROLLED

PRE-K* $0

HDST $8,315

K–12** $9,385

0   2   4   6   8   10   12   14   16   18
$ THOUSANDS

■ State Contributions   ■ Federal Contributions
■ Local Contributions   ■ TANF Spending

Nebraska

PERCENT OF STATE POPULATION ENROLLED

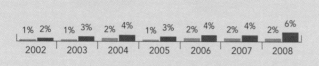

■ 3-year-olds ■ 4-year-olds

STATE SPENDING PER CHILD ENROLLED
(2008 DOLLARS)

In 1992, the Nebraska Early Childhood Education Grant Program began as a pilot program and was expanded in 2001. Although children may be enrolled as early as 6 weeks of age, the program's focus is on serving 3- and 4-year-old children at risk. State funds are distributed to public schools and educational service units, but services are also offered through partnerships with private child care centers, family resource centers, and Head Start agencies. As collaborative funding efforts are required by the state, all grantees must cover at least half of their program costs using other federal, state or local sources.

At least 70 percent of each program's funding must be used to serve children having at least one of four risk factors set by the state. These priority areas are: children eligible for free or reduced-price lunch, English Language Learners, children born prematurely or with low birth weight, and children of teen parents who have not completed high school. Children who do not meet the eligibility requirement are permitted to enroll, with a sliding payment scale used for tuition.

Nebraska passed legislation in 2005 allowing 4-year-olds in approved school-based prekindergarten programs to be included in the K–12 state aid formula. Additional school districts became eligible for state aid for the 4-year-olds they served. As a result, the total number of young children served by state funding grew by approximately 600 children in the 2007-2008 program year.

ACCESS RANKINGS		RESOURCES RANKINGS	
4-YEAR-OLDS	3-YEAR-OLDS	STATE SPENDING	ALL REPORTED SPENDING
33	16	32	13

NEBRASKA EARLY CHILDHOOD EDUCATION GRANT PROGRAM

ACCESS

Total state program enrollment ....2,221[1]

School districts that offer state program 23%

Income requirement ....185% FPL[2]

Hours of operation ....Determined locally[3]

Operating schedule ....Academic year

Special education enrollment 3,076

Federally funded Head Start enrollment 4,326

State-funded Head Start enrollment 0

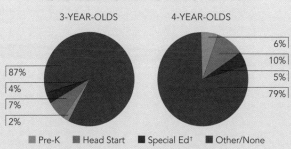

STATE PRE-K AND HEAD START ENROLLMENT AS PERCENTAGE OF TOTAL POPULATION

3-YEAR-OLDS: 87%, 4%, 7%, 2%

4-YEAR-OLDS: 6%, 10%, 5%, 79%

■ Pre-K ■ Head Start ■ Special Ed† ■ Other/None

† This number represents children in special education who are not enrolled in Head Start but may be enrolled in state-funded pre-K.

QUALITY STANDARDS CHECKLIST

POLICY	STATE PRE-K REQUIREMENT	BENCHMARK	DOES REQUIREMENT MEET BENCHMARK?
Early learning standards	Comprehensive	Comprehensive	☑
Teacher degree	BA	BA	☑
Teacher specialized training	Certification and EC endorsement	Specializing in pre-K	☑
Assistant teacher degree	12 cr. hours in CD or ECE or equivalent	CDA or equivalent	☑
Teacher in-service	12 clock hours	At least 15 hours/year	☑
Maximum class size		20 or lower	☑
3-year-olds	20		
4-year-olds	20		
Staff-child ratio		1:10 or better	☑
3-year-olds	1:10		
4-year-olds	1:10		
Screening/referral and support services	Support services only[4]	Vision, hearing, health; and at least 1 support service	☐
Meals	Snack	At least 1/day	☐
Monitoring	Site visits and other monitoring	Site visits	☑

TOTAL BENCHMARKS MET

8

RESOURCES

Total state pre-K spending $6,200,647

Local match required? ....Yes, 100% of state funding

State spending per child enrolled $2,792

All reported spending per child enrolled* $6,748

* Pre-K programs may receive additional funds from federal or local sources that are not included in this figure.

**K–12 expenditures include capital spending as well as current operating expenditures.

Data are for the '07-'08 school year, unless otherwise noted.

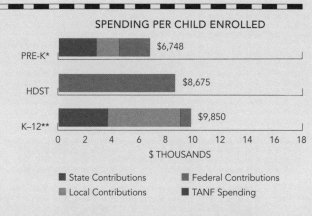

SPENDING PER CHILD ENROLLED

PRE-K*: $6,748

HDST: $8,675

K–12**: $9,850

$ THOUSANDS (0 2 4 6 8 10 12 14 16 18)

■ State Contributions ■ Federal Contributions
■ Local Contributions ■ TANF Spending

---

[1] This total includes 111 children younger than age 3.

[2] Seventy percent of each program's funding must be used to serve children having at least one of four risk factors, one of which is family income. The other risk factors are non-English speaking family members, teen parent, low birth weight or other child health risk.

[3] Most programs operate part day, 3.5 to 4 hours per day, 4 days per week.

[4] Screenings and referrals are determined locally. Support services include two parent conferences and two home visits, parenting support or training, parent involvement activities, transition to kindergarten activities, family development and support based on the family's needs and interest, and other locally determined services.

Nevada

PERCENT OF STATE POPULATION ENROLLED

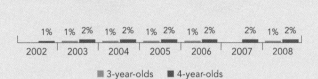

	2002	2003	2004	2005	2006	2007	2008
3-year-olds	1%	1%	1%	1%	1%		1%
4-year-olds		2%	2%	2%	2%	2%	2%

■ 3-year-olds   ■ 4-year-olds

STATE SPENDING PER CHILD ENROLLED
(2008 DOLLARS)

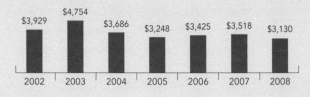

2002	2003	2004	2005	2006	2007	2008
$3,929	$4,754	$3,686	$3,248	$3,425	$3,518	$3,130

The Nevada State PreKindergarten Education Program began in 2001 as the Early Childhood Education Comprehensive Plan. The program provides funds to launch new preschool education programs and expand existing programs. The focus is on providing preschool for 3- to 5-year-olds, with eligibility criteria determined by individual grantees. In determining eligibility criteria, programs are required to identify needs in their communities. Priority for enrollment is given to 4- and 5-year-olds who will be eligible for kindergarten the following year. Children may also be eligible if they are from low-income families, are English Language Learners, or have an IEP.

The quality of the program is controlled by the state through the requirements of a competitive grant process rather than through explicit program policy. Grantees may include school districts or community organizations. Funding is based on the needs expressed by the grantees through their grant application.

In an attempt to assess the learning gains of children identified as Limited English Proficient (43 percent of enrollment), the program has implemented a statewide pilot project using the PreLAS, a measure of oral language proficiency and pre-literacy skills. The state is also working to adopt a program quality assessment protocol that includes classroom observation instruments such as the ECERS-R and the ELLCO.

ACCESS RANKINGS		RESOURCES RANKINGS	
4-YEAR-OLDS	3-YEAR-OLDS	STATE SPENDING	ALL REPORTED SPENDING
37	24	27	32

NEVADA STATE PREKINDERGARTEN EDUCATION PROGRAM

ACCESS

Total state program enrollment 1,039

School districts that offer state program 53%

Income requirement ....None[1]

Hours of operation ....Determined locally[2]

Operating schedule ....Academic year

Special education enrollment 3,210

Federally funded Head Start enrollment.........................2,769

State-funded Head Start enrollment 0

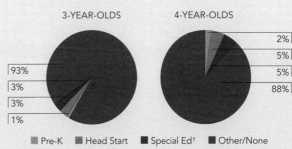

STATE PRE-K AND HEAD START ENROLLMENT AS PERCENTAGE OF TOTAL POPULATION

3-YEAR-OLDS: 93%, 3%, 3%, 1%

4-YEAR-OLDS: 2%, 5%, 5%, 88%

■ Pre-K   ■ Head Start   ■ Special Ed[†]   ■ Other/None

[†] This number represents children in special education who are not enrolled in Head Start, but includes children who are enrolled in state-funded pre-K.

QUALITY STANDARDS CHECKLIST

POLICY	STATE PRE-K REQUIREMENT	BENCHMARK	DOES REQUIREMENT MEET BENCHMARK?
Early learning standards	Comprehensive	Comprehensive	☑
Teacher degree	BA[3]	BA	☑
Teacher specialized training	ECE license - Birth–K or Birth–Grade 2[3]	Specializing in pre-K	☑
Assistant teacher degree	HSD	CDA or equivalent	☐
Teacher in-service	6 credit hours/5 years	At least 15 hours/year	☑
Maximum class size		20 or lower	☑
3-year-olds	16		
4-year-olds	20		
Staff-child ratio		1:10 or better	☑
3-year-olds	1:8		
4-year-olds	1:10		
Screening/referral and support services	Support services only[4]	Vision, hearing, health; and at least 1 support service	☐
Meals	None	At least 1/day	☐
Monitoring	Site visits and other monitoring	Site visits	☑

TOTAL BENCHMARKS MET

7

RESOURCES

Total state pre-K spending $3,251,671

Local match required?...No

State spending per child enrolled $3,130

All reported spending per child enrolled* $3,130

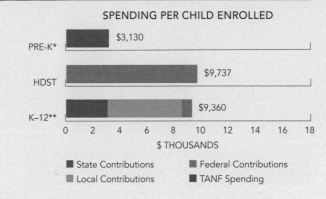

SPENDING PER CHILD ENROLLED

PRE-K*: $3,130

HDST: $9,737

K–12**: $9,360

$ THOUSANDS (0 2 4 6 8 10 12 14 16 18)

■ State Contributions   ■ Federal Contributions
■ Local Contributions   ■ TANF Spending

* Pre-K programs may receive additional funds from federal or local sources that are not included in this figure.

**K–12 expenditures include capital spending as well as current operating expenditures.

Data are for the '07-'08 school year, unless otherwise noted.

[1] Although there is no income requirement, all programs give priority to children who are English Language Learners, have an IEP, or are from low-income families.

[2] Programs are required to operate a minimum of 10 hours per week. Full days are allowed, but all programs operate 2.5-3 hours per day, 4 or 5 days per week due to limited funding.

[3] Classroom on Wheels (COW) teachers already employed as of 2003-2004 were grandfathered in and do not have to meet these requirements currently, but are expected to work toward meeting them. All new hires must be credentialed teachers, and most COW classrooms now have a credentialed teacher.

[4] Screening and referral requirements are decided at the local level. Support services include parenting support or training and parent involvement activities that typically encompass home visits, classroom volunteering, literacy nights, parenting classes, workshops, ESL classes, and parent conferences.

New Hampshire

NO PROGRAM

ACCESS RANKINGS		RESOURCES RANKINGS	
4-YEAR-OLDS	3-YEAR-OLDS	STATE SPENDING	ALL REPORTED SPENDING
No Program		No Program	

ACCESS

Total state program enrollment 0

School districts that offer state program.......................NA

Income requirement ....NA

Hours of operation ....NA

Operating schedule ....NA

Special education enrollment 1,389

Federally funded Head Start enrollment...................1,375

State-funded Head Start enrollment ....0 [1]

STATE PRE-K AND HEAD START ENROLLMENT AS PERCENTAGE OF TOTAL POPULATION

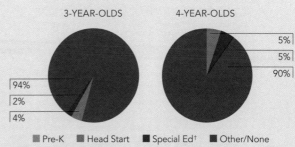

3-YEAR-OLDS

4-YEAR-OLDS

94%
2%
4%

5%
5%
90%

■ Pre-K ■ Head Start ■ Special Ed[†] ■ Other/None

[†] This number represents children in special education who are not enrolled in Head Start.

QUALITY STANDARDS CHECKLIST

TOTAL BENCHMARKS MET
No Program

RESOURCES

Total state pre-K spending...$0

Local match required? ....NA

State Head Start spending ....$331,337 [1]

State spending per child enrolled $0

All reported spending per child enrolled*......................$0

* Pre-K programs may receive additional funds from federal or local sources that are not included in this figure.

**K–12 expenditures include capital spending as well as current operating expenditures.

Data are for the '07-'08 school year, unless otherwise noted.

SPENDING PER CHILD ENROLLED

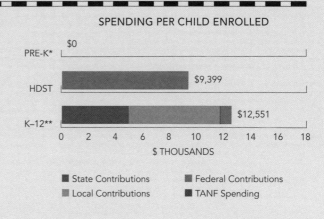

PRE-K* $0

HDST $9,399

K–12** $12,551

0 2 4 6 8 10 12 14 16 18
$ THOUSANDS

■ State Contributions ■ Federal Contributions
■ Local Contributions ■ TANF Spending

---

[1] New Hampshire's state Head Start funds are allocated for transportation and teacher salaries.

New Jersey

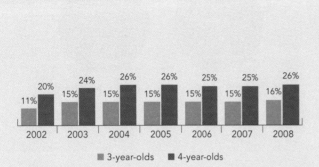

■ 3-year-olds ■ 4-year-olds

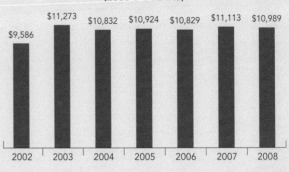

I n 1998, New Jersey's Supreme Court mandated the provision of preschool for all 3- and 4-year-olds in the state's highest poverty districts. This mandate resulted in the development of the Abbott Preschool Program, which is offered in the 31 school districts where at least 40 percent of children qualify for free or reduced-price lunch. Funds are distributed directly from the state Department of Education to school districts, which may in turn contract with Head Start or private child care centers to provide services. In addition to DOE funding, Abbott districts and/or providers may receive funding from the state Department of Human Services (DHS) to provide extended-day, extended-year services. Although the funds formerly provided services for all children enrolled in an Abbott preschool program, effective with the 2007-2008 school year, DHS vouchers are available only to families with incomes up to 300 percent of the poverty level.

As part of a separate initiative, Early Childhood Program Aid (ECPA) is provided to 101 school districts, known as non-Abbott ECPA districts, in which 20 to 40 percent of children qualify for free or reduced-price lunch. Through ECPA funding, non-Abbott ECPA districts operate full-day kindergarten, offer at least a half-day preschool program for 4-year-olds, and improve services for children in pre-K through third grade. Preschool programs typically operate in public schools, but some districts choose to contract with Head Start or private child care centers to offer services.

A third state-funded preschool initiative, the Early Launch to Learning Initiative (ELLI), was established in 2004 as part of New Jersey's efforts to provide access to high-quality preschool education to all the state's 4-year-olds. All non-Abbott districts are encouraged to apply for funding, including school districts that already provide preschool but need additional funding to serve more income-eligible children, extend program hours, or improve program quality. Districts already receiving ECPA funding may apply for ELLI funds as well, to be used to improve program quality or extend program hours. ELLI funding levels are based on the projected number of low-income 4-year-old children the district plans to serve and the length of the program day.

Under the School Funding Reform Act of 2008, the state plans to fund full-day preschool for at-risk 3- and 4-year-olds in districts throughout the state. The expansion will be phased in over six years, beginning in the 2008-2009 program year, with the goal of providing preschool for an additional 30,000 children by the 2013-2014 school year.

In order to document the contributions New Jersey makes to preschool through its separate initiatives, we first present summary information reflecting the state's overall commitment to preschool. Enrollment and state spending for the Abbott, ECPA, and ELLI initiatives are taken into account. Next, we present specific details about each initiative in the state. The third page of this profile focuses exclusively on the Abbott program; the fourth page focuses exclusively on the ECPA program; and the final page focuses exclusively on the ELLI program.

STATE OVERVIEW

Total state program enrollment 47,004

Total state spending $516,541,421

State spending per child enrolled $10,989

All reported spending per child enrolled $10,989

STATE PRE-K AND HEAD START ENROLLMENT AS PERCENTAGE OF TOTAL POPULATION

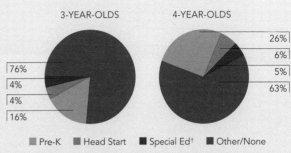

3-YEAR-OLDS

76%
4%
4%
16%

4-YEAR-OLDS

26%
6%
5%
63%

■ Pre-K ■ Head Start ■ Special Ed† ■ Other/None

† This number represents children in special education who are not enrolled in Head Start but may be enrolled in state-funded pre-K.

SPENDING PER CHILD ENROLLED

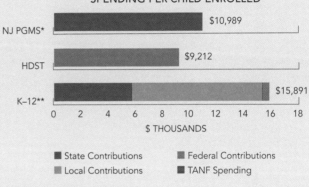

NJ PGMS* $10,989

HDST $9,212

K–12** $15,891

0 2 4 6 8 10 12 14 16 18
$ THOUSANDS

■ State Contributions ■ Federal Contributions
■ Local Contributions ■ TANF Spending

* Pre-K programs may receive additional funds from federal or local sources that are not included in this figure.

**K–12 expenditures include capital spending as well as current operating expenditures.

Data are for the '07-'08 school year, unless otherwise noted.

State per-child spending in New Jersey appears to be higher for state prekindergarten programs than for K–12 education, but in fact this is not the case in the districts that offer state pre-K. More than 80 percent of state prekindergarten enrollment is in Abbott districts, which also have a K–12 state aid payment that is nearly 3 times the statewide average per child. In other words, state spending per child is also much higher for K–12 in the Abbott districts.

ACCESS RANKINGS	
4-YEAR-OLDS	3-YEAR-OLDS
15	4

RESOURCES RANKINGS	
STATE SPENDING	ALL REPORTED SPENDING
1	1

NEW JERSEY ABBOTT PRESCHOOL PROGRAM

ACCESS

Total state program enrollment 38,818

School districts that offer state program 5%

Income requirement ....None[1]

Hours of operation............................6 hours/day, 5 days/week[2]

Operating schedule ....Academic year[2]

Special education enrollment 11,034

Federally funded Head Start enrollment.......................12,229

State-funded Head Start enrollment 0

STATE PRE-K AND HEAD START ENROLLMENT AS PERCENTAGE OF TOTAL POPULATION

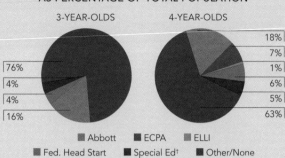

3-YEAR-OLDS
- 76%
- 4%
- 4%
- 16%

4-YEAR-OLDS
- 18%
- 7%
- 1%
- 6%
- 5%
- 63%

■ Abbott ■ ECPA ■ ELLI
■ Fed. Head Start ■ Special Ed[†] ■ Other/None

[†] This number represents children in special education who are not enrolled in Head Start but may be enrolled in state-funded pre-K.

QUALITY STANDARDS CHECKLIST

POLICY	STATE PRE-K REQUIREMENT	BENCHMARK	DOES REQUIREMENT MEET BENCHMARK?
Early learning standards	Comprehensive	Comprehensive	☑
Teacher degree	BA	BA	☑
Teacher specialized training	Certification in Pre-K–3	Specializing in pre-K	☑
Assistant teacher degree	HSD[3]	CDA or equivalent	☐
Teacher in-service	100 clock hours/5 years	At least 15 hours/year	☑
Maximum class size		20 or lower	☑
3-year-olds	15		
4-year-olds	15		
Staff-child ratio		1:10 or better	☑
3-year-olds	2:15		
4-year-olds	2:15		
Screening/referral and support services	Vision, hearing, health, developmental; and support services[4]	Vision, hearing, health; and at least 1 support service	☑
Meals	Breakfast, lunch and snack	At least 1/day	☑
Monitoring	Site visits and other monitoring	Site visits	☑

TOTAL BENCHMARKS MET

9

RESOURCES

Total state pre-K spending............................$477,356,871

Local match required? ....No

State spending per child enrolled.........................$12,297

All reported spending per child enrolled* $12,297

SPENDING PER CHILD ENROLLED

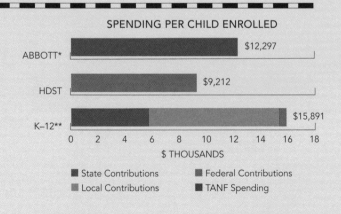

ABBOTT* $12,297

HDST $9,212

K–12** $15,891

0 2 4 6 8 10 12 14 16 18
$ THOUSANDS

■ State Contributions ■ Federal Contributions
■ Local Contributions ■ TANF Spending

* Pre-K programs may receive additional funds from federal or local sources that are not included in this figure.

** K–12 expenditures include capital spending as well as current operating expenditures.

Data are for the '07-'08 school year, unless otherwise noted.

[1] Only districts where at least 40 percent of children qualify for free or reduced-price lunch receive funding through this initiative. All 3- and 4-year-old children within those districts are eligible to participate.

[2] Due to a change in regulations from the Department of Children and Families, the before- and after-care program moved to a voucher system. As a result of this change, providers are only required by the Department of Education to provide a 6-hour educational program for the 180 day academic year. Providers can choose to operate a before- and after-care program and/or a full-year (245

day) program. If they chose to do so, all children meeting income requirements are paid for through the DCF.

[3] Assistant teachers in public schools supported by Title I funding must meet the education/degree requirements specified in NCLB.

[4] Dental screenings and referrals are determined locally. Support services include parenting support or training, parent involvement activities, health services for children, information about nutrition, referral to social services, and transition to kindergarten activities.

NEW JERSEY NON-ABBOTT EARLY CHILDHOOD PROGRAM AID

ACCESS

Total state program enrollment 7,526

School districts that offer state program 17%

Income requirement ....None[1]

Hours of operation ....At least 2.75 hours/day,
5 days/week[2]

Operating schedule ....Academic year

Special education enrollment 11,034

Federally funded Head Start enrollment..........................12,229

State-funded Head Start enrollment 0

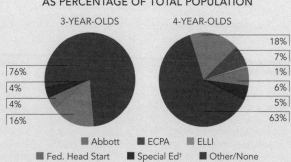

STATE PRE-K AND HEAD START ENROLLMENT AS PERCENTAGE OF TOTAL POPULATION

3-YEAR-OLDS

76%
4%
4%
16%

4-YEAR-OLDS

18%
7%
1%
6%
5%
63%

■ Abbott ■ ECPA ■ ELLI
■ Fed. Head Start ■ Special Ed[†] ■ Other/None

[†] This number represents children in special education who are not enrolled in Head Start but may be enrolled in state-funded pre-K.

QUALITY STANDARDS CHECKLIST

POLICY	STATE PRE-K REQUIREMENT	BENCHMARK	DOES REQUIREMENT MEET BENCHMARK?
Early learning standards	Comprehensive	Comprehensive	☑
Teacher degree	BA	BA	☑
Teacher specialized training	Certification in Pre-K–3	Specializing in pre-K	☑
Assistant teacher degree	HSD[3]	CDA or equivalent	☐
Teacher in-service	100 clock hours/5 years	At least 15 hours/year	☑
Maximum class size		20 or lower	☐
3-year-olds	25[4]		
4-year-olds	25[4]		
Staff-child ratio		1:10 or better	☐
3-year-olds	1:25[4]		
4-year-olds	1:25[4]		
Screening/referral and support services	Vision, hearing, health, developmental; and support services[5]	Vision, hearing, health; and at least 1 support service	☑
Meals	Depend on length of program day[6]	At least 1/day	☐
Monitoring	Site visits and other monitoring	Site visits	☑

TOTAL BENCHMARKS MET

6

RESOURCES

Total state pre-K spending ....$36,500,000[7]

Local match required? ....No

State spending per child enrolled $4,850

All reported spending per child enrolled* $4,850

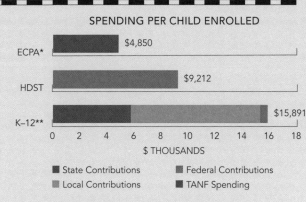

SPENDING PER CHILD ENROLLED

ECPA* $4,850

HDST $9,212

K–12** $15,891

$ THOUSANDS

■ State Contributions ■ Federal Contributions
■ Local Contributions ■ TANF Spending

* Pre-K programs may receive additional funds from federal or local sources that are not included in this figure.

** K–12 expenditures include capital spending as well as current operating expenditures.

Data are for the '07-'08 school year, unless otherwise noted.

[1] Only districts where 20 to 40 percent of children qualify for free or reduced-price lunch receive funding through this initiative. All 3- and 4-year-old children within those districts are eligible to participate. However, the program is only open to 3-year-olds once the district has offered full-day kindergarten to all age-eligible children, and either half- or full-day preschool to all 4-year-olds.

[2] Half-day programs must be at least 2.75 hours per day; full-day programs must be at least 6 hours per day. Length of program day varies by districts. In some cases, both half- and full-day programs are offered.

[3] Assistant teachers in public schools supported by Title I funding must meet the education/degree requirements specified in NCLB.

[4] Beginning July 1, 2008 the maximum class size changed to 18 and the staff-child ratio requirement changed to 1:9.

[5] Dental screenings and referrals are determined locally. Support services include education services or job training for parents, parent involvement activities, and transition to kindergarten activities.

[6] Meals are required in full-day programs.

[7] This figure is an estimate of state funds directed to services for preschool-age children.

NEW JERSEY EARLY LAUNCH TO LEARNING INITIATIVE

ACCESS

Total state program enrollment 660

School districts that offer state program 5%

Income requirement ....185% FPL[1]

Hours of operation ....2.75 hours/day (part-day),
6 hours/day (full-day), 5 days/week[2]

Operating schedule ....Academic year

Special education enrollment 11,034

Federally funded Head Start enrollment.......................12,229

State-funded Head Start enrollment 0

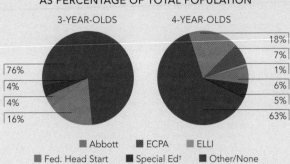

STATE PRE-K AND HEAD START ENROLLMENT AS PERCENTAGE OF TOTAL POPULATION

3-YEAR-OLDS: 76%, 4%, 4%, 16%

4-YEAR-OLDS: 18%, 7%, 1%, 6%, 5%, 63%

■ Abbott ■ ECPA ■ ELLI
■ Fed. Head Start ■ Special Ed[†] ■ Other/None

[†] This number represents children in special education who are not enrolled in Head Start but may be enrolled in state-funded pre-K.

QUALITY STANDARDS CHECKLIST

POLICY	STATE PRE-K REQUIREMENT	BENCHMARK	DOES REQUIREMENT MEET BENCHMARK?
Early learning standards	Comprehensive	Comprehensive	☑
Teacher degree	BA	BA	☑
Teacher specialized training	Certification in Pre-K–3	Specializing in pre-K	☑
Assistant teacher degree	HSD[3]	CDA or equivalent	☐
Teacher in-service	100 clock hours/5 years	At least 15 hours/year	☑
Maximum class size		20 or lower	☑
3-year-olds	NA		
4-year-olds	20		
Staff-child ratio		1:10 or better	☑
3-year-olds	NA		
4-year-olds	1:10		
Screening/referral and support services	Vision, hearing, health developmental; and support services[4]	Vision, hearing, health; and at least 1 support service	☑
Meals	Depend on length of program day[5]	At least 1/day	☐
Monitoring	Site visits and other monitoring	Site visits	☑

TOTAL BENCHMARKS MET

8

RESOURCES

Total state pre-K spending $2,684,550

Local match required? ....Yes[6]

State spending per child enrolled.................................$4,068

All reported spending per child enrolled* $4,068

* Pre-K programs may receive additional funds from federal or local sources that are not included in this figure.

** K–12 expenditures include capital spending as well as current operating expenditures.

Data are for the '07-'08 school year, unless otherwise noted.

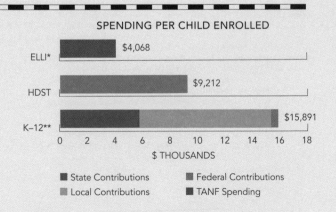

SPENDING PER CHILD ENROLLED

ELLI*: $4,068

HDST: $9,212

K–12**: $15,891

$ THOUSANDS

■ State Contributions ■ Federal Contributions
■ Local Contributions ■ TANF Spending

---

[1] Districts may enroll other students in unusual circumstances.

[2] Districts may offer either a half day (2 hours, 45 minutes) or full day (6 hours), and for 5 days per week.

[3] Assistant teachers in public schools supported by Title I funding must meet the education/degree requirements specified in NCLB.

[4] Dental screenings and referrals are determined locally. Support services include parent involvement activities and transition to kindergarten activities.

[5] Full-day programs must offer breakfast and lunch.

[6] Special education and local funding or tuition must be used to meet costs beyond DOE funding.

New Mexico

PERCENT OF STATE POPULATION ENROLLED

STATE SPENDING PER CHILD ENROLLED
(2008 DOLLARS)

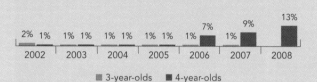

■ 3-year-olds ■ 4-year-olds

The 2007-2008 school year was the third year of operation for the state's prekindergarten education program, New Mexico PreK. New Mexico PreK's exclusive purpose is to provide center-based early childhood services for 4-year-olds. Half of the enrolled children are served in public schools while the other half are served in nonpublic settings such as community and municipal child care centers, Head Start programs, universities, a Bureau of Indian Affairs school, and family child care homes. New Mexico PreK does not have a specific income requirement for eligibility but two-thirds of enrolled children at each site must live in the attendance zone of a Title I elementary school. All staff members are trained to use the New Mexico PreK Observational Assessment, which was implemented program-wide during the 2006-2007 school year and is now available in Spanish.

Funding for New Mexico PreK is awarded on a competitive basis with priority for funding given to programs in areas with schools with the highest percentages of children failing to meet No Child Left Behind's adequate yearly progress in math and reading. Half-day slots are funded based on half of the funding level for kindergarten slots. The New Mexico PreK initiative continued to be entirely state-funded during its third year of operation, with a budget of $10.9 million serving more than 3,500 children. Increases in funding led to increases in enrollment for the 2007-2008 and 2008-2009 school years.

Another state-funded preschool initiative, the Child Development Program, offers services including family support services, home visits, and preschool education programs to at-risk children from birth to age 3 who do not qualify for other eligibility-based programs. However, programs can limit eligibility to specific risk factors based on locally determined needs such as homelessness, poverty, or having a teen parent. Funding cuts over the past few years have resulted in a decrease in the number of preschool-age children served by the program, and during the 2007-2008 school year the Child Development Program did not serve any 4-year-olds. Because the Child Development Program no longer serves 4-year-olds and serves less than one percent of New Mexico's 3-year-olds, NIEER no longer considers the program to primarily focus on providing center-based early childhood education to 3- and 4-year-olds.

New Mexico also allocated $1,496,915 in state funds to supplement services in federal Head Start classrooms.

ACCESS RANKINGS		RESOURCES RANKINGS	
4-YEAR-OLDS	3-YEAR-OLDS	STATE SPENDING	ALL REPORTED SPENDING
25	None Served	28	33

NEW MEXICO PREK

ACCESS

Total state program enrollment 3,570

School districts that offer state program 54%

Income requirement ....None

Hours of operation ....Determined locally[1]

Operating schedule ....Academic year

Special education enrollment 3,679

Federally funded Head Start enrollment 6,758

State-funded Head Start enrollment ....0[2]

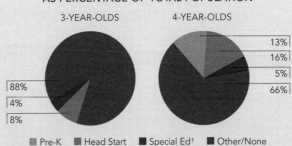

STATE PRE-K AND HEAD START ENROLLMENT AS PERCENTAGE OF TOTAL POPULATION

3-YEAR-OLDS
- 88%
- 4%
- 8%

4-YEAR-OLDS
- 13%
- 16%
- 5%
- 66%

■ Pre-K ■ Head Start ■ Special Ed[†] ■ Other/None

† This number represents children in special education who are not enrolled in Head Start, but includes children who are enrolled in state-funded pre-K.

QUALITY STANDARDS CHECKLIST

POLICY	STATE PRE-K REQUIREMENT	BENCHMARK	DOES REQUIREMENT MEET BENCHMARK?
Early learning standards	Comprehensive	Comprehensive	☑
Teacher degree	BA[3]	BA	☑
Teacher specialized training	Licensure in ECE Birth–grade 3	Specializing in pre-K	☑
Assistant teacher degree	AA[4]	CDA or equivalent	☑
Teacher in-service	At least 45 clock hours	At least 15 hours/year	☑
Maximum class size		20 or lower	☑
3-year-olds	NA		
4-year-olds	20		
Staff-child ratio		1:10 or better	☑
3-year-olds	NA		
4-year-olds	1:10		
Screening/referral and support services	Vision, hearing, health, dental developmental; and support services[5]	Vision, hearing, health; and at least 1 support service	☑
Meals	Snack[6]	At least 1/day	☐
Monitoring	Site visits and other monitoring	Site visits	☑

TOTAL BENCHMARKS MET

9

RESOURCES

Total state pre-K spending ....$10,909,000[7]

Local match required? ....No

State Head Start spending ....$1,496,915[2]

State spending per child enrolled $3,056

All reported spending per child enrolled* $3,056

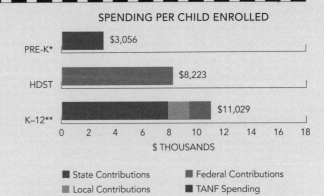

SPENDING PER CHILD ENROLLED

- PRE-K*: $3,056
- HDST: $8,223
- K–12**: $11,029

($ THOUSANDS, scale 0 to 18)

■ State Contributions ■ Federal Contributions
■ Local Contributions ■ TANF Spending

* Pre-K programs may receive additional funds from federal or local sources that are not included in this figure.

**K–12 expenditures include capital spending as well as current operating expenditures.

Data are for the '07-'08 school year, unless otherwise noted.

[1] Schedules are determined locally but the majority of programs operate 2.5-3 hours daily for 5 days per week. Programs must provide 450 hours of classroom instruction plus 90 hours of parent/family activities each year.

[2] State Head Start funds are used to provide extended-day services to Head Start children whose families are participating in the TANF program.

[3] For each classroom, the lead teacher must hold a New Mexico Early Childhood Teacher License: Birth through Third Grade (requires a BA) within five years of the program starting.

[4] Assistant teachers in public and nonpublic schools are expected to obtain an AA in early childhood education within five years of a program starting.

[5] Support services include four annual parent conferences or home visits, parent education or job training, parenting support or training, parent involvement activities, health services for children, information about nutrition, referral to social services, and transition to kindergarten activities.

[6] All programs must offer a snack. If operating more than 3.5 hours per day, programs must also offer a meal. Beginning in the 2008-2009 school year, all programs will be required to provide at least one meal per day.

[7] Additional funds not counted in these figures are $327,000 for a program evaluation, $1,835,600 for professional development and technical assistance, and $1,000,000 for program start-up equipment.

New York

PERCENT OF STATE POPULATION ENROLLED

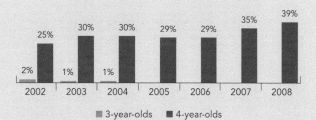

■ 3-year-olds   ■ 4-year-olds

STATE SPENDING PER CHILD ENROLLED
(2008 DOLLARS)

New York's Universal Prekindergarten (UPK) program began providing prekindergarten services in 1998. The program aims to serve all 4-year-olds in the state, regardless of income, but has not received sufficient funding to meet this goal. As a result, UPK served about 40 percent of the state's 4-year-olds during the 2007-2008 school year. Districts offering UPK slots use a random lottery system to select children for enrollment. Funds are distributed directly to school districts to operate prekindergarten programs, but districts are required to use at least 10 percent of their funding to subcontract with Head Start, private child care centers, or other community agencies. More than half of UPK funding was subcontracted to local providers for the 2007-2008 school year. UPK teachers in public schools must hold a New York state teaching certification. Teachers in nonpublic UPK settings are not required to be certified as long as they are supervised by a certified teacher.

Prior to the creation of the UPK initiative, New York offered preschool education through the Targeted Prekindergarten (TPK) program. This program was originally established as the Experimental Prekindergarten (EPK) program in 1966 and was one of the earliest state-funded preschool education programs in the nation. TPK funding was used to provide family activities and social services in addition to half-day preschool.

In January 2006, the New York State Board of Regents recommended that the UPK and TPK programs be combined into the New York Universal Prekindergarten program. The goal is for this program to receive adequate funding to serve all 4-year-olds in New York. As a result, the TPK program ceased operating after the 2006-2007 school year and UPK's funding was increased by 50 percent for the 2007-2008 school year. As a result of the new UPK funding formula in 2007-2008, all school districts in the state were eligible to receive UPK funding for the first time. Fifty-nine percent of school districts offered the program in 2007-2008, including 142 districts that did so for the first time. The state will offer planning grants to assist in the expansion of UPK.

New York will adopt prekindergarten standards during the 2008-2009 school year. New UPK regulations will emphasize the alignment of curricula and instruction with the learning standards and assessment.

ACCESS RANKINGS		RESOURCES RANKINGS	
4-YEAR-OLDS	3-YEAR-OLDS	STATE SPENDING	ALL REPORTED SPENDING
8	25	18	24

NEW YORK UNIVERSAL PREKINDERGARTEN

ACCESS

Total state program enrollment 91,517

School districts that offer state program ....58%[1]

Income requirement ....None

Hours of operation ....2.5 hours/day (part-day),
5 hours/day (full-day), 5 days/week

Operating schedule ....Academic year

Special education enrollment 44,222

Federally funded Head Start enrollment 43,316

State-funded Head Start enrollment 0

STATE PRE-K AND HEAD START ENROLLMENT AS PERCENTAGE OF TOTAL POPULATION

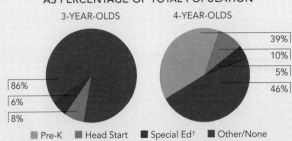

3-YEAR-OLDS

4-YEAR-OLDS

86% | 6% | 8%

39% | 10% | 5% | 46%

■ Pre-K ■ Head Start ■ Special Ed† ■ Other/None

† This number represents children in special education who are not enrolled in state-funded pre-K or Head Start.

QUALITY STANDARDS CHECKLIST

POLICY	STATE PRE-K REQUIREMENT	BENCHMARK	DOES REQUIREMENT MEET BENCHMARK?
Early learning standards	Not comprehensive	Comprehensive	☐
Teacher degree	BA prior to 1978; MA after (public); AA or CDA (nonpublic)[2]	BA	☐
Teacher specialized training	Certification in Birth–Grade 2 (public); AA in ECE or meets CDA requirements (nonpublic)[3]	Specializing in pre-K	☑
Assistant teacher degree	Level I certification (public); HSD (nonpublic)[4]	CDA or equivalent	☐
Teacher in-service	175 clock hours/5 years	At least 15 hours/year	☑
Maximum class size		20 or lower	☑
3-year-olds	NA		
4-year-olds	20		
Staff-child ratio		1:10 or better	☑
3-year-olds	NA		
4-year-olds	1:9		
Screening/referral and support services	Vision, hearing, health, dental, developmental; and support services[5]	Vision, hearing, health; and at least 1 support service	☑
Meals	Depend on length of program day[6]	At least 1/day	☐
Monitoring	Site visits and other monitoring	Site visits	☑

TOTAL BENCHMARKS MET

6

RESOURCES

Total state pre-K spending $361,293,769

Local match required? ....No

State spending per child enrolled $3,948

All reported spending per child enrolled* $3,948

SPENDING PER CHILD ENROLLED

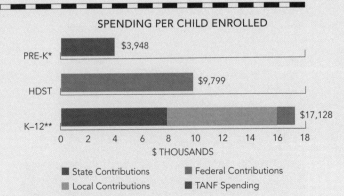

PRE-K* $3,948

HDST $9,799

K–12** $17,128

$ THOUSANDS

■ State Contributions ■ Federal Contributions
■ Local Contributions ■ TANF Spending

* Pre-K programs may receive additional funds from federal or local sources that are not included in this figure.

** K–12 expenditures include capital spending as well as current operating expenditures.

Data are for the '07-'08 school year, unless otherwise noted.

1 2007-2008 was the first year that funding was made available to all school districts in New York state. Of the 677 districts, 396 chose to participate in UPK during the 2007-2008 school year.

2 Since 2004, programs in nonpublic school settings have been required to meet the same certification requirements as those in public settings. However, a legislative amendment allowed certain community-based organizations to be exempt from this requirement until at least 2010, as long as uncertified teachers receive on-site supervision by certified teachers.

3 Teachers in community-based organizations are currently exempt from certification if they have on-site supervision by a certified teacher.

4 Level I certification requires a high school diploma or equivalent and passing of the Assessment of Teaching Assistant Skills Test. Assistant teachers employed by nonpublic schools must meet the standards of the licensing or registering agency.

5 Support services include parent education or job training, parenting support or training, parent involvement activities, health services for parents and children, referral to social services, and transition to kindergarten activities. The number of required annual parent conferences or home visits is determined locally.

6 Programs operating fewer than 3 hours must provide a nutritional meal or snack. Programs operating more than 3 hours must provide appropriate meals and snacks to ensure that nutritional needs of children are met.

North Carolina

PERCENT OF STATE POPULATION ENROLLED

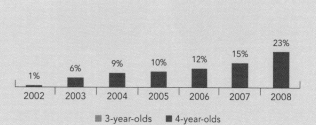

1% 2002
6% 2003
9% 2004
10% 2005
12% 2006
15% 2007
23% 2008

■ 3-year-olds ■ 4-year-olds

STATE SPENDING PER CHILD ENROLLED
(2008 DOLLARS)

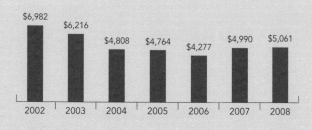

$6,982 2002
$6,216 2003
$4,808 2004
$4,764 2005
$4,277 2006
$4,990 2007
$5,061 2008

North Carolina began offering its *More at Four* Pre-Kindergarten Program in 2001. The program is targeted to at-risk 4-year-old children who are served through *More at Four* in Head Start agencies, private child care centers, and public schools. Nonpublic program settings can receive state funding only if they receive high quality ratings under the state child care licensing system and match the teacher credentialing requirements of public schools, which involve holding a bachelor's degree and a birth–kindergarten license. Nonpublic settings have up to four years to phase in these high-quality standards.

Children are eligible for *More at Four* if they come from families with incomes below 75 percent of the state median income or if they have other risk factors including limited English proficiency, educational or developmental delay, a chronic health condition, or an identified disability. Additionally, children of active duty military personnel are eligible for the program. Since the 2005-2006 school year, *More at Four* programs have been required to follow early learning standards. The North Carolina Office of School Readiness is currently finalizing recommendations for curricula that are aligned with the state's early learning standards, including providing opportunities to develop behaviors, competencies and knowledge.

More at Four has been funded through the state lottery, which has allowed for rapid expansion. The state added 10,000 slots that became available during the 2007-2008 school year, expanding the program by more than one-third. In the 2008-2009 school year, an additional $30 million will be provided to continue to expand the program for at-risk 4-year-olds, with a significant amount of the money being used to increase per-child spending.

North Carolina also contributed to the advancement of preschool education in the state with the creation of the Smart Start program in 1993. Smart Start supports collaboration and local planning to provide comprehensive early childhood services for children from birth to age 5. The goals of the program are to support early care and education programs, provide family support services, improve child health outcomes, and increase the overall quality of child care. This report focuses only on data from the *More at Four* program.

ACCESS RANKINGS		RESOURCES RANKINGS	
4-YEAR-OLDS	3-YEAR-OLDS	STATE SPENDING	ALL REPORTED SPENDING
16	None Served	10	11

NORTH CAROLINA MORE AT FOUR

ACCESS

Total state program enrollment 27,788

School districts that offer state program ....100% (counties)

Income requirement ....80% of children must be
be at or below 75% SMI

Hours of operation ....6-6.5 hours/day, 5 days/week

Operating schedule ....Academic year

Special education enrollment 10,683

Federally funded Head Start enrollment 17,564

State-funded Head Start enrollment 0

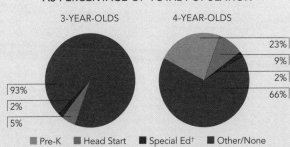

**STATE PRE-K AND HEAD START ENROLLMENT
AS PERCENTAGE OF TOTAL POPULATION**

3-YEAR-OLDS

4-YEAR-OLDS

93%
2%
5%

23%
9%
2%
66%

■ Pre-K   ■ Head Start   ■ Special Ed[†]   ■ Other/None

[†] This number represents children in special education
who are not enrolled in state-funded pre-K or Head Start.

QUALITY STANDARDS CHECKLIST

POLICY	STATE PRE-K REQUIREMENT	BENCHMARK	DOES REQUIREMENT MEET BENCHMARK?
Early learning standards	Comprehensive	Comprehensive	☑
Teacher degree	BA[1]	BA	☑
Teacher specialized training	Birth–K license[1]	Specializing in pre-K	☑
Assistant teacher degree	CDA or meets NCLB requirements (public), CDA (nonpublic)[2]	CDA or equivalent	☑
Teacher in-service	15 clock hours/5 years	At least 15 hours/year	☑
Maximum class size		20 or lower	☑
3-year-olds	NA		
4-year-olds	18		
Staff-child ratio		1:10 or better	☑
3-year-olds	NA		
4-year-olds	1:9		
Screening/referral and support services	Vision, hearing, health, dental, developmental; and support services[3]	Vision, hearing, health; and at least 1 support service	☑
Meals	Lunch and either breakfast or snack	At least 1/day	☑
Monitoring	Site visits and other monitoring	Site visits	☑

TOTAL BENCHMARKS MET

10

RESOURCES

Total state pre-K spending $140,635,709

Local match required?......................Yes, amount not specified

State spending per child enrolled $5,061

All reported spending per child enrolled* $6,954

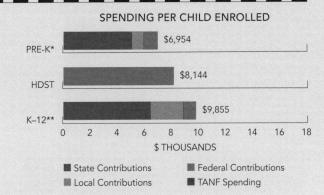

SPENDING PER CHILD ENROLLED

PRE-K* $6,954

HDST $8,144

K–12** $9,855

0 2 4 6 8 10 12 14 16 18
$ THOUSANDS

■ State Contributions   ■ Federal Contributions
■ Local Contributions   ■ TANF Spending

---

* Pre-K programs may receive additional funds from federal or local sources
that are not included in this figure.

**K–12 expenditures include capital spending as well as current operating
expenditures.

Data are for the '07-'08 school year, unless otherwise noted.

[1] All lead teachers in a *More at Four* classroom are required to hold a bachelor's
degree in early childhood education or a related field and a North Carolina
Birth–Kindergarten Teacher Licensure. Teachers in nonpublic settings must have
a minimum of an associate's degree and work to obtain a bachelor's degree and
birth–kindergarten license within four years of the program being recognized as
a *More at Four* Program. In some circumstances, exceptions to this timeline may
be granted if the provider appears to be working in good faith to reach this
level of credential.

[2] NCLB generally requires assistant teachers to have a 2-year degree. *More at
Four* requires that assistant teachers who meet NCLB requirements but do not
hold a CDA have 6 semester hours of EC coursework or two years experience in
an early childhood classroom. An associate's degree is highly encouraged for
assistant teachers in nonpublic settings.

[3] Support services include parent involvement activities and transition to
kindergarten activities. Programs must also provide information on medical
homes and health insurance. Parent conferences and home visits are
recommended but are not required.

North Dakota

NO PROGRAM

ACCESS RANKINGS	
4-YEAR-OLDS	3-YEAR-OLDS
No Program	

RESOURCES RANKINGS	
STATE SPENDING	ALL REPORTED SPENDING
No Program	

ACCESS

Total state program enrollment 0

School districts that offer state program........................NA

Income requirement ....NA

Hours of operation ....NA

Operating schedule ....NA

Special education enrollment 883

Federally funded Head Start enrollment....................2,869

State-funded Head Start enrollment 0

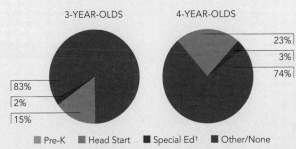

**STATE PRE-K AND HEAD START ENROLLMENT
AS PERCENTAGE OF TOTAL POPULATION**

3-YEAR-OLDS   4-YEAR-OLDS

23%
3%
74%

83%
2%
15%

■ Pre-K   ■ Head Start   ■ Special Ed†   ■ Other/None

† This number represents children in special education
who are not enrolled in Head Start.

QUALITY STANDARDS CHECKLIST

RESOURCES

Total state pre-K spending...............................$0

Local match required? ....NA

State Head Start spending................................$0

State spending per child enrolled $0

All reported spending per child enrolled*.....................$0

* Pre-K programs may receive additional funds from federal or local sources
   that are not included in this figure.

** K–12 expenditures include capital spending as well as current operating
    expenditures.

Data are for the '07-'08 school year, unless otherwise noted.

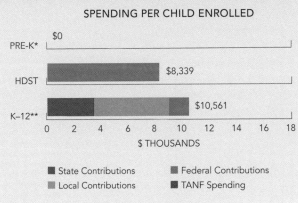

SPENDING PER CHILD ENROLLED

PRE-K* $0

HDST $8,339

K–12** $10,561

0   2   4   6   8   10   12   14   16   18
$ THOUSANDS

■ State Contributions   ■ Federal Contributions
■ Local Contributions   ■ TANF Spending

Ohio

PERCENT OF STATE POPULATION ENROLLED

STATE SPENDING PER CHILD ENROLLED
(2008 DOLLARS)

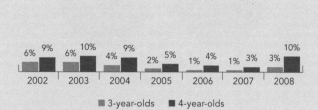

2002: 6% 9%
2003: 6% 10%
2004: 4% 9%
2005: 2% 5%
2006: 1% 4%
2007: 1% 3%
2008: 3% 10%

■ 3-year-olds ■ 4-year-olds

$6,680 (2002)
$5,823 (2003)
$5,461 (2004)
$7,426 (2005)
$2,578 (2006)
$2,663 (2007)
$7,260 (2008)

After a successful four-year pilot program, the Ohio Public School Preschool Program (PSP) was established in 1990. Now known as Early Childhood Education (ECE), the program serves 3- and 4-year-olds from families with incomes up to 200 percent of the federal poverty level. A sliding fee scale is used for children from families above 100 percent of FPL. Children from families above 200 percent of FPL can also attend the program using district funds or parent tuition, if space permits. Funds are distributed directly to public schools, which may in turn subcontract with Head Start programs or private child care centers. During the 2006-2007 school year, an increase in per-child spending led to a decrease in the number of funded children. With the new biennium starting July 1, 2009, additional funding for Early Childhood Education increased the number of districts receiving funds from 112 to 205. This funding provided services for a total of 6,092 children.

Beginning in 2005, Ohio decreased supplemental state funding for the federal Head Start program in favor of providing state funds to the Early Learning Initiative (ELI). The program is a companion to the ECE program and requires the same educational and comprehensive services. The purpose of ELI is to provide education experiences that address school readiness and provide full-day, year-round services to children of working families. Agencies that receive funding directly are public schools, Head Start agencies, and private and faith-based child care centers. These agencies can in turn subcontract with the same types of agencies as well as with family child care providers. Eligibility for the ELI program is dependent on family income. Children with family incomes under 185 percent of FPL are eligible for the program. Formerly, eligibility was reassessed every six months and unless other funding was available, services were discontinued for families who began earning incomes above 185 percent of FPL. Effective with the 2007-2008 school year, children are assured of continuous enrollment for a full year after initially being determined eligible for ELI services. This change means that the ELI program now fits NIEER's definition of a state-funded preschool education program.

The first two pages of this state profile document Ohio's overall contributions and commitment to state prekindergarten, including state spending and enrollment for both the Early Childhood Education initiative and the Early Learning Initiative. The third page focuses exclusively on the Early Childhood Education initiative and the final page presents specific details about the Early Learning Initiative.

STATE OVERVIEW

Total state program enrollment 19,215

Total state spending $139,509,323

State spending per child enrolled $7,260

All reported spending per child enrolled $7,260

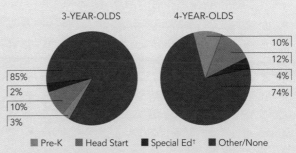

STATE PRE-K AND HEAD START ENROLLMENT AS PERCENTAGE OF TOTAL POPULATION

3-YEAR-OLDS

- 85%
- 2%
- 10%
- 3%

4-YEAR-OLDS

- 10%
- 12%
- 4%
- 74%

■ Pre-K ■ Head Start ■ Special Ed† ■ Other/None

† This number represents children in special education who are not enrolled in Head Start or ECE.

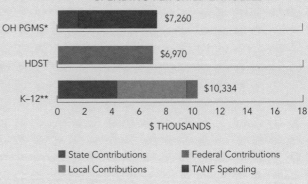

SPENDING PER CHILD ENROLLED

OH PGMS* — $7,260

HDST — $6,970

K–12** — $10,334

0 2 4 6 8 10 12 14 16 18

$ THOUSANDS

■ State Contributions ■ Federal Contributions
■ Local Contributions ■ TANF Spending

* Pre-K programs may receive additional funds from federal or local sources that are not included in this figure.

** K–12 expenditures include capital spending as well as current operating expenditures.

Data are for the '07-'08 school year, unless otherwise noted.

ACCESS RANKINGS	
4-YEAR-OLDS	**3-YEAR-OLDS**
29	15

RESOURCES RANKINGS	
STATE SPENDING	**ALL REPORTED SPENDING**
4	9

OHIO EARLY CHILDHOOD EDUCATION

ACCESS

Total state program enrollment ....6,166[1]

School districts that offer state program 28%

Income requirement ....200% FPL

Hours of operation ....Determined locally[2]

Operating schedule ....Academic year[2]

Special education enrollment 13,433

Federally funded Head Start enrollment 32,651

State-funded Head Start enrollment 0

STATE PRE-K AND HEAD START ENROLLMENT AS PERCENTAGE OF TOTAL POPULATION

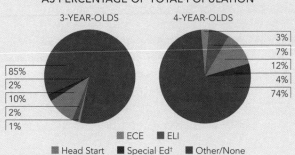

3-YEAR-OLDS
- 85%
- 2%
- 10%
- 2%
- 1%

4-YEAR-OLDS
- 3%
- 7%
- 12%
- 4%
- 74%

■ ECE   ■ ELI
■ Head Start   ■ Special Ed[†]   ■ Other/None

[†] This number represents children in special education who are not enrolled in Head Start or ECE.

QUALITY STANDARDS CHECKLIST

POLICY	STATE PRE-K REQUIREMENT	BENCHMARK	DOES REQUIREMENT MEET BENCHMARK?
Early learning standards	Not comprehensive[3]	Comprehensive	☐
Teacher degree	AA (public), CDA (nonpublic)[4]	BA	☐
Teacher specialized training	Pre-K associate level teaching cert., Pre-K, K, or EC license (public); Meets CDA requirements (nonpublic)	Specializing in pre-K	☑
Assistant teacher degree	HSD	CDA or equivalent	☐
Teacher in-service	20 clock hours/2 years[5]	At least 15 hours/year	☐
Maximum class size		20 or lower	☐
3-year-olds	24		
4-year-olds	28		
Staff-child ratio		1:10 or better	☐
3-year-olds	1:12		
4-year-olds	1:14		
Screening/referral and support services	Vision, hearing, health, dental, developmental; and support services[6]	Vision, hearing, health; and at least 1 support service	☑
Meals	Depend on length of program day[7]	At least 1/day	☐
Monitoring	Site visits and other monitoring	Site visits	☑

TOTAL BENCHMARKS MET

3

RESOURCES

Total state pre-K spending $28,705,839

Local match required? ....No

State spending per child enrolled $4,656

All reported spending per child enrolled* $4,656

SPENDING PER CHILD ENROLLED

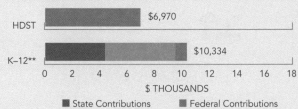

ECE* $4,656

HDST $6,970

K–12** $10,334

$ THOUSANDS

■ State Contributions   ■ Federal Contributions
■ Local Contributions   ■ TANF Spending

* Pre-K programs may receive additional funds from federal or local sources that are not included in this figure.

** K–12 expenditures include capital spending as well as current operating expenditures.

Data are for the '07–'08 school year, unless otherwise noted.

[1] An additional 1,250 children from families with income above 200 percent FPL paid full tuition; these children are not counted in the enrollment total.

[2] Most programs operate between 3 and 3.5 hours per day, 4 days per week. Operating schedules are generally coordinated with district calendars. The funded annual operating schedule is technically the academic year, but schools may choose year-long services.

[3] In addition to its Early Learning Content Standards, Ohio also has Program Guidelines that address child health and development, which have been reviewed and sanctioned by the state Board of Education.

[4] For nonpublic settings, at least 50 percent of their teachers must have an AA or

higher. All other teachers must be enrolled in an AA or higher degree program. By July 1, 2009 all teachers in programs that began in 2006 must have an AA.

[5] Effective in 2007-2008, teachers now have two years to complete 20 hours of in-service instead of one year.

[6] Screening and referrals for lead and hematocrit are also required. Support services include two annual parent conferences or home visits, parenting support or training, parent involvement activities, child health services, information about nutrition, referral to social services, and transition to kindergarten activities.

[7] Lunch must be provided for children in attendance beyond part-day hours and snack is also provided for children who attend full-day sessions.

OHIO EARLY LEARNING INITIATIVE

ACCESS

Total state program enrollment ....13,049[1]

School districts that offer state program ....91% (counties)

Income requirement ....165-185% FPL[2]

Hours of operation ....Determined locally[3]

Operating schedule ....Calendar year

Special education enrollment 13,433

Federally funded Head Start enrollment 32,651

State-funded Head Start enrollment 0

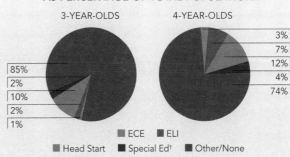

STATE PRE-K AND HEAD START ENROLLMENT AS PERCENTAGE OF TOTAL POPULATION

3-YEAR-OLDS

85%
2%
10%
2%
1%

4-YEAR-OLDS

3%
7%
12%
4%
74%

■ ECE ■ ELI ■ Head Start ■ Special Ed[†] ■ Other/None

[†] This number represents children in special education who are not enrolled in Head Start or ECE.

QUALITY STANDARDS CHECKLIST

POLICY	STATE PRE-K REQUIREMENT	BENCHMARK	DOES REQUIREMENT MEET BENCHMARK?
Early learning standards	Not comprehensive[4]	Comprehensive	☐
Teacher degree	HSD (public and nonpublic)[5]	BA	☐
Teacher specialized training	Pre-K associate level teaching cert., Pre-K–3 license (public); Pre-K associate level teaching cert. (nonpublic)	Specializing in pre-K	☑
Assistant teacher degree	HSD	CDA or equivalent	☐
Teacher in-service	20 clock hours/2 years[5]	At least 15 hours/year	☐
Maximum class size 3-year-olds 4-year-olds	 20 20	20 or lower	☑
Staff-child ratio 3-year-olds 4-year-olds	 1:10 1:10	1:10 or better	☑
Screening/referral and support services	Vision, hearing, health, dental, developmental; and support services[6]	Vision, hearing, health; and at least 1 support service	☑
Meals	Depends on length of program day[7]	At least 1/day	☐
Monitoring	Site visits and other monitoring	Site visits	☑

TOTAL BENCHMARKS MET

5

RESOURCES

Total state pre-K spending $110,803,484

Local match required? ....No

State spending per child enrolled ....$8,491[8]

All reported spending per child enrolled* ....$8,491[8]

SPENDING PER CHILD ENROLLED

ELI* — $8,491

HDST — $6,970

K–12** — $10,334

0 2 4 6 8 10 12 14 16 18
$ THOUSANDS

■ State Contributions ■ Federal Contributions
■ Local Contributions ■ TANF Spending

---

* Pre-K programs may receive additional funds from federal or local sources that are not included in this figure.

**K–12 expenditures include capital spending as well as current operating expenditures.

Data are for the '07-'08 school year, unless otherwise noted.

[1] Initial enrollment can occur at any point throughout the year. This number represents the average monthly enrollment.

[2] Families enter the program at up to 165 percent FPL and exit the program at 185 percent FPL.

[3] Programs are reimbursed by the number of hours of attendance based on hourly, part-time or full-time rates. Full-day reimbursement is based on100 or more hours per 4 weeks and part-day is based on 55 to 99.5 hours per 4 weeks. Programs operate 5 days per week.

[4] In addition to its Early Learning Content Standards, Ohio also has Program Guidelines that address child health and development, which have been reviewed and sanctioned by the state Board of Education.

[5] At least 50 percent of teachers must have an AA degree or higher. All other teachers must be working toward an AA degree.

[6] Screening and referrals for hematocrit are also required. Support services include two annual parent conferences or home visits, parenting support or training, parent involvement activities, child health services, information about nutrition, referral to social services, transition to kindergarten activities, and other support services.

[7] Programs must provide meals or snacks depending on the hours of attendance.

[8] This number is based on the average monthly enrollment and total spending. Each contracted agency is awarded approximately $10,438 per slot which could be for multiple children, who may enroll on a full-time, part-time or hourly basis.

Oklahoma

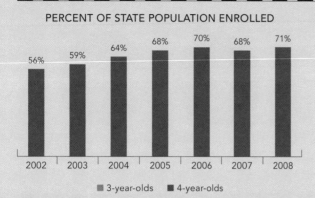

PERCENT OF STATE POPULATION ENROLLED

2002	2003	2004	2005	2006	2007	2008
56%	59%	64%	68%	70%	68%	71%

■ 3-year-olds ■ 4-year-olds

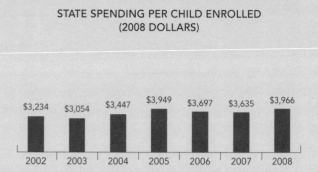

STATE SPENDING PER CHILD ENROLLED
(2008 DOLLARS)

2002	2003	2004	2005	2006	2007	2008
$3,234	$3,054	$3,447	$3,949	$3,697	$3,635	$3,966

In 1980, Oklahoma established a pilot preschool education program, the Early Childhood Four-Year-Old Program, aiming to eventually serve all 4-year-olds. In 1990 the program received statewide funding, but the state limited prekindergarten funding to only 4-year-olds eligible for Head Start, although districts could provide the program to other children using local funds or tuition. In 1998, Oklahoma offered free, voluntary access to state-funded preschool for all of its 4-year-olds, becoming the second state in the nation to do so.

Enrollment in the Early Childhood Four-Year-Old Program has steadily increased over the years with 99 percent of school districts now choosing to offer the program. Starting with the 2003-2004 school year, Oklahoma has ranked first in the nation every year for the percentage of 4-year-olds enrolled. In addition, greater proportions of 4-year-olds are now attending full-day programs.

Public school districts receive funding for the Early Childhood Four-Year-Old Program directly through the state's school finance formula. Districts are reimbursed at the district's per-pupil rate, with specific funding amounts or weights based on whether prekindergarten is offered for a half or full day. While districts receive funding directly, they may subcontract by placing a public school teacher with another type of provider, including Head Start programs, child care centers, and other community-based programs. During the 2007-2008 school year, more than 4,100 children were enrolled in collaboration programs. Children enrolled in these collaboration programs are considered public school enrollees and therefore receive the same services as children served at public schools.

Recently, the Early Childhood Four-Year-Old Program formed partnerships between public schools and child care facilities that receive the highest rating in the state's quality rating system for child care (three stars). Oklahoma anticipates that more three-star facilities will participate as more incentives are expected to be offered.

Through a separate initiative, Oklahoma also supplements the federal Head Start program to expand services and enrollment, offer family services, and develop early intervention strategies. Head Start programs received $2,905,602 in state funds in fiscal year 2008.

In addition, Oklahoma established the Pilot Early Childhood Program during the 2006-2007 school year. This program is available to at-risk children from birth through age 3. The program is funded by public and private funds to provide a year-round program. Enrollment in the pilot program continues to expand each year, with 219 3-year-olds served in the 2007-2008 school year.

ACCESS RANKINGS		RESOURCES RANKINGS	
4-YEAR-OLDS	3-YEAR-OLDS	STATE SPENDING	ALL REPORTED SPENDING
1	None Served	17	8

OKLAHOMA EARLY CHILDHOOD FOUR-YEAR-OLD PROGRAM

ACCESS

Total state program enrollment...35,231

School districts that offer state program 99%

Income requirement ....None

Hours of operation...........................2.5 hours/day (part-day) or
6 hours/day (full-day); 5 days/week[1]

Operating schedule ....Academic year

Special education enrollment 3,771

Federally funded Head Start enrollment........................15,022

State-funded Head Start enrollment ....0[2]

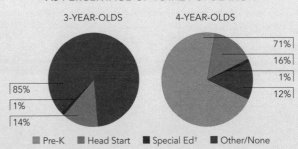

STATE PRE-K AND HEAD START ENROLLMENT AS PERCENTAGE OF TOTAL POPULATION

3-YEAR-OLDS

85%
1%
14%

4-YEAR-OLDS

71%
16%
1%
12%

■ Pre-K   ■ Head Start   ■ Special Ed[†]   ■ Other/None

[†] This number represents children in special education who are not enrolled in state-funded pre-K or Head Start.

QUALITY STANDARDS CHECKLIST

POLICY	STATE PRE-K REQUIREMENT	BENCHMARK	DOES REQUIREMENT MEET BENCHMARK?
Early learning standards	Comprehensive	Comprehensive	☑
Teacher degree	BA/BS	BA	☑
Teacher specialized training	EC certification for birth–3	Specializing in pre-K	☑
Assistant teacher degree	See footnotes[3]	CDA or equivalent	☐
Teacher in-service	75 clock hours/5years	At least 15 hours/year	☑
Maximum class size		20 or lower	☑
3-year-olds	NA		
4-year-olds	20		
Staff-child ratio		1:10 or better	☑
3-year-olds	NA		
4-year-olds	1:10		
Screening/referral and support services	Vision, hearing, health, developmental; and support services[4]	Vision, hearing, health; and at least 1 support service	☑
Meals	At least 1 meal[5]	At least 1/day	☑
Monitoring	Site visits and other monitoring	Site visits	☑

TOTAL BENCHMARKS MET

9

RESOURCES

Total state pre-K spending ....$139,735,129[6]

Local match required? ....No

State Head Start spending ....$2,905,602[2]

State spending per child enrolled $3,966

All reported spending per child enrolled* $7,484

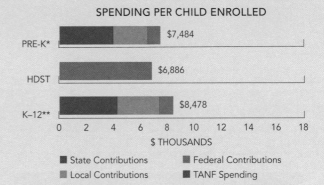

SPENDING PER CHILD ENROLLED

PRE-K* $7,484

HDST $6,886

K–12** $8,478

0   2   4   6   8   10   12   14   16   18
$ THOUSANDS

■ State Contributions   ■ Federal Contributions
■ Local Contributions   ■ TANF Spending

* Pre-K programs may receive additional funds from federal or local sources that are not included in this figure.

** K–12 expenditures include capital spending as well as current operating expenditures.

Data are for the '07-'08 school year, unless otherwise noted.

[1] Providers may choose from either of two program options: a half-day program with 2.5 instructional hours daily, a full-day program with 6 instructional hours daily, or a combination of both options. All programs operate 5 days per week.

[2] State Head Start funds are used to expand services, offer family services, develop early intervention strategies, and expand enrollment, although it is unknown how many additional slots are funded.

[3] Assistant teachers must meet federal requirements to be highly qualified under NCLB. They must have an AA, or 48 credit hours of college coursework, or pass one of two state-approved tests that do not have specific educational requirements. One test is the Oklahoma General Education Test (an exam required for pre-K–12 public school teachers) and the other is a national test for para-professional status.

[4] Dental services are determined locally. Support services include two parent conferences or home visits annually, parent involvement activities, health services for children, information about nutrition, referral to social services, and transition to kindergarten activities. Programs must also offer or make referrals for other services including mental health services, and all other typical public school program services (such as early intervention, transition programs or literacy coaches).

[5] At least one meal is provided through the Federal Child Nutrition Program, but specific meals depend on the length of the program. This federal program does not provide snacks for students, so snacks are determined locally.

[6] State spending was calculated on a percentage of the total program spending amount provided.

Oregon

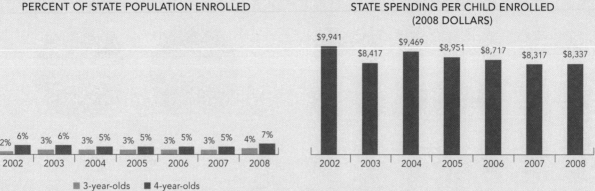

PERCENT OF STATE POPULATION ENROLLED

2002	2003	2004	2005	2006	2007	2008
2% 6%	3% 6%	3% 5%	3% 5%	3% 5%	3% 5%	4% 7%

■ 3-year-olds ■ 4-year-olds

STATE SPENDING PER CHILD ENROLLED
(2008 DOLLARS)

2002	2003	2004	2005	2006	2007	2008
$9,941	$8,417	$9,469	$8,951	$8,717	$8,317	$8,337

Established in 1987, the Oregon Head Start Prekindergarten program provides comprehensive child development services to 3- and 4-year-old children from low-income families. All programs must meet the federal Head Start Performance Standards and monitoring requirements in order to receive funding. State pre-K funding is awarded to any non-sectarian organizations through a competitive grant process. All federal Head Start grantees are jointly funded with both federal and state funding to expand their enrollment. Additionally, state funding is allocated to other entities such as public schools, private agencies, and universities meeting Head Start Performance Standards but not receiving federal Head Start funding. A state/federal partnership supporting a collaborative federal Head Start and state prekindergarten system has been established by a formal Memorandum of Understanding between the Oregon Department of Education and the Region X Office of Head Start.

In recent years, the Oregon Head Start Prekindergarten program has faced reductions in enrollment as a result of fluctuating funding. In an attempt to move toward access for all 3- and 4-year-olds, a $39 million expansion provided an additional 3,068 slots for eligible children during the 2007-2009 biennium. During the 2007-2008, school year, 1,732 children were added to the program and another 1,300 children are expected to be enrolled in the 2008-2009 school year.

ACCESS RANKINGS		RESOURCES RANKINGS	
4-YEAR-OLDS	3-YEAR-OLDS	STATE SPENDING	ALL REPORTED SPENDING
31	14	2	4

OREGON HEAD START PREKINDERGARTEN

ACCESS

Total state program enrollment 5,098

School districts that offer state program ....100% (counties)

Income requirement ....80% to 90% of children must
be at or below 100% FPL[1]

Hours of operation ....Determined locally[2]

Operating schedule ....Determined locally[2]

Special education enrollment 5,375

Federally funded Head Start enrollment 10,390

State-funded Head Start enrollment ....4,884[3]

STATE PRE-K AND HEAD START ENROLLMENT AS PERCENTAGE OF TOTAL POPULATION

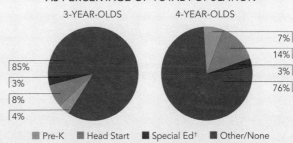

3-YEAR-OLDS — 85%, 3%, 8%, 4%

4-YEAR-OLDS — 7%, 14%, 3%, 76%

■ Pre-K ■ Head Start ■ Special Ed† ■ Other/None

† This number represents children in special education
who are not enrolled in state-funded pre-K or Head Start.

QUALITY STANDARDS CHECKLIST

POLICY	STATE PRE-K REQUIREMENT	BENCHMARK	DOES REQUIREMENT MEET BENCHMARK?
Early learning standards	Comprehensive	Comprehensive	☑
Teacher degree	BA (public), CDA (nonpublic)[4]	BA	☐
Teacher specialized training	License + 15 hrs. ECE cr. (public); Meets CDA requirement (nonpublic)[4]	Specializing in pre-K	☑
Assistant teacher degree	HSD or GED	CDA or equivalent	☐
Teacher in-service	15 clock hours/year[5]	At least 15 hours/year	☑
Maximum class size		20 or lower	☑
3-year-olds	17		
4-year-olds	20		
Staff-child ratio		1:10 or better	☑
3-year-olds	2:17		
4-year-olds	1:10		
Screening/referral and support services	Vision, hearing, health, dental, developmental, immunizations; and support services[6]	Vision, hearing, health; and at least 1 support service	☑
Meals	Lunch and either breakfast or snack[7]	At least 1/day	☑
Monitoring	Site visits and other monitoring	Site visits	☑

TOTAL BENCHMARKS MET

8

RESOURCES

Total state pre-K spending ....$42,500,000[8]

Local match required? ....No

State Head Start spending ....$42,500,000[8]

State spending per child enrolled $8,337

All reported spending per child enrolled* $8,337

* Pre-K programs may receive additional funds from federal or local sources
that are not included in this figure.

**K–12 expenditures include capital spending as well as current operating
expenditures.

Data are for the '07–'08 school year, unless otherwise noted.

SPENDING PER CHILD ENROLLED

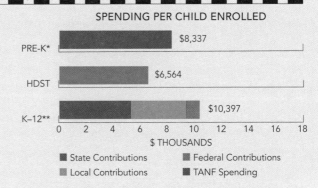

PRE-K* — $8,337
HDST — $6,564
K–12** — $10,397

$ THOUSANDS

■ State Contributions ■ Federal Contributions
■ Local Contributions ■ TANF Spending

1 If a grantee has both federal Head Start and state pre-K funding, 90% of children
must meet the income requirement. If a grantee only has state pre-K funding, 80%
of children must meet the income requirement. In addition, effective December
2007, 35% of enrollment may be children whose family incomes are between
100% and 130% FPL after meeting the needs of children at 100% or below FPL.

2 Programs must be offered for at least 3.5 hours per day. Most programs operate
3 or 4 days per week. All programs must operate a minimum of 32 weeks and
474 hours per year.

3 This number represents enrollment in the Oregon Head Start Prekindergarten
program. All state-funded Head Start enrollment is through this program.

4 In nonpublic school grantee settings, half of grantee teachers must have at least
an AA or higher degree in ECE or a related degree with a minimum of 15 ECE
college credits. Requirements for public school teachers do not apply to classrooms
run by agencies other than public schools, even if located in public schools.

5 Fifteen hours of teacher in-service per year are required in the new Head Start
Reauthorization Act as of December 2007.

6 Support services include four annual parent conferences or home visits, parent
education or job training, parenting support or training, parent involvement
activities, health services for parents and children, information about nutrition,
referral to social services, transition to kindergarten activities, mental health
services, and community partnerships.

7 Programs are required to offer meals and snacks that provide at least one-third
of the child's daily nutritional needs. In addition to lunches for all children,
morning programs offer breakfast to all children and afternoon programs offer
snacks to all children.

8 This figure represents the state contribution to the Oregon Head Start
Prekindergarten program, which is a state-funded Head Start model. All
state pre-K spending is therefore directed toward Head Start programs.

115

Pennsylvania

PERCENT OF STATE POPULATION ENROLLED

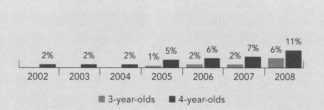

■ 3-year-olds ■ 4-year-olds

STATE SPENDING PER CHILD ENROLLED
(2008 DOLLARS)

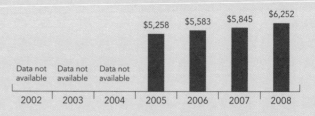

Pennsylvania did not have a state-funded preschool education program that was considered such under state law until 2004. However, school districts could offer prekindergarten services to 4-year-old children through Pennsylvania's Kindergarten for Four-Year-Olds (K4) program. Children enrolled in K4 are included in the districts' daily membership counts for public school attendance and are partially funded through the state's basic instructional subsidy formula. A combination of local taxes, public school funds, Title I, and Head Start partnerships is used to fund the program but data on funding levels is not collected.

During the 2004-2005 school year, Pennsylvania established the prekindergarten option through the Education Accountability Block Grant (EABG) with the goal of increasing children's academic success through provision of high-quality early childhood programs. Children are eligible for EABG prekindergarten programs two years prior to the locally determined kindergarten eligibility age, but districts can choose other requirements such as low income or academic readiness to limit eligibility. School districts decide how to allocate their EABG funds, which can be used for a number of programs and improvements, including preschool education, full-day kindergarten, and reducing class sizes in kindergarten through third grade.

Pennsylvania's third prekindergarten initiative, the Head Start Supplemental Assistance Program (HSSAP), was established in the 2004-2005 school year with an initial investment of $15 million. Enrollment and state funding for this program increased to 5,780 children and $40 million in the 2007-2008 school year. Through this initiative, supplemental funds are used for new Head Start slots or to provide extended-day services. Federal Head Start grantees may participate in this state-funded program and are required to follow the federal Head Start Performance Standards. In addition, beginning in 2007-2008 child care centers must achieve a level of STAR 2 or higher in the Keystone STARS continuous quality improvement system to be eligible to partner with Head Start programs.

In the 2007-2008 program year, Pennsylvania launched a fourth preschool education initiative, the Pennsylvania Pre-K Counts program. The Pennsylvania Department of Education funds Pre-K Counts and grantees receive funding through a competitive award system. Grantees include school districts, Head Start, and licensed nursery schools or child care centers participating in Keystone STARS that are designated at a STAR 2 or higher. Eligibility for Pre-K Counts is determined by the age of the child (two years before their locally determined kindergarten eligibility) as well as other locally determined risk factors.

All guidance for K4, EABG, Pre-K Counts and state Head Start funding currently includes reference to the Keystone STARS standards. This document serves as a framework for quality service delivery, along with the Early Learning Standards.

The first two pages of this state profile present information on Pennsylvania's overall commitment and contribution to state-funded preschool, including state spending and enrollment for all four of Pennsylvania's preschool education programs. The third page focuses exclusively on EABG, the fourth page describes K4, the fifth page provides specific details about HSSAP, and the last page highlights the Pre-K Counts program.

STATE OVERVIEW

Total state program enrollment......................................23,937[1]

Total state spending...$130,548,078[2]

State Head Start spending.....................................$40,000,000

State spending per child enrolled................................$6,252[2]

All reported spending per child enrolled.......................$6,252[2]

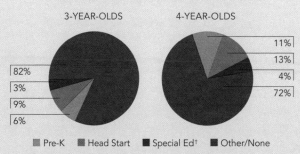

STATE PRE-K AND HEAD START ENROLLMENT AS PERCENTAGE OF TOTAL POPULATION

3-YEAR-OLDS

82%
3%
9%
6%

4-YEAR-OLDS

11%
13%
4%
72%

■ Pre-K ■ Head Start ■ Special Ed[†] ■ Other/None

[†] This number represents children in special education
who are not enrolled in Head Start, Pre-K Counts, or HSSAP.

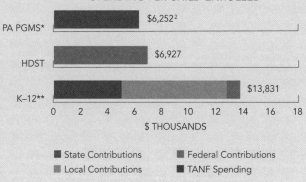

SPENDING PER CHILD ENROLLED

PA PGMS* $6,252[2]

HDST $6,927

K–12** $13,831

0   2   4   6   8   10 12 14 16 18

$ THOUSANDS

■ State Contributions   ■ Federal Contributions
■ Local Contributions   ■ TANF Spending

* Pre-K programs may receive additional funds from federal or local sources
 that are not included in this figure.

** K–12 expenditures include capital spending as well as current operating
 expenditures.

Data are for the '07-'08 school year, unless otherwise noted.

ACCESS RANKINGS	
4-YEAR-OLDS	3-YEAR-OLDS
28	8

RESOURCES RANKINGS	
STATE SPENDING	ALL REPORTED SPENDING
8	14

[1] The state did not break EABG enrollment into a specific number of 3- or 4-year-olds. As a result, age breakdowns used in the Access pie chart were estimated, using the
 proportions of enrollees who were ages 3 or 4 in state programs that served 3-year-olds and provided age breakdowns for 2007-2008.

[2] These figures do not include the K4 program, as the state was unable to provide spending information for this program.

PENNSYLVANIA EDUCATION ACCOUNTABILITY BLOCK GRANT

ACCESS

Total state program enrollment ....4,155[1]

School districts that offer state program 9%

Income requirement ....None[2]

Hours of operation ....Determined locally[3]

Operating schedule ....Determined locally[3]

Special education enrollment 18,368

Federally funded Head Start enrollment.......................31,536

State-funded Head Start enrollment 5,780

STATE PRE-K AND HEAD START ENROLLMENT AS PERCENTAGE OF TOTAL POPULATION

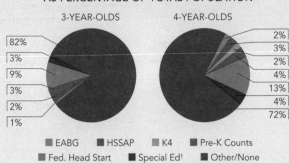

3-YEAR-OLDS

82%
3%
9%
3%
2%
1%

4-YEAR-OLDS

2%
3%
2%
4%
13%
4%
72%

■ EABG　■ HSSAP　■ K4　■ Pre-K Counts
■ Fed. Head Start　■ Special Ed[†]　■ Other/None

[†] This number represents children in special education who are not enrolled in Head Start, Pre-K Counts, or HSSAP.

QUALITY STANDARDS CHECKLIST

POLICY	STATE PRE-K REQUIREMENT	BENCHMARK	DOES REQUIREMENT MEET BENCHMARK?
Early learning standards	Comprehensive	Comprehensive	☑
Teacher degree	BA and ECE certification (public); AA (community partners)[4]	BA	☐
Teacher specialized training	Certification in EC, N–3 (public); None (community partners)[4]	Specializing in pre-K	☐
Assistant teacher degree	None[5]	CDA or equivalent	☐
Teacher in-service	180 clock hours/5 years	At least 15 hours/year	☑
Maximum class size		20 or lower	☑
3-year-olds	20		
4-year-olds	20		
Staff-child ratio		1:10 or better	☑
3-year-olds	1:10		
4-year-olds	1:10		
Screening/referral and support services	Determined locally	Vision, hearing, health; and at least 1 support service	☐
Meals	None	At least 1/day	☐
Monitoring	Site visits and other monitoring	Site visits	☑

TOTAL BENCHMARKS MET

5

RESOURCES

Total state pre-K spending $15,548,078

Local match required? ....No

State Head Start spending $40,000,000

State spending per child enrolled $3,742

All reported spending per child enrolled* $3,742

* Pre-K programs may receive additional funds from federal or local sources that are not included in this figure.

**K–12 expenditures include capital spending as well as current operating expenditures.

Data are for the '07-'08 school year, unless otherwise noted.

SPENDING PER CHILD ENROLLED

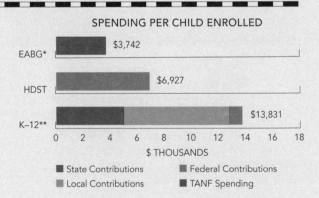

EABG*　$3,742

HDST　$6,927

K–12**　$13,831

0　2　4　6　8　10　12　14　16　18

$ THOUSANDS

■ State Contributions　■ Federal Contributions
■ Local Contributions　■ TANF Spending

[1] The state did not break EABG enrollment into a specific number of 3- or 4-year-olds. As a result, age breakdowns used in the Access pie charts were estimated, using the proportions of enrollees who were ages 3 or 4 in state programs that served 3-year-olds and provided age breakdowns for 2007-2008.

[2] Eligibility requirements are locally determined.

[3] Most programs operate 2.5 hours or 5 hours per day, 5 days per week, 180 days per year.

[4] Regulations finalized in December 2006 mandate that teachers in programs operated by community providers must have at least an AA. In 2011, all teachers regardless of setting will need ECE certification.

[5] In public school settings, assistant teachers must meet the NCLB requirements for highly qualified. For non-public settings, programs follow their regulatory requirements. By 2009-2010, all aides will have completed at least two years of postsecondary study, possess an AA or higher, or pass a rigorous state or local assessment of knowledge of and ability to assist in instruction.

PENNSYLVANIA KINDERGARTEN FOR FOUR-YEAR-OLDS

ACCESS

Total state program enrollment 3,057

School districts that offer state program 17%

Income requirement ....None

Hours of operation ....Determined locally[1]

Operating schedule ....Academic year

Special education enrollment 18,368

Federally funded Head Start enrollment.........................31,536

State-funded Head Start enrollment 5,780

STATE PRE-K AND HEAD START ENROLLMENT AS PERCENTAGE OF TOTAL POPULATION

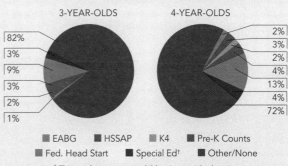

3-YEAR-OLDS   4-YEAR-OLDS

82% / 3% / 9% / 3% / 2% / 1%

2% / 3% / 2% / 4% / 13% / 4% / 72%

■ EABG ■ HSSAP ■ K4 ■ Pre-K Counts
■ Fed. Head Start ■ Special Ed[†] ■ Other/None

[†] This number represents children in special education
who are not enrolled in Head Start, Pre-K Counts, or HSSAP.

QUALITY STANDARDS CHECKLIST

POLICY	STATE PRE-K REQUIREMENT	BENCHMARK	DOES REQUIREMENT MEET BENCHMARK?
Early learning standards	Comprehensive	Comprehensive	☑
Teacher degree	BA	BA	☑
Teacher specialized training	EE or ECE certification	Specializing in pre-K	☐
Assistant teacher degree	Meet NCLB requirements (Title 1 schools); None (all other schools)[2]	CDA or equivalent	☐
Teacher in-service	180 clock hours/5 years	At least 15 hours/year	☑
Maximum class size		20 or lower	☑
3-year-olds	NA		
4-year-olds	20		
Staff-child ratio		1:10 or better	☑
3-year-olds	NA		
4-year-olds	1:10		
Screening/referral and support services	Determined locally	Vision, hearing, health; and at least 1 support service	☐
Meals	None	At least 1/day	☐
Monitoring	None	Site visits	☐

TOTAL BENCHMARKS MET

5

RESOURCES

Total state pre-K spending ....Not available

Local match required? ....No

State Head Start spending $40,000,000

State spending per child enrolled.........................Not available

All reported spending per child enrolled*............Not available

SPENDING PER CHILD ENROLLED

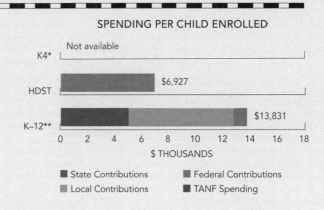

K4* Not available

HDST $6,927

K–12** $13,831

0 2 4 6 8 10 12 14 16 18
$ THOUSANDS

■ State Contributions ■ Federal Contributions
■ Local Contributions ■ TANF Spending

* Pre-K programs may receive additional funds from federal or local sources
  that are not included in this figure.

** K–12 expenditures include capital spending as well as current operating
  expenditures.

Data are for the '07-'08 school year, unless otherwise noted.

[1] The minimum requirement is 2.5 hours/day, 5 days/week, 180 days/year.

[2] Assistant teachers in Title I schools must meet the NCLB requirements for highly qualified teachers. There are no specific degree requirements for assistant teachers in
  other schools. By 2009-2010, all assistant teachers will be required to meet the highly qualified requirements of NCLB.

PENNSYLVANIA HEAD START SUPPLEMENTAL ASSISTANCE PROGRAM

ACCESS

Total state program enrollment 5,780

School districts that offer state program..................75% (Head Start grantees)

Income requirement....................At least 90% of children must be at or below 100% FPL

Hours of operation ....Determined locally[1]

Operating schedule ....Determined locally[1]

Special education enrollment 18,368

Federally funded Head Start enrollment 31,536

State-funded Head Start enrollment 5,780

STATE PRE-K AND HEAD START ENROLLMENT AS PERCENTAGE OF TOTAL POPULATION

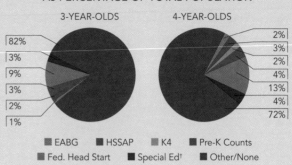

3-YEAR-OLDS

82%
3%
9%
3%
2%
1%

4-YEAR-OLDS

2%
3%
2%
4%
13%
4%
72%

■ EABG   ■ HSSAP   ■ K4   ■ Pre-K Counts
■ Fed. Head Start   ■ Special Ed[†]   ■ Other/None

† This number represents children in special education who are not enrolled in Head Start, Pre-K Counts, or HSSAP.

QUALITY STANDARDS CHECKLIST

POLICY	STATE PRE-K REQUIREMENT	BENCHMARK	DOES REQUIREMENT MEET BENCHMARK?
Early learning standards	Comprehensive	Comprehensive	☑
Teacher degree	CDA[2]	BA	☐
Teacher specialized training	Meets CDA requirements[2]	Specializing in pre-K	☑
Assistant teacher degree	HSD	CDA or equivalent	☐
Teacher in-service	15 clock hours[3]	At least 15 hours/year	☑
Maximum class size		20 or lower	☑
3-year-olds	17		
4-year-olds	20		
Staff-child ratio		1:10 or better	☑
3-year-olds	2:17		
4-year-olds	2:17		
Screening/referral and support services	Vision, hearing, health, dental, developmental; and support services[4]	Vision, hearing, health; and at least 1 support service	☑
Meals	Lunch and either breakfast or snack	At least 1/day	☑
Monitoring	Site visits and other monitoring	Site visits	☑

TOTAL BENCHMARKS MET

8

RESOURCES

Total state pre-K spending ....$40,000,000[5]

Local match required?..........................Yes, following Head Start performance standards

State Head Start spending ....$40,000,000[5]

State spending per child enrolled $6,920

All reported spending per child enrolled* ....$6,920[6]

* Pre-K programs may receive additional funds from federal or local sources that are not included in this figure.

**K–12 expenditures include capital spending as well as current operating expenditures.

Data are for the '07-'08 school year, unless otherwise noted.

SPENDING PER CHILD ENROLLED

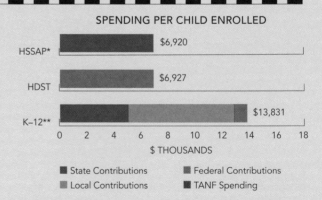

HSSAP* $6,920

HDST $6,927

K–12** $13,831

0   2   4   6   8   10   12   14   16   18
$ THOUSANDS

■ State Contributions   ■ Federal Contributions
■ Local Contributions   ■ TANF Spending

[1] The operating schedule is determined locally, but the minimum follows federal Head Start requirements of 3.5 hours per day, 4 days per week, and 128 days per year.

[2] Federal Head Start requirements state that 50 percent of teachers must have an AA in ECE. If teachers are employed by a school district, ECE certification is required.

[3] In December 2007, the requirement changed to 15 clock hours of professional development per year as specified in the federal Head Start reauthorization.

[4] Support services include two annual parent conferences or home visits and comprehensive services as required by federal Head Start Performance Standards that include parent education or job training, parenting support or training, parent involvement activities, health services for children, information about nutrition, referral for social services, and transition to kindergarten activities.

[5] All spending through this initiative is directed toward Head Start programs.

[6] Additional funds not counted in this figure include $433,500 ($75 per child) in federal Head Start dollars for grantees specifically for technical assistance.

PENNSYLVANIA PRE-K COUNTS

ACCESS

Total state program enrollment 10,945

School districts that offer state program ....85% (counties)

Income requirement ....300% FPL[1]

Hours of operation ....2.5 instructional hours/day (part-day),
5 instructional hours/day (full-day),
5 days/week

Operating schedule ....Academic year

Special education enrollment 18,368

Federally funded Head Start enrollment........................31,536

State-funded Head Start enrollment 5,780

STATE PRE-K AND HEAD START ENROLLMENT AS PERCENTAGE OF TOTAL POPULATION

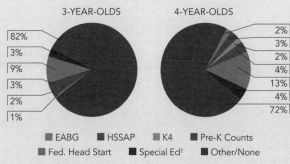

3-YEAR-OLDS

82%
3%
9%
3%
2%
1%

4-YEAR-OLDS

2%
3%
2%
4%
13%
4%
72%

■ EABG ■ HSSAP ■ K4 ■ Pre-K Counts
■ Fed. Head Start ■ Special Ed[†] ■ Other/None

[†] This number represents children in special education
who are not enrolled in Head Start, Pre-K Counts, or HSSAP.

QUALITY STANDARDS CHECKLIST

POLICY	STATE PRE-K REQUIREMENT	BENCHMARK	DOES REQUIREMENT MEET BENCHMARK?
Early learning standards	Comprehensive	Comprehensive	☑
Teacher degree	BA in ECE (public); AA in ECE or CD or ECE cert. and 18 credits (nonpublic)[2]	BA	☐
Teacher specialized training	ECE certification (public); AA in ECE or ECE cert., and 18 credits in ECE (nonpublic)[2]	Specializing in pre-K	☑
Assistant teacher degree	None	CDA or equivalent	☐
Teacher in-service	180 clock hours/5 years	At least 15 hours/year	☑
Maximum class size 3-year-olds 4-year-olds	20 20	20 or lower	☑
Staff-child ratio 3-year-olds 4-year-olds	1:10 1:10	1:10 or better	☑
Screening/referral and support services	Determined locally	Vision, hearing, health; and at least 1 support service	☐
Meals	Snack[3]	At least 1/day	☐
Monitoring	Site visits and other monitoring	Site visits	☑

TOTAL BENCHMARKS MET

6

RESOURCES

Total state pre-K spending 75,000,000

Local match required? ....No

State Head Start spending $40,000,000

State spending per child enrolled $6,852

All reported spending per child enrolled* $6,852

SPENDING PER CHILD ENROLLED

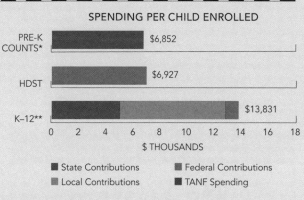

PRE-K COUNTS* — $6,852

HDST — $6,927

K–12** — $13,831

0 2 4 6 8 10 12 14 16 18
$ THOUSANDS

■ State Contributions ■ Federal Contributions
■ Local Contributions ■ TANF Spending

* Pre-K programs may receive additional funds from federal or local sources
that are not included in this figure.

**K–12 expenditures include capital spending as well as current operating
expenditures.

Data are for the '07-'08 school year, unless otherwise noted.

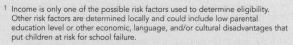

[1] Income is only one of the possible risk factors used to determine eligibility.
Other risk factors are determined locally and could include low parental
education level or other economic, language, and/or cultural disadvantages that
put children at risk for school failure.

[2] Teachers in child care or Head Start are required to have at least an AA in early
childhood education or child development. Teachers in nursery schools are

required to have ECE certification and 18 credits. If a teacher has a degree that
is not in ECE, they must have at least 18 credits in ECE and apply for a waiver.
Beginning in December 2011, all teachers will be required to have a BA and
ECE certification.

[3] Half-day programs are required to provide a snack. Full-day programs are
required to provide a snack and one meal.

Rhode Island

NO PROGRAM

During the 2007-2008 school year, Rhode Island did not have a distinct state-funded preschool initiative meeting the criteria used in this report, though it offered initiatives with the goal of expanding access to early childhood education. One initiative, the Comprehensive Child Care Services Program (CCCSP), began providing comprehensive services to 3- and 4-year-olds in child care settings in 2001, but was eliminated in an effort to close the state budget deficit for fiscal year 2009.

Through another initiative, Rhode Island provides state funding to supplement the federal Head Start program. The state spent $2.97 million to fund additional services for 400 children in Head Start during the 2007-2008 school year. The 2008-2009 school year saw cuts in this program, and a total of 142 children were served with $1 million in state funds. However, a compromise over these cutbacks resulted in a legislative bill requiring the Rhode Island Department of Education to begin planning for a prekindergarten demonstration project. After two years of operation, the demonstration project is expected to grow into a statewide preschool initiative.

ACCESS RANKINGS	
4-YEAR-OLDS	3-YEAR-OLDS
No Program	

RESOURCES RANKINGS	
STATE SPENDING	ALL REPORTED SPENDING
No Program	

ACCESS

Total state program enrollment 0

School districts that offer state program.......................NA

Income requirement ....NA

Hours of operation ....NA

Operating schedule ....NA

Special education enrollment 1,724

Federally funded Head Start enrollment...................2,386

State-funded Head Start enrollment 400

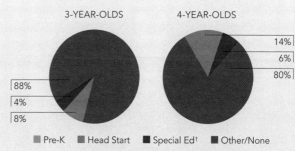

STATE PRE-K AND HEAD START ENROLLMENT AS PERCENTAGE OF TOTAL POPULATION

3-YEAR-OLDS   4-YEAR-OLDS

88%
4%
8%

14%
6%
80%

■ Pre-K   ■ Head Start   ■ Special Ed†   ■ Other/None

† This number represents children in special education
who are not enrolled in Head Start.

QUALITY STANDARDS CHECKLIST

TOTAL BENCHMARKS MET
No Program

RESOURCES

Total state pre-K spending..$0

Local match required? ....NA

State Head Start spending................................$2,970,000

State spending per child enrolled $0

All reported spending per child enrolled*......................$0

* Pre-K programs may receive additional funds from federal or local sources
that are not included in this figure.

**K–12 expenditures include capital spending as well as current operating
expenditures.

Data are for the '07-'08 school year, unless otherwise noted.

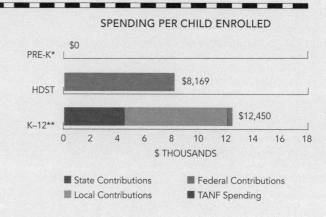

SPENDING PER CHILD ENROLLED

PRE-K* $0

HDST $8,169

K–12** $12,450

0   2   4   6   8   10   12   14   16   18
$ THOUSANDS

■ State Contributions   ■ Federal Contributions
■ Local Contributions   ■ TANF Spending

South Carolina

PERCENT OF STATE POPULATION ENROLLED

STATE SPENDING PER CHILD ENROLLED
(2008 DOLLARS)

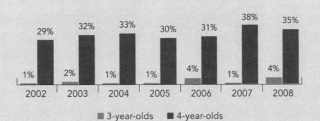

■ 3-year-olds ■ 4-year-olds

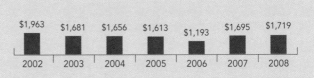

In 1984, the South Carolina Education Improvement Act established the Half-Day Child Development Program, known as 4K, with the primary purpose of improving school readiness. Each district in the state is required to have at least one 4K class, which provides half-day preschool education to at-risk 4-year-olds. Child eligibility requirements are selected according to local need, based on a list of state-specified risk factors. Examples of risk factors include having single parents or parents with low educational attainment, being homeless, or having a low family income.

State funds are distributed to 4K programs based on the number of kindergartners per district eligible for free or reduced-price lunch. Additional funding sources are used in about 15 percent of programs to provide full-day services to preschool children. Although some districts partner with Head Start or private child care centers to provide services, the majority of children are served in public school settings.

In 2006, another state initiative, the Child Development Education Pilot Program (CDEPP), was created as a result of the lawsuit *Abbeville County School District v. South Carolina*. The court decision mandated that full-day preschool be provided in certain circumstances. Only counties named in the lawsuit that choose to offer 4K services are required to provide full-day preschool for children residing in the county who are eligible for free or reduced-price lunch or Medicaid. Public school programs must be approved by the state Department of Education while private child centers must obtain approval from the Office of First Steps.

The First Steps to School Readiness program is an additional state initiative, although it is not the focus of this report. Funds are distributed through First Steps County Partnerships for use at the local level for a variety of services for children and their families. Although First Steps is separate from 4K and CDEPP, some communities use funds from this initiative in collaboration with 4K and CDEPP for such purposes as extending services to a full day or providing additional slots in existing programs.

The first two pages of this state profile document South Carolina's overall contributions and commitment to state prekindergarten, including state spending and enrollment for both the Half-Day Child Development Program and the Child Development Education Pilot Program initiatives. The third page focuses exclusively on the Half-Day Child Development Program initiative and the final page presents specific details about the CDEPP initiative.

STATE OVERVIEW

Total state program enrollment 22,590

Total state spending $38,821,515

State spending per child enrolled $1,719

All reported spending per child enrolled* $2,134

STATE PRE-K AND HEAD START ENROLLMENT AS PERCENTAGE OF TOTAL POPULATION

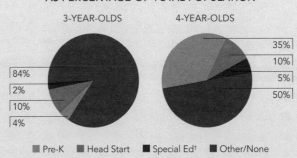

3-YEAR-OLDS

84%
2%
10%
4%

4-YEAR-OLDS

35%
10%
5%
50%

■ Pre-K   ■ Head Start   ■ Special Ed†   ■ Other/None

† This number represents children in special education who are not enrolled in Head Start, but includes children who are enrolled in state-funded pre-K.

SPENDING PER CHILD ENROLLED

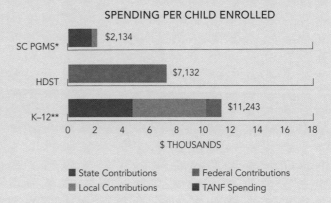

SC PGMS* $2,134

HDST $7,132

K–12** $11,243

$ THOUSANDS

■ State Contributions   ■ Federal Contributions
■ Local Contributions   ■ TANF Spending

* Pre-K programs may receive additional funds from federal or local sources that are not included in this figure.

** K–12 expenditures include capital spending as well as current operating expenditures.

Data are for the '07-'08 school year, unless otherwise noted.

ACCESS RANKINGS	
4-YEAR-OLDS	3-YEAR-OLDS
10	13

RESOURCES RANKINGS	
STATE SPENDING	ALL REPORTED SPENDING
37	38

SOUTH CAROLINA HALF-DAY CHILD DEVELOPMENT PROGRAM

ACCESS

Total state program enrollment 18,398

School districts that offer state program 59%

Income requirement ....185% FPL[1]

Hours of operation ....2.5 hours/day, 5 days/week

Operating schedule ....Academic year

Special education enrollment 5,285

Federally funded Head Start enrollment.......................11,681

State-funded Head Start enrollment 0

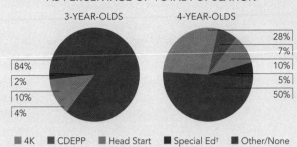

STATE PRE-K AND HEAD START ENROLLMENT AS PERCENTAGE OF TOTAL POPULATION

3-YEAR-OLDS

- 84%
- 2%
- 10%
- 4%

4-YEAR-OLDS

- 28%
- 7%
- 10%
- 5%
- 50%

■ 4K ■ CDEPP ■ Head Start ■ Special Ed[†] ■ Other/None

† This number represents children in special education who are not enrolled in Head Start, but includes children who are enrolled in state-funded pre-K.

QUALITY STANDARDS CHECKLIST

POLICY	STATE PRE-K REQUIREMENT	BENCHMARK	DOES REQUIREMENT MEET BENCHMARK?
Early learning standards	Comprehensive	Comprehensive	☑
Teacher degree	BA	BA	☑
Teacher specialized training	EC certification for pre-K–3	Specializing in pre-K	☑
Assistant teacher degree	HSD	CDA or equivalent	☐
Teacher in-service	15 clock hours/year	At least 15 hours/year	☑
Maximum class size		20 or lower	☑
3-year-olds	20		
4-year-olds	20		
Staff-child ratio		1:10 or better	☑
3-year-olds	1:10		
4-year-olds	1:10		
Screening/referral and support services	Vision, hearing, health, developmental, dental; and support services[2]	Vision, hearing, health; and at least 1 support service	☑
Meals	Snack	At least 1/day	☐
Monitoring	Site visits and other monitoring	Site visits	☑

TOTAL BENCHMARKS MET

8

RESOURCES

Total state pre-K spending $21,832,678

Local match required? ....No

State spending per child enrolled $1,187

All reported spending per child enrolled* $1,697

* Pre-K programs may receive additional funds from federal or local sources that are not included in this figure.

**K–12 expenditures include capital spending as well as current operating expenditures.

Data are for the '07-'08 school year, unless otherwise noted.

SPENDING PER CHILD ENROLLED

4K*	$1,697
HDST	$7,132
K–12**	$11,243

0 2 4 6 8 10 12 14 16 18
$ THOUSANDS

■ State Contributions ■ Federal Contributions
■ Local Contributions ■ TANF Spending

---

[1] Children are eligible for the program if they are determined to be educationally at-risk.

[2] Support services include four annual parent conferences or home visits, education services or job training for parents, parenting support or training, parent involvement activities, health services for children, referral to social services, transition to kindergarten activities, and other locally determined services.

SOUTH CAROLINA CHILD DEVELOPMENT EDUCATION PILOT PROGRAM

ACCESS

Total state program enrollment 4,192

School districts that offer state program 41%

Income requirement ....185% FPL[1]

Hours of operation ....6.5 hours/day, 5 days/week

Operating schedule ....Academic year

Special education enrollment 5,285

Federally funded Head Start enrollment 11,681

State-funded Head Start enrollment 0

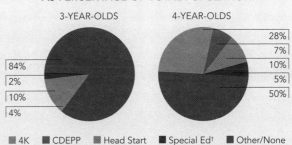

STATE PRE-K AND HEAD START ENROLLMENT
AS PERCENTAGE OF TOTAL POPULATION

3-YEAR-OLDS

84%
2%
10%
4%

4-YEAR-OLDS

28%
7%
10%
5%
50%

■ 4K   ■ CDEPP   ■ Head Start   ■ Special Ed[†]   ■ Other/None

[†] This number represents children in special education who are not enrolled in Head Start, but includes children who are enrolled in state-funded pre-K.

QUALITY STANDARDS CHECKLIST

POLICY	STATE PRE-K REQUIREMENT	BENCHMARK	DOES REQUIREMENT MEET BENCHMARK?
Early learning standards	Comprehensive	Comprehensive	☑
Teacher degree	BA (public), AA in ECE (nonpublic)[2]	BA	☐
Teacher specialized training	EC certification for pre-K–3 (public); AA in ECE (nonpublic)[2]	Specializing in pre-K	☑
Assistant teacher degree	HSD[3]	CDA or equivalent	☐
Teacher in-service	15 clock hours/year	At least 15 hours/year	☑
Maximum class size		20 or lower	☑
3-year-olds	20		
4-year-olds	20		
Staff-child ratio		1:10 or better	☑
3-year-olds	1:10		
4-year-olds	1:10		
Screening/referral and support services	Vision, hearing, health, developmental; and support services[4]	Vision, hearing, health; and at least 1 support service	☑
Meals	Breakfast and lunch	At least 1/day	☑
Monitoring	Site visits and other monitoring	Site visits	☑

TOTAL BENCHMARKS MET

8

RESOURCES

Total state pre-K spending $16,988,837

Local match required? ....No

State spending per child enrolled $4,053

All reported spending per child enrolled* $4,053

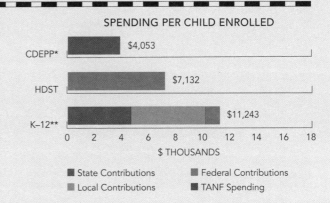

SPENDING PER CHILD ENROLLED

CDEPP* $4,053

HDST $7,132

K–12** $11,243

0 2 4 6 8 10 12 14 16 18
$ THOUSANDS

■ State Contributions   ■ Federal Contributions
■ Local Contributions   ■ TANF Spending

* Pre-K programs may receive additional funds from federal or local sources that are not included in this figure.

** K–12 expenditures include capital spending as well as current operating expenditures.

Data are for the '07-'08 school year, unless otherwise noted.

[1] Children are also eligible if they receive Medicaid services.

[2] In the First Steps program, the requirement for the AA degree may be waived. In public school settings, all teachers must have a BA degree or higher and be certified in early childhood.

[3] The teaching assistant must complete one course of ECD 101 within the calendar year if they do not have an AA degree.

[4] Dental screenings and referrals are determined locally. Support services include two annual parent conferences or home visits, parenting support or training, and parent involvement activities, health services for children and transition to kindergarten activities.

South Dakota

NO PROGRAM

ACCESS RANKINGS		RESOURCES RANKINGS	
4-YEAR-OLDS	3-YEAR-OLDS	STATE SPENDING	ALL REPORTED SPENDING
No Program		No Program	

ACCESS

Total state program enrollment	0
School districts that offer state program	NA
Income requirement	NA
Hours of operation	NA
Operating schedule	NA
Special education enrollment	1,537
Federally funded Head Start enrollment	3,596
State-funded Head Start enrollment	0

STATE PRE-K AND HEAD START ENROLLMENT AS PERCENTAGE OF TOTAL POPULATION

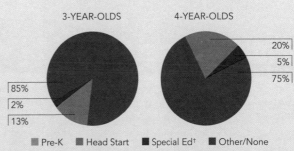

3-YEAR-OLDS

85%
2%
13%

4-YEAR-OLDS

20%
5%
75%

■ Pre-K ■ Head Start ■ Special Ed† ■ Other/None

† This number represents children in special education who are not enrolled in Head Start.

QUALITY STANDARDS CHECKLIST

TOTAL BENCHMARKS MET

No Program

RESOURCES

Total state pre-K spending	$0
Local match required?	NA
State Head Start spending	$0
State spending per child enrolled	$0
All reported spending per child enrolled*	$0

* Pre-K programs may receive additional funds from federal or local sources that are not included in this figure.

**K–12 expenditures include capital spending as well as current operating expenditures.

Data are for the '07-'08 school year, unless otherwise noted.

SPENDING PER CHILD ENROLLED

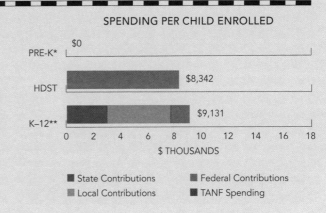

PRE-K* $0

HDST $8,342

K–12** $9,131

0 2 4 6 8 10 12 14 16 18
$ THOUSANDS

■ State Contributions   ■ Federal Contributions
■ Local Contributions   ■ TANF Spending

Tennessee

PERCENT OF STATE POPULATION ENROLLED

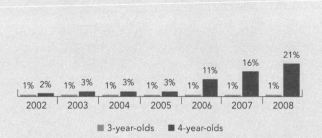

■ 3-year-olds   ■ 4-year-olds

STATE SPENDING PER CHILD ENROLLED
(2008 DOLLARS)

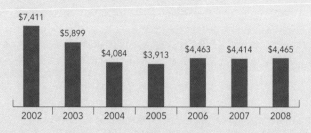

In 1998, Tennessee began funding the Early Childhood Education (ECE) Pilot Project, which offered competitive grants to public schools, Head Start agencies, private child care agencies, institutes of higher education, and public housing authorities to provide preschool. The Tennessee Voluntary Pre-K (VPK) program began in the 2005-2006 school year and includes the pilot pre-K program. The VPK program allows only school systems to compete for state grants, but public schools can subcontract with Head Start agencies, private child care agencies, institutes of higher education, and public housing authorities. Enrollment priority is given to 3- and 4-year-old children who are eligible for free or reduced-price lunch. Enrollment is also open to children who meet other state-specified risk factors, which include being in state custody, English Language Learner status, having a history of abuse or neglect, having an IEP, and other locally determined risk factors such as having a parent on active military duty.

Until 2003, Tennessee's preschool program relied partially on TANF funding. In 2005, the state began using excess lottery funds to expand its state prekindergarten program, resulting in an additional 6,000 at-risk children being served in the 2005-2006 school year. Tennessee then tripled its general revenue allocation for preschool, enabling 232 new VPK programs to serve more than 4,500 additional at-risk children during the 2006-2007 school year. In 2007-2008, an additional $25 million enabled VPK to serve more than 4,700 additional at-risk children.

The Office of Early Learning (OEL) was established in 2005 to administer the VPK program. OEL also includes the Even Start State Coordinator Office, Family Resources Centers, Head Start State Collaboration Office, and School Administered Child Care Program Evaluation. It is responsible for program administration, oversight, monitoring, data collection, technical assistance, and training. To provide information and best practices in support of preschool education, OEL coordinates and collaborates with intra-state agencies, local school systems, and community providers.

ACCESS RANKINGS		RESOURCES RANKINGS	
4-YEAR-OLDS	3-YEAR-OLDS	STATE SPENDING	ALL REPORTED SPENDING
17	22	13	17

TENNESSEE VOLUNTARY PRE-K

ACCESS

Total state program enrollment 17,916

School districts that offer state program 99%

Income requirement ....185% FPL[1]

Hours of operation ....5.5 hours/day, 5 days/week[2]

Operating schedule ....Academic year

Special education enrollment 6,363

Federally funded Head Start enrollment 15,469

State-funded Head Start enrollment 0

STATE PRE-K AND HEAD START ENROLLMENT AS PERCENTAGE OF TOTAL POPULATION

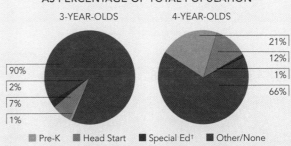

3-YEAR-OLDS: 90%, 2%, 7%, 1%
4-YEAR-OLDS: 21%, 12%, 1%, 66%

■ Pre-K   ■ Head Start   ■ Special Ed[†]   ■ Other/None

[†] This number represents children in special education who are not enrolled in state-funded pre-K or Head Start.

QUALITY STANDARDS CHECKLIST

POLICY	STATE PRE-K REQUIREMENT	BENCHMARK	DOES REQUIREMENT MEET BENCHMARK?
Early learning standards	Comprehensive	Comprehensive	☑
Teacher degree	BA	BA	☑
Teacher specialized training	Teacher license and certification in Early Childhood Pre-K endorsement[3]	Specializing in pre-K	☑
Assistant teacher degree	CDA (ECE pilot); HSD + pre-K experience (VPK)[4]	CDA or equivalent	☐
Teacher in-service	18 clock hours	At least 15 hours/year	☑
Maximum class size		20 or lower	☑
3-year-olds	16		
4-year-olds	20		
Staff-child ratio		1:10 or better	☑
3-year-olds	1:8		
4-year-olds	1:10		
Screening/referral and support services	Vision, hearing, health, developmental; and support services[5]	Vision, hearing, health; and at least 1 support service	☑
Meals	Lunch and either breakfast or snack	At least 1/day	☑
Monitoring	Site visits and other monitoring	Site visits	☑

TOTAL BENCHMARKS MET

9

RESOURCES

Total state pre-K spending $80,000,000

Local match required?..Yes[6]

State spending per child enrolled $4,465

All reported spending per child enrolled* $5,578

SPENDING PER CHILD ENROLLED

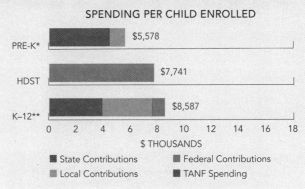

PRE-K*: $5,578
HDST: $7,741
K–12**: $8,587

$ THOUSANDS (0 to 18)

■ State Contributions   ■ Federal Contributions
■ Local Contributions   ■ TANF Spending

* Pre-K programs may receive additional funds from federal or local sources that are not included in this figure.

**K–12 expenditures include capital spending as well as current operating expenditures.

Data are for the '07-'08 school year, unless otherwise noted.

[1] Children who meet the income criteria receive highest priority for enrollment. In 2007-2008, 86 percent of children enrolled in the program met the income requirement.

[2] Naptime cannot be counted in the 5.5 hour minimum.

[3] Permissible types of pre-K certifications include: Pre-K–3, Pre-K–4, Pre-K–K, Pre-K–1 Special Education, and Pre-K–3 Special Education.

[4] In the ECE pilot, all assistant teachers are required to have a CDA. In the VPK program, the LEA is required to hire an assistant teacher with a CDA if one is available, but if not, the LEA may hire one with a high school diploma and relevant experience working with ECE programs.

[5] Dental screening and referrals are locally determined. Support services include two annual parent conferences or home visits, parenting support or training, parent involvement activities, referral for social services, and transition to pre-K and kindergarten activities. Some other comprehensive services are required, but specific services are determined locally.

[6] The state provides each LEA with their state share of the Basic Education Plan (BEP) amount of the cost per classroom unit, which varies by county. The LEA must identify a local funding match to add to their BEP funds that equals the amount per classroom unit set by the commissioner.

Texas

PERCENT OF STATE POPULATION ENROLLED

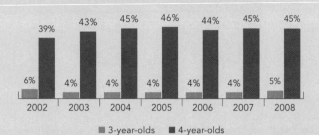

■ 3-year-olds ■ 4-year-olds

STATE SPENDING PER CHILD ENROLLED
(2008 DOLLARS)

In the 1985-1986 school year, the Texas Public School Prekindergarten initiative began providing half-day prekindergarten to at-risk 4-year-old children. At-risk eligibility factors include eligibility for free or reduced-price lunch, homelessness, limited English proficiency, and having parents who are on active military duty or have been injured or killed on duty. Children who are or were in foster care are also eligible for the program as of the 2007-2008 school year. Children who do not meet eligibility requirements may still participate in the program if their families choose to pay tuition and if districts choose to serve ineligible children. Any district that serves 15 or more eligible 4-year-old children is required to offer the Texas Public School Prekindergarten program. With any additional state and district funds, programs can also serve 3-year-olds. Over the past several years, enrollment in the program has steadily increased with more than 190,000 children being served in the 2007-2008 school year.

Using the Foundation School Program, Texas Public School Prekindergarten is supported by state and local funds and is part of the K–12 system. While districts are encouraged to offer services through Head Start programs or private child care centers, funding is distributed directly to school districts. The Foundation School Program provides funding for half-day services only. However, programs can apply for funding for full-day services from the Prekindergarten Expansion Grant Program, which awards competitive grants annually. Typically, school districts with low third grade reading scores have priority for receiving the grants.

In the 2007-2008 school year, more than 43,000 preschool children and their teachers in 170 school districts participated in the Texas Early Education Model (TEEM). TEEM encourages public schools, child care centers, and Head Start programs to coordinate services and share resources. The program is administered through the State Center for Early Childhood Development and is grant-funded to programs that use a research-based pre-reading instructional program and serve at least 75 percent low-income students.

Beginning in 2007-2008, the Texas Education Code amended its reporting requirements for purposes of the Texas School Readiness Certification System, which is a quality rating system designed to improve the academic achievement of prekindergarten students through a diverse delivery system. In addition, in the spring of 2008, the Texas Prekindergarten Curriculum Guidelines were revised and were distributed in the fall of 2008. The guidelines were incorporated into Proclamation 2011 for Instructional Materials and will be adopted by the state in 2010 and provided to prekindergarten classrooms beginning in the 2011-2012 school year.

ACCESS RANKINGS		RESOURCES RANKINGS	
4-YEAR-OLDS	3-YEAR-OLDS	STATE SPENDING	ALL REPORTED SPENDING
5	10	21	27

TEXAS PUBLIC SCHOOL PREKINDERGARTEN

ACCESS

Total state program enrollment 193,869

School districts that offer state program 82%

Income requirement ....185% FPL[1]

Hours of operation............................3 hours/day, 5 days/week[2]

Operating schedule ....Academic year

Special education enrollment 20,373

Federally funded Head Start enrollment 65,618

State-funded Head Start enrollment 0

STATE PRE-K AND HEAD START ENROLLMENT AS PERCENTAGE OF TOTAL POPULATION

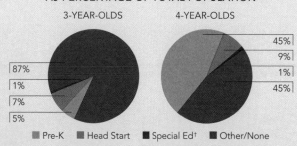

3-YEAR-OLDS

87%
1%
7%
5%

4-YEAR-OLDS

45%
9%
1%
45%

■ Pre-K ■ Head Start ■ Special Ed[†] ■ Other/None

[†] This number represents children in special education who are not enrolled in state-funded pre-K or Head Start.

QUALITY STANDARDS CHECKLIST

POLICY	STATE PRE-K REQUIREMENT	BENCHMARK	DOES REQUIREMENT MEET BENCHMARK?
Early learning standards	Comprehensive	Comprehensive	☑
Teacher degree	BA	BA	☑
Teacher specialized training	Generalist (EC–Grade 4) Teaching Certificate[3]	Specializing in pre-K	☑
Assistant teacher degree	HSD	CDA or equivalent	☐
Teacher in-service	150 clock hours/5 years	At least 15 hours/year	☑
Maximum class size		20 or lower	☐
3-year-olds	No limit[4]		
4-year-olds	No limit[4]		
Staff-child ratio		1:10 or better	☐
3-year-olds	No limit		
4-year-olds	No limit		
Screening/referral and support services	Determined locally[5]	Vision, hearing, health; and at least 1 support service	☐
Meals	Depend on length of program day[6]	At least 1/day	☐
Monitoring	None	Site visits	☐

TOTAL BENCHMARKS MET

4

RESOURCES

Total state pre-K spending ....$694,211,195[7]

Local match required? ....No

State spending per child enrolled $3,581

All reported spending per child enrolled* $3,581

SPENDING PER CHILD ENROLLED

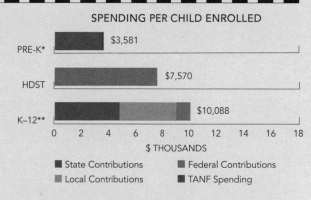

PRE-K* $3,581

HDST $7,570

K–12** $10,088

$ THOUSANDS

■ State Contributions   ■ Federal Contributions
■ Local Contributions   ■ TANF Spending

* Pre-K programs may receive additional funds from federal or local sources that are not included in this figure.

** K–12 expenditures include capital spending as well as current operating expenditures.

Data are for the '07-'08 school year, unless otherwise noted.

1 During the 2007-2008 program year, 73 percent of children enrolled qualified based on income. Children may also qualify if they are homeless, have a history of foster care, have a parent on active military duty, or have non-English speaking family members.

2 School districts that receive Prekindergarten Expansion Grant funding are required to offer 6 hours of services per day.

3 The Generalist Teaching Certificate covers early childhood through fourth grade. The pedagogy is based on developmental levels for children and appropriate teaching methods for each grade level. Texas standards no longer specify a number of semester hours in early childhood education.

4 Prekindergarten classes no larger than 15 (for 3-year-olds) or 18 (for 4-year-olds) are preferred but not required.

5 Vision, hearing, health, developmental, and dental screening and referrals are determined locally. Some support services are required, but specific services are determined locally. The number of annual parent conferences or home visits is also determined locally.

6 School districts are not required to serve meals to prekindergarten students. However, most school districts do serve either breakfast or lunch, and some offer both meals. All districts offering full-day programs provide lunch.

7 State funding under the Foundation School Program, distributed on the basis of aggregated average daily attendance, totaled $610,528,200. The Prekindergarten Expansion Grant Program contributed an additional $74,502,995 and TANF MOE money is included in the total amount.

Utah

NO PROGRAM

ACCESS RANKINGS		RESOURCES RANKINGS	
4-YEAR-OLDS	3-YEAR-OLDS	STATE SPENDING	ALL REPORTED SPENDING
No Program		No Program	

ACCESS

Total state program enrollment 0

School districts that offer state program.......................NA

Income requirement ....NA

Hours of operation ....NA

Operating schedule ....NA

Special education enrollment 4,857

Federally funded Head Start enrollment...................5,461

State-funded Head Start enrollment 0

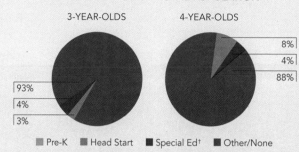

STATE PRE-K AND HEAD START ENROLLMENT
AS PERCENTAGE OF TOTAL POPULATION

3-YEAR-OLDS   4-YEAR-OLDS

8%
4%
88%

93%
4%
3%

■ Pre-K   ■ Head Start   ■ Special Ed†   ■ Other/None

† This number represents children in special education
who are not enrolled in Head Start.

QUALITY STANDARDS CHECKLIST

TOTAL
BENCHMARKS
MET

No
Program

RESOURCES

Total state pre-K spending...$0

Local match required? ....NA

State Head Start spending...$0

State spending per child enrolled $0

All reported spending per child enrolled*......................$0

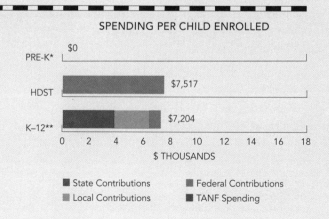

SPENDING PER CHILD ENROLLED

PRE-K* $0

HDST $7,517

K–12** $7,204

0   2   4   6   8   10   12   14   16   18
$ THOUSANDS

■ State Contributions   ■ Federal Contributions
■ Local Contributions   ■ TANF Spending

---

* Pre-K programs may receive additional funds from federal or local sources
   that are not included in this figure.

** K–12 expenditures include capital spending as well as current operating
   expenditures.

Data are for the '07-'08 school year, unless otherwise noted.

Vermont

PERCENT OF STATE POPULATION ENROLLED

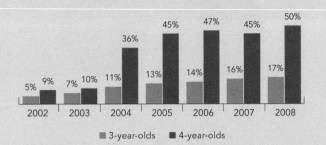

■ 3-year-olds ■ 4-year-olds

STATE SPENDING PER CHILD ENROLLED
(2008 DOLLARS)

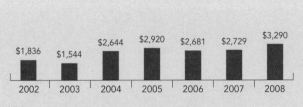

A iming to increase access to preschool education programs for at-risk 3- and 4-year-olds, Vermont established the Vermont Early Education Initiative (EEI) in 1987. Eligibility is limited to children from families with incomes below 185 percent of the federal poverty level or who exhibit risk factors such as developmental delay, limited English proficiency, social isolation, or abuse or neglect. Through this initiative, grants are awarded to public schools, private child care centers, Parent-Child Centers, faith-based and family child care centers, and Head Start programs to provide preschool education. Although funding for EEI has remained stable over the past few years it is still below the level of funding seen in fiscal year 1996 and the value of grants has decreased steadily, when accounting for inflation, since the program began. EEI programs may collaborate with other community resources for additional funding and to provide services.

Vermont increased support and funding for preschool education in 2003 with a second state initiative, the Vermont Publicly Funded Prekindergarten using Average Daily Membership (PFP-ADM) census data. Eligibility is open to all 3- and 4-year-olds within communities choosing to participate in the program. Through this initiative, approximately 80 percent of Vermont's local education agencies receive state education funds to provide up to 10 hours per week of preschool education. PFP-ADM funds are distributed to local schools, which may in turn contract with other providers such as Head Start and private child care centers. Forty percent of the K–6 education funding level is allocated to preschool education programs through a funding formula, and the local education agencies may supplement their budgets with funds from other sources. Teachers in the PFP-ADM program receive support, including professional development opportunities, to help them meet the Vermont Early Learning Standards. As of the 2007-2008 school year, PFP-ADM became known as Vermont Prekindergarten Education-Act 62. Effective with the 2008-2009 school year, programs in nonpublic settings will be required to have one BA teacher at each center, rather than one in every classroom.

The first two pages of Vermont's profile describe the state's overall contribution and commitment to preschool education with enrollment and state spending information for both initiatives. The next two pages provide specific details about each of Vermont's preschool initiatives with the Vermont Prekindergarten Education-Act 62 program detailed on the third page and the EEI program detailed on the following page.

STATE OVERVIEW

Total state program enrollment 4,438

Total state spending $14,602,206

State spending per child enrolled $3,290

All reported spending per child enrolled $3,290

STATE PRE-K AND HEAD START ENROLLMENT AS PERCENTAGE OF TOTAL POPULATION

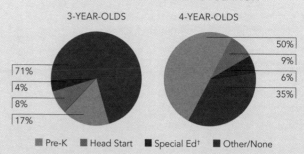

3-YEAR-OLDS

71%
4%
8%
17%

4-YEAR-OLDS

50%
9%
6%
35%

■ Pre-K   ■ Head Start   ■ Special Ed†   ■ Other/None

† This number represents children in special education who are not enrolled in Head Start but may be enrolled in state-funded pre-K.

SPENDING PER CHILD ENROLLED

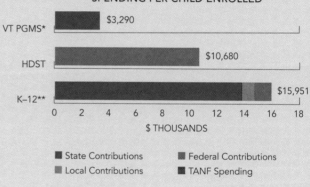

VT PGMS* $3,290

HDST $10,680

K–12** $15,951

0   2   4   6   8   10   12   14   16   18

$ THOUSANDS

■ State Contributions   ■ Federal Contributions
■ Local Contributions   ■ TANF Spending

* Pre-K programs may receive additional funds from federal or local sources that are not included in this figure.

**K–12 expenditures include capital spending as well as current operating expenditures.

Data are for the '07-'08 school year, unless otherwise noted.

ACCESS RANKINGS	
4-YEAR-OLDS	3-YEAR-OLDS
4	3

RESOURCES RANKINGS	
STATE SPENDING	ALL REPORTED SPENDING
25	30

VERMONT PREKINDERGARTEN EDUCATION - ACT 62

ACCESS

Total state program enrollment 3,507

School districts that offer state program......63% (communities)[1]

Income requirement ....None

Hours of operation ....Determined locally[2]

Operating schedule ....Academic year

Special education enrollment ....1,014[3]

Federally funded Head Start enrollment 1,205

State-funded Head Start enrollment 0

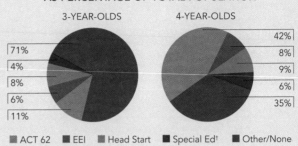

STATE PRE-K AND HEAD START ENROLLMENT AS PERCENTAGE OF TOTAL POPULATION

3-YEAR-OLDS: 71%, 4%, 8%, 6%, 11%

4-YEAR-OLDS: 42%, 8%, 9%, 6%, 35%

■ ACT 62　■ EEI　■ Head Start　■ Special Ed[†]　■ Other/None

[†] This number represents children in special education who are not enrolled in Head Start but may be enrolled in state-funded pre-K.

QUALITY STANDARDS CHECKLIST

POLICY	STATE PRE-K REQUIREMENT	BENCHMARK	DOES REQUIREMENT MEET BENCHMARK?
Early learning standards	Comprehensive	Comprehensive	☑
Teacher degree	BA[4]	BA	☑
Teacher specialized training	ECE or ECSE endorsement	Specializing in pre-K	☑
Assistant teacher degree	Determined locally[5]	CDA or equivalent	☐
Teacher in-service	9 credit hours/7 years	At least 15 hours/year	☑
Maximum class size		20 or lower	☑
3-year-olds	20		
4-year-olds	20		
Staff-child ratio		1:10 or better	☑
3-year-olds	1:10		
4-year-olds	1:10		
Screening/referral and support services	Vision, hearing, health, developmental; and support services[6]	Vision, hearing, health; and at least 1 support service	☑
Meals	No meals are required[7]	At least 1/day	☐
Monitoring	None	Site visits	☐

TOTAL BENCHMARKS MET

7

RESOURCES

Total state pre-K spending ....$13,300,000[8]

Local match required? ....No

State spending per child enrolled $3,792

All reported spending per child enrolled* ....$3,792[9]

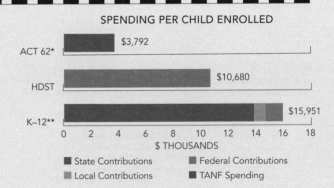

SPENDING PER CHILD ENROLLED

ACT 62*: $3,792
HDST: $10,680
K–12**: $15,951

$ THOUSANDS

■ State Contributions　■ Federal Contributions
■ Local Contributions　■ TANF Spending

* Pre-K programs may receive additional funds from federal or local sources that are not included in this figure.

**K–12 expenditures include capital spending as well as current operating expenditures.

Data are for the '07-'08 school year, unless otherwise noted.

[1] This is an approximate number of communities; statewide data on pre-K programs were not collected in 2007-2009.

[2] Programs are funded to operate 6-10 hours per week, with a "full-time" child attending 10 hours per week. The most common school-based model is between 3-4 hours/day, 2-3 days/week.

[3] Vermont did not report special education enrollment. It was estimated based on the percentage of 3- and 4-year-olds in special education in 2006-2007.

[4] New requirements related to Act 62 take effect in July 2008, which removes the BA requirement for lead teachers in programs in nonpublic settings. Nonpublic centers will be permitted to have one licensed teacher per center rather than one per classroom, and registered child care homes will require only brief supervision by a licensed teacher.

[5] Assistant teachers must have an AA or equivalent in public settings and a minimum of 6 credits in ECE in nonpublic settings. Other required assistant teacher training is not specified in Act 62 and depends on the type of pre-K provider.

[6] Dental screenings and referrals are determined locally. Support services include two annual home visits or parent conferences, parenting support or training, parent involvement activities, health services for children, information about nutrition, referral to social services, and transition to kindergarten activities.

[7] There is no requirement for meals. However, most programs are half day and offer a snack. If the program is part of Head Start or a child care program, meals will be offered.

[8] This figure is an estimate of total spending. In previous years, the state could not separate out the specific amount of spending for pre-K. In the 2007-2008 school year, the state collected spending information for the program separately for the first time.

[9] The state did not break Act 62 enrollment into specific numbers of 3- and 4-year-olds. As a result, these calculations are estimates based on proportions of enrollees who were ages 3 or 4 in state programs that served 3-year-olds and provided age breakdowns for 2007-2008.

VERMONT EARLY EDUCATION INITIATIVE

ACCESS

Total state program enrollment 931

School districts that offer....................46% (supervisory unions)[1]
state program

Income requirement ....185% FPL[2]

Hours of operation ....Determined locally[3]

Operating schedule ....Academic year

Special education enrollment ....1,014[4]

Federally funded Head Start enrollment..........................1,205

State-funded Head Start enrollment 0

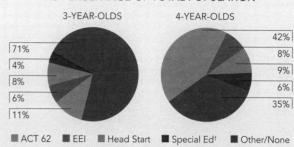

STATE PRE-K AND HEAD START ENROLLMENT AS PERCENTAGE OF TOTAL POPULATION

3-YEAR-OLDS
- 71%
- 4%
- 8%
- 6%
- 11%

4-YEAR-OLDS
- 42%
- 8%
- 9%
- 6%
- 35%

■ ACT 62   ■ EEI   ■ Head Start   ■ Special Ed†   ■ Other/None

† This number represents children in special education who are not enrolled in Head Start but may be enrolled in state-funded pre-K.

QUALITY STANDARDS CHECKLIST

POLICY	STATE PRE-K REQUIREMENT	BENCHMARK	DOES REQUIREMENT MEET BENCHMARK?
Early learning standards	Comprehensive	Comprehensive	☑
Teacher degree	BA[5]	BA	☑
Teacher specialized training	Early Childhood Educator (public and nonpublic)	Specializing in pre-K	☑
Assistant teacher degree	Determined locally[6]	CDA or equivalent	☐
Teacher in-service	9 credit hours/7 years (public)	At least 15 hours/year	☐
Maximum class size		20 or lower	☑
3-year-olds	16		
4-year-olds	16		
Staff-child ratio		1:10 or better	☑
3-year-olds	1:8		
4-year-olds	1:10		
Screening/referral and support services	Vision, hearing, health, developmental; and support services[7]	Vision, hearing, health; and at least 1 support service	☑
Meals	No meals are required	At least 1/day	☐
Monitoring	None[8]	Site visits	☐

TOTAL BENCHMARKS MET

6

RESOURCES

Total state pre-K spending $1,302,206

Local match required? ....No

State spending per child enrolled $1,399

All reported spending per child enrolled* $1,399

* Pre-K programs may receive additional funds from federal or local sources that are not included in this figure.

** K–12 expenditures include capital spending as well as current operating expenditures.

Data are for the '07-'08 school year, unless otherwise noted.

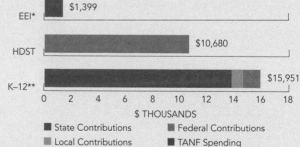

SPENDING PER CHILD ENROLLED

- EEI* — $1,399
- HDST — $10,680
- K–12** — $15,951

$ THOUSANDS (0 2 4 6 8 10 12 14 16 18)

■ State Contributions   ■ Federal Contributions
■ Local Contributions   ■ TANF Spending

---

[1] EEI grants are given to supervisory unions rather than districts. In addition grants were awarded to some parent-child centers, child care centers, Head Start programs and a homeless shelter.

[2] Children may also qualify based on other risk factors such as developmental delay, risk for abuse or neglect, limited English proficiency, exposure to violence or substance abuse, social isolation, low educational attainment by parents, homelessness, teen parent, parent active military duty, or incarcerated parent. In 2007-2008, 53 percent of children met the income requirement.

[3] Programs operate an average of 3.5 hours/day and an average of 3 days/week during the academic year.

[4] Vermont did not report special education enrollment. It was estimated based on the percentage of 3- and 4-year-olds in special education in 2006-2007.

[5] State policy does not explicitly require teachers in nonpublic settings to hold a BA, but this standard is enforced as a mandatory component of the grant review process.

[6] Public schools use NCLB highly qualified teacher status or an AA in setting educational expectations for assistant teachers, but this is not a requirement. Private programs use HSD plus 6 credits in ECE in setting educational expectations, but again it is not a requirement. Requirements for assistant teachers depend on the type of program.

[7] District-wide screenings for all 3- to 5-year-olds are conducted, and referrals for services are provided to children whether or not they are EEI eligible. Dental screenings and referrals are determined locally. Support services include two annual parent conferences or home visits, education services or job training for parents, parenting support or training, parent involvement activities, health services for children, information about nutrition, referral to social services, and transition to kindergarten activities.

[8] State policy does not formally require monitoring but standard practice includes documentation of children's learning and/or child outcomes, documentation of program-level outcomes, review of program facilities and safety procedures, results of program self-assessments, and review of program records.

Virginia

PERCENT OF STATE POPULATION ENROLLED

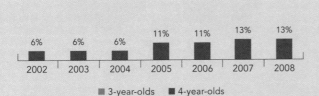

■ 3-year-olds ■ 4-year-olds

STATE SPENDING PER CHILD ENROLLED
(2008 DOLLARS)

The Virginia Preschool Initiative was established in 1995 to serve at-risk 4-year-olds not enrolled in existing preschool programs. Program eligibility is determined locally, based on risk factors such as poverty, homelessness, having parents with limited education, family unemployment, parental incarceration, or limited English proficiency.

Funds for the Virginia Preschool Initiative are distributed directly to public school districts and local departments of social services, which both may subcontract with Head Start or private child care centers to provide services. Any community receiving funding for the program is required to contribute matching funds based on a local composite index of district resources. Programs choosing to operate on a half-day schedule receive 50 percent of the full-day funding allocation.

Funding allocations were increased in the 2004-2005 school year to serve 90 percent of at-risk children not served in other preschool programs. For the 2006-2007 school year, the state increased per-pupil funding to provide services to all at-risk 4-year-olds. The per-pupil rate will increase again starting in the 2008-2009 program year due to an additional $22 million allocated to support the Virginia Preschool Initiative over the biennium.

Beginning with the 2007-2008 program year, all programs are required to follow the newly revised early learning standards, which were expanded to include science, history, social science, personal and social development, and physical and motor standards.

ACCESS RANKINGS		RESOURCES RANKINGS	
4-YEAR-OLDS	3-YEAR-OLDS	STATE SPENDING	ALL REPORTED SPENDING
24	None Served	22	16

VIRGINIA PRESCHOOL INITIATIVE

ACCESS

Total state program enrollment 13,125

School districts that offer state program 77%

Income requirement ....None

Hours of operation ....3 hours/day (half day),
6 hours/day (full day); 5 days/week[1]

Operating schedule ....Academic year

Special education enrollment 9,374

Federally funded Head Start enrollment 12,321

State-funded Head Start enrollment 0

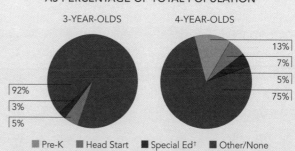

STATE PRE-K AND HEAD START ENROLLMENT AS PERCENTAGE OF TOTAL POPULATION

3-YEAR-OLDS: 92%, 3%, 5%

4-YEAR-OLDS: 13%, 7%, 5%, 75%

■ Pre-K ■ Head Start ■ Special Ed[†] ■ Other/None

[†] This number represents children in special education who are not enrolled in Head Start, but includes children who are enrolled in state-funded pre-K.

QUALITY STANDARDS CHECKLIST

POLICY	STATE PRE-K REQUIREMENT	BENCHMARK	DOES REQUIREMENT MEET BENCHMARK?
Early learning standards	Comprehensive	Comprehensive	☑
Teacher degree	BA (public), HSD (nonpublic)[2]	BA	☐
Teacher specialized training	License + certification in Pre-K–3, or –6, EC for 3- and 4-year-olds (public), None (nonpublic)[2]	Specializing in pre-K	☐
Assistant teacher degree	HSD or GED	CDA or equivalent	☐
Teacher in-service	15 clock hours	At least 15 hours/year	☑
Maximum class size		20 or lower	☑
3-year-olds	NA		
4-year-olds	18		
Staff-child ratio		1:10 or better	☑
3-year-olds	NA		
4-year-olds	1:9		
Screening/referral and support services	Vision, hearing, health; and support services[3]	Vision, hearing, health; and at least 1 support service	☑
Meals	At least breakfast and snack[4]	At least 1/day	☑
Monitoring	Site visits and other monitoring[5]	Site visits	☑

TOTAL BENCHMARKS MET

7

RESOURCES

Total state pre-K spending $46,916,828

Local match required? ....Yes, based on composite
index of local ability to pay

State spending per child enrolled $3,575

All reported spending per child enrolled* $5,639

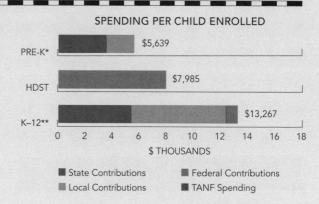

SPENDING PER CHILD ENROLLED

PRE-K*: $5,639

HDST: $7,985

K–12**: $13,267

$ THOUSANDS

■ State Contributions ■ Federal Contributions
■ Local Contributions ■ TANF Spending

* Pre-K programs may receive additional funds from federal or local sources that are not included in this figure.

**K–12 expenditures include capital spending as well as current operating expenditures.

Data are for the '07-'08 school year, unless otherwise noted.

[1] Localities may choose to offer half-day programs for 3 hours per day or full-day programs for 6 hours per day. Most programs operate on a full-day schedule. All programs operate 5 days per week.

[2] Teachers in public schools are required to hold a license with endorsements in the areas in which they are working. Teachers not located in public schools who have a minimum of high school completion must show certification of completion of 120 hours of training in the subject areas of first aid, human growth and development, health and safety issues, and behavioral management of children.

[3] Support services include parent involvement activities, child health services, and referral for social services. Other comprehensive services and the annual number of required parent conferences or home visits are determined locally.

[4] All children receive breakfast and snack regardless of full- or half-day services. All children in full-day programs receive lunch.

[5] Site visits and other monitoring activities are required every two years.

Washington

PERCENT OF STATE POPULATION ENROLLED

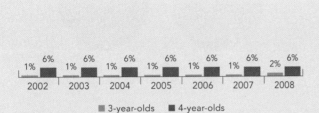

■ 3-year-olds ■ 4-year-olds

STATE SPENDING PER CHILD ENROLLED
(2008 DOLLARS)

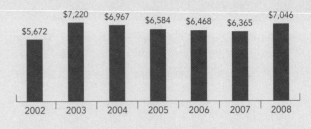

I n response to calls for early childhood education reform, the Washington Early Childhood Education and Assistance Program (ECEAP) was established in 1985. ECEAP is overseen by the state Department of Early Learning (DEL), a cabinet-level agency begun in 2006 that works with Thrive by Five Washington to fund programs and coordinate efforts to improve school readiness.

ECEAP offers health coordination, nutrition, family support, and preschool education to assist parents in raising children who are ready to learn. Four-year-olds from families at or below 110 percent of the federal poverty level are primarily served, but 3-year-olds are also enrolled based on other risk factors. In addition, up to 10 percent of slots may be filled by children who have developmental or environmental risk factors or whose families are over the income cutoff.

The DEL provides funding for ECEAP services in a variety of public and private settings, including educational service districts, school districts, local governments, nonprofit organizations, community and technical colleges, and nonsectarian organizations. The state increased its investment in ECEAP in 2007, resulting in 2,250 more children and families being served by the program during the 2007-2009 biennium. An additional rate increase has allowed for quality improvements such as increased hours of preschool education and reinforcement of teacher qualification standards. In 2008, about 8,200 children and their families in 37 counties participated in the comprehensive learning program.

ACCESS RANKINGS		RESOURCES RANKINGS	
4-YEAR-OLDS	3-YEAR-OLDS	STATE SPENDING	ALL REPORTED SPENDING
32	17	6	10

WASHINGTON EARLY CHILDHOOD EDUCATION AND ASSISTANCE PROGRAM

ACCESS

Total state program enrollment 6,801

School districts that offer state program............95% (counties)

Income requirement ....90% of children must be
at or below 110% FPL

Hours of operation ....Determined locally[1]

Operating schedule..30 weeks/year

Special education enrollment 7,656

Federally funded Head Start enrollment.......................11,502

State-funded Head Start enrollment 0

STATE PRE-K AND HEAD START ENROLLMENT AS PERCENTAGE OF TOTAL POPULATION

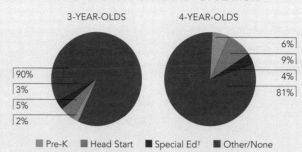

3-YEAR-OLDS: 90%, 3%, 5%, 2%

4-YEAR-OLDS: 6%, 9%, 4%, 81%

■ Pre-K ■ Head Start ■ Special Ed[†] ■ Other/None

† This number represents children in special education
who are not enrolled in state-funded pre-K or Head Start.

QUALITY STANDARDS CHECKLIST

POLICY	STATE PRE-K REQUIREMENT	BENCHMARK	DOES REQUIREMENT MEET BENCHMARK?
Early learning standards	Comprehensive	Comprehensive	☑
Teacher degree	AA or BA	BA	☐
Teacher specialized training	30 quarter units in ECE[2]	Specializing in pre-K	☑
Assistant teacher degree	CDA or 12 quarter credits in ECE	CDA or equivalent	☑
Teacher in-service	15 clock hours	At least 15 hours/year	☑
Maximum class size		20 or lower	☑
3-year-olds	20		
4-year-olds	20		
Staff-child ratio		1:10 or better	☑
3-year-olds	1:9		
4-year-olds	1:9		
Screening/referral and support services	Vision, hearing, health, dental, developmental; and support services[3]	Vision, hearing, health; and at least 1 support service	☑
Meals	At least 1 meal[4]	At least 1/day	☑
Monitoring	Site visits and other monitoring	Site visits	☑

TOTAL BENCHMARKS MET

9

RESOURCES

Total state pre-K spending $47,919,000

Local match required? ....No

State spending per child enrolled $7,046

All reported spending per child enrolled* $7,046

SPENDING PER CHILD ENROLLED

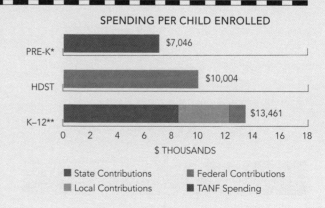

PRE-K*: $7,046
HDST: $10,004
K–12**: $13,461

$ THOUSANDS

■ State Contributions ■ Federal Contributions
■ Local Contributions ■ TANF Spending

* Pre-K programs may receive additional funds from federal or local sources
that are not included in this figure.

** K–12 expenditures include capital spending as well as current operating
expenditures.

Data are for the '07-'08 school year, unless otherwise noted.

[1] A minimum of 240 hours per year in at least 30 weeks is required. Most programs
operate 2.5 to 6 hours per day, 3 to 4 days per week, with a typical schedule
being 3 hours per day, 4 days per week.

[2] Teachers with a BA must also have an ECE endorsement.

[3] Support services include 3 hours of parent conferences, 3 hours of family support

services, parenting support or training, parent involvement activities, health
services for children, information about nutrition, referral to social services,
transition to kindergarten activities, mental health consultation, services of a
dietician, and oral/dental health services.

[4] Programs of fewer than 3 hours must provide breakfast or lunch. Programs lasting
more than 3 hours must provide breakfast or lunch and a snack.

West Virginia

PERCENT OF STATE POPULATION ENROLLED

STATE SPENDING PER CHILD ENROLLED
(2008 DOLLARS)

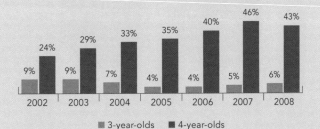

■ 3-year-olds ■ 4-year-olds

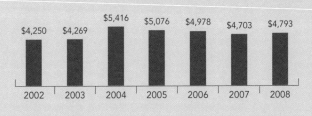

I n 1983, revisions to West Virginia's school code established the Public School Early Childhood Education initiative, allowing local school boards to offer preschool education programs for 3- and 4-year-olds. West Virginia then passed legislation in 2000 requiring the state to expand access to preschool education programs, in order to make prekindergarten available to all 4-year-olds in the state by the 2012-2013 school year. The state has been successful in increasing the number of 4-year-olds served and offers preschool education programs in all school districts. However, the increase in access for 4-year-olds over the past few years has resulted in a decrease in access for 3-year-olds. As of July 2004, only 3-year-olds who have an Individualized Education Plan (IEP) are eligible to receive state funding for West Virginia's preschool program, now called the West Virginia Universal Pre-K System. West Virginia is working with its 55 counties to ensure they have a sufficient number of classrooms and that these classrooms meet the state's quality standards. Each year, counties are required to share with the state their plan for expanding access to state-funded pre-K.

Funding for the West Virginia Universal Pre-K System initiative is allocated to public schools, which may subcontract with other agencies to offer services. West Virginia requires that half of the programs operate in collaborative settings with private prekindergarten, child care centers, or Head Start programs in order to facilitate expansion of the program. Supplementary funding for preschool education in the state is provided through federal Head Start, IDEA, Title I, and Title II.

The majority of West Virginia's Universal Pre-K programs use the Creative Curriculum in their classrooms. The state also has a web-based portfolio based on the Creative Curriculum, which allows teachers to track assessment results and progress for all students as required by the West Virginia Early Learning Standards Framework.

ACCESS RANKINGS		RESOURCES RANKINGS	
4-YEAR-OLDS	3-YEAR-OLDS	STATE SPENDING	ALL REPORTED SPENDING
6	7	12	7

WEST VIRGINIA UNIVERSAL PRE-K

ACCESS

Total state program enrollment 12,404

School districts that offer state program 100%

Income requirement ....None

Hours of operation ....Determined locally[1]

Operating schedule ....Academic year[1]

Special education enrollment 3,045

Federally funded Head Start enrollment...........................7,029

State-funded Head Start enrollment 0

STATE PRE-K AND HEAD START ENROLLMENT AS PERCENTAGE OF TOTAL POPULATION

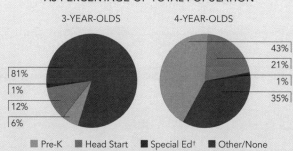

3-YEAR-OLDS

81%
1%
12%
6%

4-YEAR-OLDS

43%
21%
1%
35%

■ Pre-K   ■ Head Start   ■ Special Ed[†]   ■ Other/None

[†] This number represents children in special education
who are not enrolled in state-funded pre-K or Head Start.

QUALITY STANDARDS CHECKLIST

POLICY	STATE PRE-K REQUIREMENT	BENCHMARK	DOES REQUIREMENT MEET BENCHMARK?
Early learning standards	Comprehensive	Comprehensive	☑
Teacher degree	BA in ECE or Pre-K SpEd (pre-K only programs); AA (blended programs)[2]	BA	☐
Teacher specialized training	See footnote[3]	Specializing in pre-K	☑
Assistant teacher degree	HSD	CDA or equivalent	☐
Teacher in-service	15 clock hours per year	At least 15 hours/year	☑
Maximum class size		20 or lower	☑
3-year-olds	20		
4-year-olds	20		
Staff-child ratio		1:10 or better	☑
3-year-olds	1:10		
4-year-olds	1:10		
Screening/referral and support services	Vision, hearing, health, dental, developmental; and support services[4]	Vision, hearing, health; and at least 1 support service	☑
Meals	Depend on length of program day[5]	At least 1/day	☐
Monitoring	Site visits and other monitoring	Site visits	☑

TOTAL BENCHMARKS MET

7

RESOURCES

Total state pre-K spending $59,452,747

Local match required? ....No

State spending per child enrolled $4,793

All reported spending per child enrolled* $7,778

* Pre-K programs may receive additional funds from federal or local sources
that are not included in this figure.

** K–12 expenditures include capital spending as well as current operating
expenditures.

Data are for the '07-'08 school year, unless otherwise noted.

SPENDING PER CHILD ENROLLED

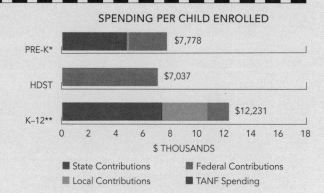

PRE-K* $7,778

HDST $7,037

K–12** $12,231

0   2   4   6   8   10   12   14   16   18

$ THOUSANDS

■ State Contributions   ■ Federal Contributions
■ Local Contributions   ■ TANF Spending

[1] Hours of operation are determined locally, but programs must operate for at
least 12 hours per week, with a maximum of 30 hours per week, and at least
108 instructional days.

[2] If the classroom is in a community collaborative site (supported by two or more
funding sources and located in a public school or community-based setting),
the teacher may acquire a permanent authorization for community programs,
provided that the teacher has at least an Associate's degree in an approved
field and has completed or is working toward an approved list of core early
childhood courses.

[3] Teachers in public school settings that are not collaboratives must be certified
in birth–5, early childhood education, preschool special needs, or elementary
education (with a pre-K–K endorsement). Teachers in community collaborative
settings must have a minimum of an Associate degree in child development/
early childhood or in occupational development with an emphasis in child
development/early childhood.

[4] Support services include two annual parent conferences or home visits,
transition to kindergarten activities, and other locally determined services.

[5] Meals must be offered if the program operates for more than 4 hours per day.

Wisconsin

PERCENT OF STATE POPULATION ENROLLED

STATE SPENDING PER CHILD ENROLLED
(2008 DOLLARS)

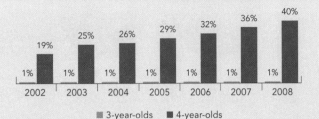

■ 3-year-olds ■ 4-year-olds

Since 1848 when Wisconsin became a state, its constitution has included commitment to provide free education for 4-year-olds. In 1873, the state established the Four-Year-Old Kindergarten (4K) program, which continues to operate today despite a suspension of state funding between 1957 and 1984. Funds are distributed to public schools, which may choose to offer preschool education programs or contract with Head Start or private child care centers to do so. Public school districts receive 50 percent of the standard state per-pupil K–12 funding amount to provide half-day slots for 4-year-olds. They may receive 60 percent if they also offer parent support programs.

Over the past few years, Wisconsin has successfully increased enrollment in its Four-Year-Old Kindergarten program by both opening new programs in districts that did not previously offer 4K and by increasing enrollment in districts with existing programs. Sixty-eight percent of elementary school districts offered 4K during the 2007-2008 school year, an increase from the previous years. State-funded programs are encouraged to follow the Wisconsin Model Early Learning Standards, although they are not required to do so.

Wisconsin has a second, separate state-funded preschool initiative, the Wisconsin Head Start program, which offers comprehensive early education for 3- and 4-year-olds with a disability or from a low-income family. Wisconsin uses state funding to supplement federal Head Start, enabling federal Head Start grantees to increase access and other preschool services. Head Start grantees and local school districts frequently collaborate to implement 4K. These partnerships have increased over the last few years and the state has offered start-up grants to encourage such collaboration. Wisconsin Head Start programs are required to follow federal Head Start Performance Standards.

The first two pages of the Wisconsin profile summarize the state's overall contribution and commitment to state-funded preschool education programs, including enrollment and state spending for both 4K and Wisconsin Head Start. The third page presents specific details on the 4K program and the fourth page focuses on the state-financed Head Start program.

STATE OVERVIEW

Total state program enrollment 29,175

Total state spending $92,212,500

State Head Start spending $7,212,500

State spending per child enrolled $3,161

All reported spending per child enrolled $4,737

STATE PRE-K AND HEAD START ENROLLMENT AS PERCENTAGE OF TOTAL POPULATION

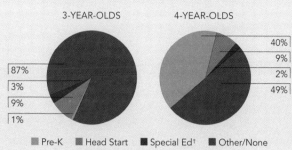

3-YEAR-OLDS

87%
3%
9%
1%

4-YEAR-OLDS

40%
9%
2%
49%

■ Pre-K   ■ Head Start   ■ Special Ed†   ■ Other/None

† This number represents children in special education
who are not enrolled in Head Start or 4K.

SPENDING PER CHILD ENROLLED

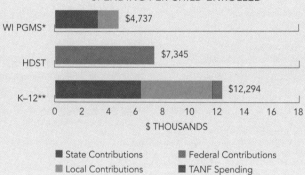

WI PGMS* $4,737

HDST $7,345

K–12** $12,294

0   2   4   6   8   10   12   14   16   18
$ THOUSANDS

■ State Contributions   ■ Federal Contributions
■ Local Contributions   ■ TANF Spending

* Pre-K programs may receive additional funds from federal or local sources
that are not included in this figure.

** K–12 expenditures include capital spending as well as current operating
expenditures.

Data are for the '07-'08 school year, unless otherwise noted.

ACCESS RANKINGS	
4-YEAR-OLDS	3-YEAR-OLDS
7	23

RESOURCES RANKINGS	
STATE SPENDING	ALL REPORTED SPENDING
26	20

WISCONSIN FOUR-YEAR-OLD KINDERGARTEN

ACCESS

Total state program enrollment 27,759

School districts that offer state program 68%

Income requirement ....None

Hours of operation ....Determined locally[1]

Operating schedule ....Determined locally[1]

Special education enrollment 8,246

Federally funded Head Start enrollment 12,913

State-funded Head Start enrollment ....1,229[2]

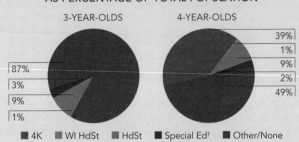

STATE PRE-K AND HEAD START ENROLLMENT AS PERCENTAGE OF TOTAL POPULATION

3-YEAR-OLDS

- 87%
- 3%
- 9%
- 1%

4-YEAR-OLDS

- 39%
- 1%
- 9%
- 2%
- 49%

■ 4K ■ WI HdSt ■ HdSt ■ Special Ed† ■ Other/None

† This number represents children in special education who are not enrolled in Head Start or 4K.

QUALITY STANDARDS CHECKLIST

POLICY	STATE PRE-K REQUIREMENT	BENCHMARK	DOES REQUIREMENT MEET BENCHMARK?
Early learning standards	Comprehensive	Comprehensive	☑
Teacher degree	BA[3]	BA	☑
Teacher specialized training	EC-level or EC to Middle Childhood-level license[3]	Specializing in pre-K	☑
Assistant teacher degree	Teacher asst. license or AA (public); 1 course in EC (nonpublic)[4]	CDA or equivalent	☐
Teacher in-service	6 credit hours/5 years	At least 15 hours/year	☑
Maximum class size		20 or lower	☐
3-year-olds	NA		
4-year-olds	Determined locally		
Staff-child ratio		1:10 or better	☐
3-year-olds	NA		
4-year-olds	Determined locally		
Screening/referral and support services	Support services only[5]	Vision, hearing, health; and at least 1 support service	☐
Meals	Depend on length of program day[6]	At least 1/day	☐
Monitoring	Site visits and other monitoring	Site visits	☑

TOTAL BENCHMARKS MET

5

RESOURCES

Total state pre-K spending $85,000,000

Local match required? ....Yes, local share of school revenue generated through property tax

State Head Start spending $7,212,500

State spending per child enrolled $3,062

All reported spending per child enrolled* $4,719

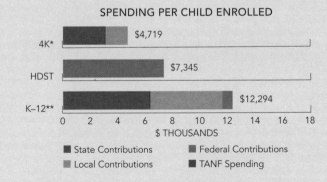

SPENDING PER CHILD ENROLLED

- 4K*: $4,719
- HDST: $7,345
- K–12**: $12,294

$ THOUSANDS

■ State Contributions ■ Federal Contributions
■ Local Contributions ■ TANF Spending

* Pre-K programs may receive additional funds from federal or local sources that are not included in this figure.

** K–12 expenditures include capital spending as well as current operating expenditures.

Data are for the '07–'08 school year, unless otherwise noted.

[1] Programs operate for a minimum of 437 hours per year, or 437 hours per year plus 87.5 hours of parent outreach, or 349.5 hours per year plus 87.5 hours of parent outreach.

[2] Wisconsin did not break this figure into specific numbers of 3- or 4-year-olds. As a result, age breakdowns used in the Access pie chart were also estimated, using proportions of federal Head Start enrollees in each age category.

[3] Teachers must hold an appropriate early childhood teacher license with the Department of Public Instruction. The pre-K, K, or EC license all require that the BA program addresses early childhood birth to third grade and includes field work and practicum with this age level. Some licenses go beyond third grade but still require early childhood-specific work.

[4] In public schools, assistant teachers may be required to have an AA if Title I standards are applicable. The requirement for assistant teachers in nonpublic settings reflects child care licensing regulations, which also require that assistant teachers be at least 18 years old.

[5] State law supports vision, hearing, immunization, and general health screenings prior to enrollment in Wisconsin's Four-Year-Old Kindergarten and they are required at kindergarten entrance for all children. Support services include parent involvement activities, health services for children, referral to social services, and school counseling. The number of annual parent conferences or home visits is determined locally.

[6] Snack and/or lunch may be provided based on the length of the program day and requirements of other community programs.

WISCONSIN HEAD START STATE SUPPLEMENT

ACCESS

Total state program enrollment ....1,416[1]

School districts that offer state program...............92% (federal Head Start grantees)

Income requirement ....90% of children must be at or below 100% FPL

Hours of operation ....Determined locally[2]

Operating schedule ....Determined locally[2]

Special education enrollment 8,246

Federally funded Head Start enrollment 12,913

State-funded Head Start enrollment ....1,229[1]

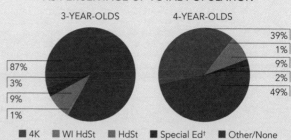

STATE PRE-K AND HEAD START ENROLLMENT AS PERCENTAGE OF TOTAL POPULATION

3-YEAR-OLDS
- 87%
- 3%
- 9%
- 1%

4-YEAR-OLDS
- 39%
- 1%
- 9%
- 2%
- 49%

■ 4K ■ WI HdSt ■ HdSt ■ Special Ed[†] ■ Other/None

[†] This number represents children in special education who are not enrolled in Head Start or 4K.

QUALITY STANDARDS CHECKLIST

POLICY	STATE PRE-K REQUIREMENT	BENCHMARK	DOES REQUIREMENT MEET BENCHMARK?
Early learning standards	Comprehensive	Comprehensive	☑
Teacher degree	BA (public); CDA (nonpublic)[3]	BA	☐
Teacher specialized training	ECE License in birth to age 8 or 12 (public); Meets CDA requirements (nonpublic)[3]	Specializing in pre-K	☑
Assistant teacher degree	Determined locally (public), 1 course in EC (nonpublic)[4]	CDA or equivalent	☐
Teacher in-service	15 clock hours[5]	At least 15 hours/year	☐
Maximum class size		20 or lower	☑
3-year-olds	17		
4-year-olds	20		
Staff-child ratio		1:10 or better	☑
3-year-olds	2:17		
4-year-olds	1:10		
Screening/referral and support services	Vision, hearing, health, dental, developmental; and support services[6]	Vision, hearing, health; and at least 1 support service	☑
Meals	Lunch and snack[7]	At least 1/day	☑
Monitoring	None[8]	Site visits	☐

TOTAL BENCHMARKS MET

6

RESOURCES

Total state pre-K spending $7,212,500

Local match required? ....No

State Head Start spending ....$7,212,500[9]

State spending per child enrolled $5,094

All reported spending per child enrolled* $5,094

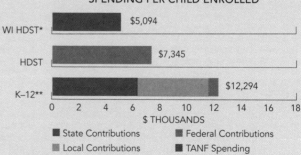

SPENDING PER CHILD ENROLLED

- WI HDST*: $5,094
- HDST: $7,345
- K–12**: $12,294

$ THOUSANDS (0 2 4 6 8 10 12 14 16 18)

■ State Contributions ■ Federal Contributions ■ Local Contributions ■ TANF Spending

* Pre-K programs may receive additional funds from federal or local sources that are not included in this figure.

** K–12 expenditures include capital spending as well as current operating expenditures.

Data are for the '07-'08 school year, unless otherwise noted.

[1] Wisconsin did not break this figure into specific numbers of 3- or 4-year-olds. As a result, age breakdowns used in the Access pie chart and Resources section were also estimated, using proportions of federal Head Start enrollees in each age category.

[2] As required by federal Head Start Performance Standards, programs must operate a minimum of 3.5 hours per day, 4 days per week, and 32 weeks per year, unless approved as a federal Head Start alternative. Programs may partner with child care or 4K to extend hours, days or weeks.

[3] School districts that are federal Head Start grantees may require lead teachers to have a BA and appropriate licensure. Head Start requires teachers to have at least a CDA.

[4] This requirement for assistant teachers in nonpublic settings reflects child care licensing regulations, which also require that assistant teachers be at least 18 years old. School districts that are federal Head Start grantees may require assistant teachers to have an AA and assistant teacher license. Title I standards apply in some districts.

[5] In December 2007, the Head Start reauthorization changed the requirement to 15 clock hours of professional development per year.

[6] Support services include two annual parent conferences or home visits, education services or job training for parents, parenting support or training, parent involvement activities, health services for parents and children, information about nutrition, referral to social services, transition to kindergarten activities, and others as per federal Head Start Performance Standards.

[7] The federal Head Start Performance Standards require that part-day programs provide children with at least one-third of their daily nutritional needs, and full-day programs provide one-half to two-thirds of daily nutritional needs, depending on the length of the program day.

[8] The state mandates that all programs follow federal Head Start monitoring requirements. The state itself does not conduct monitoring of these programs.

[9] All spending through this initiative is directed toward Head Start programs.

Wyoming

NO PROGRAM

ACCESS RANKINGS	
4-YEAR-OLDS	3-YEAR-OLDS
No Program	

RESOURCES RANKINGS	
STATE SPENDING	ALL REPORTED SPENDING
No Program	

ACCESS

Total state program enrollment 0

School districts that offer state program........................NA

Income requirement ....NA

Hours of operation ....NA

Operating schedule ....NA

Special education enrollment 1,829

Federally funded Head Start enrollment...................1,611

State-funded Head Start enrollment 0

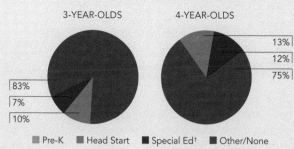

STATE PRE-K AND HEAD START ENROLLMENT AS PERCENTAGE OF TOTAL POPULATION

3-YEAR-OLDS

4-YEAR-OLDS

83%

7%

10%

13%

12%

75%

■ Pre-K   ■ Head Start   ■ Special Ed†   ■ Other/None

† This number represents children in special education who are not enrolled in Head Start.

QUALITY STANDARDS CHECKLIST

TOTAL
BENCHMARKS
MET

No
Program

RESOURCES

Total state pre-K spending..$0

Local match required? ....NA

State Head Start spending..$0

State spending per child enrolled $0

All reported spending per child enrolled*......................$0

* Pre-K programs may receive additional funds from federal or local sources that are not included in this figure.

** K–12 expenditures include capital spending as well as current operating expenditures.

Data are for the '07-'08 school year, unless otherwise noted.

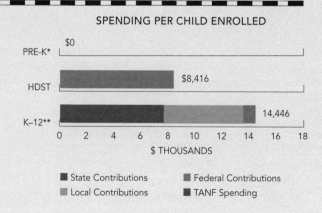

SPENDING PER CHILD ENROLLED

PRE-K* $0

HDST $8,416

K–12**   14,446

0   2   4   6   8   10   12   14   16   18
$ THOUSANDS

■ State Contributions   ■ Federal Contributions
■ Local Contributions   ■ TANF Spending

METHODOLOGY

The data in this report were collected primarily through surveys of state prekindergarten administrators and focus on the 2007-2008 program year. During July of 2008, links to a web-based survey were sent to administrators of the state-funded preschool initiatives covered in NIEER's 2007 *State Preschool Yearbook*. We also checked with other sources to determine whether any comparable new initiatives had been started since the 2006-2007 program year, or whether we had omitted any initiatives in our previous report. All initiatives included in the current report meet the criteria outlined in the survey, which defines state prekindergarten programs as initiatives that are funded and directed by the state to support group learning experiences for preschool-age children, usually ages 3 and 4. For more information about these criteria, please see "What Qualifies as a State Preschool Program" on page 21.

This report covers the same initiatives as our 2007 report, with five exceptions. During the 2007-2008 program year, new programs were launched in three states with existing programs, Iowa, Ohio and Pennsylvania. In all three states, the previous programs remain as distinct state preschool programs, and in this report the existing programs are profiled separately from the new initiatives. Iowa began the Statewide Voluntary Preschool Program (SVPP), which aims to expand access to preschool education for all 4-year-olds in the state by providing a sustainable source of funding. Ohio's Early Learning Initiative (ELI) updated their eligibility policy so that children are ensured a full year of preschool education through ELI, even if changes occur in their parents' employment and/or economic status. This change means that the ELI program now fits NIEER's definition of a state-funded preschool education program. Pennsylvania launched a fourth preschool education initiative, the Pre-K Counts program, which provides access to prekindergarten programs through funds from the state DOE.

In addition, two state initiatives that were included in the 2007 report are not included in the 2008 report. New York's Targeted Prekindergarten (TPK) program was subsumed by the state's Universal Prekindergarten (UPK) program as a result of a 2006 recommendation by the New York State Board of Regents. This resulted in an almost 50 percent increase in UPK's funding for the 2007-2008 school year, which nearly doubled the number of districts offering the program. Beginning with the 2007-2008 program year, New Mexico's Child Development Program now focuses only on children from birth to age 3. The program no longer serves 4-year-olds and served less than 1 percent of the state's 3-year-olds. Four-year-olds are served by New Mexico's PreK initiative, which is now the only state-funded preschool education program profiled in this report for that state. The District of Columbia also funds a pre-K program but is not included in the 2008 report because the District did not respond to the survey despite repeated requests.

Our survey included yes or no questions, questions that asked state administrators to select which of several choices best described their program, and open-ended questions. Where data were already available in the 2007 *State Preschool Yearbook* we provided the answer from our previous report and asked the administrators to verify that the information was still accurate for the 2007-2008 program year.

In terms of topics, the survey included questions on access, child eligibility and retention, program standards, statewide early learning standards, personnel, resources, quality improvement and accountability, and important changes to the program since the last survey. Most of the questions addressed the same issues as last year's survey, although administrators were asked to report policies that were in place for the 2007-2008 program year. A few additional questions were added to provide more information on the initiatives. The wording of some questions—such as those on special education enrollment, quality improvement, and accountability—was revised to make them clearer and to gather more precise data. Due to formatting revisions to the survey, in some cases the data gathered this year are not completely comparable to data in last year's report, although largely similar information was collected.

After the surveys were completed, we followed up with state administrators to clarify any questions about their responses. Later, we contacted them again to provide them with an opportunity to verify the data we had gathered. At that time, we asked them to review a table with all of the data from their state survey, as well as a narrative about their program. Administrators' responses to our survey, including answers for items not covered in the state profiles, are shown in Appendix A. For the first time, Appendix A (as well as Appendices B, C, D, and E) is online only and can be accessed at http://www.nieer.org/yearbook.

Although most of the data in this report were collected through surveys, there are a few exceptions. Total federal, state and local expenditures on K–12 education in 2007-2008 were calculated by NIEER based on data from the National Education Association's report, "Rankings and Estimates: Rankings of the States 2007 and Estimates of School Statistics 2008." Total K–12 spending for each state includes current operating expenditures plus annual capital outlays and interest on school debt. This provides a more complete picture of the full cost of K–12 than including only current operating expenditures, which underestimate the full cost. Our estimate of K–12 expenditures is also more comparable to total prekindergarten spending per child because this funding generally must cover all costs, including facilities. Expenditure per child was calculated for each state by dividing total expenditures by fall 2007 enrollment. We estimated the breakdown of expenditure per child by source, based on reported revenue receipts for pre-K from federal, state and local sources in each state.

The Administration for Children and Families and the Head Start Bureau of the U.S. Department of Health and Human Services were the sources of data on federal Head Start spending and enrollment. Additional Head Start data are provided in Appendix B.

Populations of 3- and 4-year-olds in each state were obtained from the Census Bureau's Population Estimates datasets and are shown in Appendix D. July estimates of populations at each single year of age are available from the Census Bureau's web site for each year from 2002-2007. Estimates for the July immediately preceding the program year (e.g., July 2007 for the 2007-2008 program year) were used to calculate percentages of 3- and 4-year-olds enrolled in state preschool, federal Head Start, and special education.

The U.S. Office of Special Education Programs provided data on special education enrollment in the Individuals with Disabilities Education Act Preschool Grants program (IDEA Section 619 of Part B) in the 2007-2008 program year. These data are provided in Appendix E.

In the 2008 *Yearbook*, we attempt to provide a more accurate estimate of unduplicated enrollments, whether in state preschool, Head Start, special education, or other settings, through a series of calculations. Because many children who are counted in special education enrollments are also enrolled in state pre-K or Head Start programs, it is important to ensure that those children are not counted twice. Twenty-eight states reported including children in special education in their state pre-K enrollment figures. Only 21 of those states were able to provide the number of 3- and 4-year-olds in special education who were also counted in their enrollment. Those children were subtracted from the special education enrollment figure for the state but remain in the state pre-K enrollment figure in the enrollment pie charts and when calculating total enrollment across both programs. The seven remaining states were unable to report special education enrollment numbers and therefore may have duplicated counts of children in their total state pre-K and special education enrollment figures (See Table 4). It should be noted that Kentucky, Mississippi, Oklahoma and West Virginia served the majority of their 3- and/or 4-year-olds with disabilities in their state pre-K programs. Therefore, it appears that their total enrollment across both programs dropped dramatically compared to last year's report, when in fact it is because children in special education who attend pre-K are no longer double counted.

Where it was not possible to estimate the percentage of 3- or 4-year-old special education students enrolled in state programs, estimates were based on the percentage of children reported to be served in environments other than early childhood settings.[1] Three- and 4-year-olds enrolled in Head Start with an IEP or IFSP, as reported in the 2007-2008 PIR, were also removed from the special education enrollment total used in the enrollment pie charts. Since the PIR does not report a breakdown of special education students by age, estimates were based on total special education enrollment and the percentage of all Head Start enrollees who were 3 or 4 years old. Three-year-olds enrolled in Early Head Start were not included in this estimate.

States are given rankings in four areas: the percentage of 4-year-olds enrolled in state prekindergarten (Access Rankings–4s), the percentage of 3-year-olds enrolled (Access Rankings–3s), state spending per child enrolled (Resources Ranking–State Spending) and all reported spending per child enrolled (Resources Ranking–All Reported Spending). The measures of access for 3- and 4-year-olds were calculated, as described above, using state data on enrollment in the prekindergarten initiatives and Census population data. When a state did not report separate enrollment numbers for 3-year-olds and 4-year-olds, the age breakdown was estimated by other means, such as using the average proportion of children enrolled in state pre-K at each age in states that served both 3- and 4-year-olds and did provide data by age. State per-child spending was calculated by dividing state prekindergarten spending (including TANF spending directed toward the state preschool initiative) by enrollment. All reported spending per child was calculated by dividing the sum of reported state, federal and local spending (including TANF) by enrollment. All states that provided data were ranked, starting with "1" for the state with the greatest percentage of its children enrolled in the state preschool education program or the state initiative that spent the most per child. States that did not serve children at age 3 receive notations of "None Served" on the rankings of access for 3-year-olds. The 12 states that did not fund a preschool education initiative are omitted from all rankings and instead receive notations of "No Program" on their state profile pages.

Additionally, this is the second year we have looked at whether states were funding their state preschool education initiatives at adequate levels to meet the NIEER quality benchmarks. For this analysis, state estimates were constructed from a national estimate in the Institute for Women's Policy Research report, "Meaningful Investments in Pre-K: Estimating the Per-Child Costs of Quality Programs,"[2] and adjusted for state cost of education differences using the state cost index from the Institute of Education Sciences report, "A Comparable Wage Approach to Geographic Cost Adjustment."[3] A state's per-child spending from all reported sources was compared to the per-child spending estimate for a full- or half-day program depending on the operating schedule of the state's program. If the program's operating schedule was determined locally, the half-day estimate was typically used. For states that were determined to be not adequately funding their preschool education initiative(s), we also provide an estimate of how much more money they would need to spend to do so. This estimate was calculated by taking the estimate of how much it would cost to adequately fund preschool education in that state and subtracting per-child spending from all reported sources.

[1] U.S. Department of Education, Office of Special Education and Rehabilitative Services, Office of Special Education Programs, *28th Annual Report to Congress on the Implementation of the Individuals with Disabilities Education Act*, 2006, vol. 1, Washington, D.C., 2009.

[2] Gault, B., Mitchell, A.W., & Williams, E. (2008). *Meaningful Investments in Pre-K: Estimating the Per-Child Costs of Quality Programs*. Washington, DC: Institute for Women's Policy Research.

[3] Taylor, L. & Fowler, W. (2006). *A Comparable Wage Approach to Geographic Cost Adjustment*. Washington, DC: IES, U.S. Department of Education.

Appendices Table of Contents

**TO DIRECTLY VIEW AND DOWNLOAD THE APPENDICES,
VISIT OUR WEBSITE WWW.NIEER.ORG/YEARBOOK**